**Other Books about the Sea and Water
by John Rousmaniere**

A Glossary of Modern Sailing Terms
No Excuse to Lose (with Dennis Conner)
The Enduring Great Lakes (editor)
"Fastnet, Force 10"
The Luxury Yachts
America's Cup Book, 1851–1983
The Annapolis Book of Seamanship
*The Student and Instructor Workbook
for The Annapolis Book of Seamanship*

THE SAILING LIFESTYLE

A Guide to Sailing and Cruising for Pleasure

by JOHN ROUSMANIERE

Illustrations by Mark Smith

Simon and Schuster
New York

Book-of-the-Month Records® offers a wide range of
opera, classical and jazz recordings. For information
and catalog write to BOMR, Camp Hill, PA 17012.

Published by Simon and Schuster
A Division of Simon & Schuster, Inc.
Simon & Schuster Building
Rockefeller Center
1230 Avenue of the Americas
New York, New York 10020
SIMON AND SCHUSTER and colophon are registered trademarks of
Simon & Schuster, Inc.
Designed by Barbara M. Marks
Manufactured in the United States of America
1 3 5 7 9 10 8 6 4 2
Library of Congress Cataloging in Publication Data
Rousmaniere, John.
The sailing lifestyle.

Includes index.
1. Sailing. 2. Sailboat living. I. Title.
GV811.R594 1985   797.1'24   85-1782
ISBN: 0-671-50887-3

Acknowledgments

The idea for this book was suggested by my editor, Fred Hills, who, after *The Annapolis Book of Seamanship* was finally in his hands, with his typically economical acuity simply asked for a book that would tell people how to cool a bottle of wine on a boat. The rest has fit more or less comfortably around that goal (which I trust is satisfactorily met in Chapter 13), but only due to the generous help of many friends and acquaintances, some of whom are acknowledged in the text but several of whom deserve special attention here.

Since my attempts at gracious eating on a boat have usually been limited to pouring a bit of wine into the canned stew, I felt sadly deficient when it came to recommending stylish cooking routines. So I asked some highly experienced sea chefs to tell me what they knew about galleys, cooking, and the good life below. The following people, whose cumulative galley experience must total close to three centuries, kindly waded through my long questionnaire and provided enough information to fill a book, much less to be the basis for Chapters 12, 13, and 14: Linda and Steve Dashew, Mimi and Dan Dyer, Dorothy Greenlee, Adra Kober, Harvey Loomis, Faith McCurdy, daughter Sheila McCurdy, Carol Nicklaus, Betty Noyes, Susie Page, Bill and Jane Robinson, Diana Russell, Pat and Spencer Smith, Brooke and Eric Swenson, and Marcia Wiley.

Chapter 15 never would have been written without the cooperation of my father and mother, Jim and Jessie Rousmaniere, who introduced me to sailing as a child, and my sons, Will and Dana, who introduced me to sailing as a father.

A shorter version of Chapter 2 was published in the May 1984 issue of *Sail,* an early draft of Chapter 18 first saw light as an address I presented to the United States Naval Academy's Safety at Sea Seminar, in January 1984, and part of Chapter 9 (on the limits of electronic navigation instruments) was written for *Sailor* magazine.

Thanks to Mark Smith and Brad Dellenbaugh for their drawings, to Peg Haller for copyediting, and to Barbara Marks, the designer.

John Rousmaniere
Stamford, Connecticut

For C. T., a Harbor Master

Table of Contents

Part II: Welcome Aboard

Part III: Cooking and Gracious Living Afloat

Part IV: When Sailing Gets Difficult

Foreword

This book is for anybody who is fascinated by the sailing life and yet is a bit intimidated by it. That's lots of people, not all of them beginners. They include the seasoned skipper who has fallen into bad habits and stopped enjoying the pastime, the person who hasn't been in a boat for years and who needs to relearn some skills before heading off on a Caribbean cruise, and the new sailor eager to get out there and do it correctly *now* without first spending a lifetime acquiring the necessary rules of thumb and helpful tricks of the trade.

I wish that a book like this had been available when I first got seriously interested in sailing, some twenty-five years ago. It would have saved me considerable time and frustration. Typical of many sailors, I think, is my sister-in-law Katherine Perls Rousmaniere. Like many people, Katherine has come to sailing in her thirties and has quickly fallen in love with it. While she doesn't think of herself as very athletic or technical-minded, she is intrigued by and eager to learn more about the complicated relationships between boat, water, and wind. Though she likes steering and sail trimming, what she enjoys most is relaxing in nature.

But Katherine has her reservations about sailing. When I asked her to describe them, she laughed and started in:

> Sunburn, that's what worries me the most. And of course whether the boat will sink. It doesn't help much when people explain why it won't tip over. Before I first went cruising I worried whether I'd be able to take a shower on the boat, and I learned quickly enough that I wouldn't—at least on *that* boat, which was fairly small. I don't like being cold, either, so I always try to prepare as well as I can for it. At first I didn't know what kinds of clothes to take so I would be both warm and functioning.

This book addresses those and many other, often unspoken, concerns about the "people side" of seafaring for pleasure and especially about that most delightful side of sailing, cruising. After more than twenty years of going out in just about every kind of boat —after racing, cruising, and daysailing in all sorts of places in weather ranging from the idyllic to the appalling—I've finally realized that I most enjoy what just about every other sailor most enjoys: a two- or three-day weekend cruise in a boat large enough to hold me and three or four friends but also small enough so that I and one other good sailor can handle her safely in tough conditions. In my experience, that means a boat whose length lies somewhere between 30 and 40 feet. Since that size range also seems to be most popular among the many sailors I know (as well as America's boat-buyers), almost everything in these pages deals directly with them. However, that's not to say that somebody heading off on a Bermuda Race in a 50-footer or for a round-the-world voyage in a 25-footer, or out for just a couple of hours on a daysailer won't find something of interest here.

Where my big sailing manual, *The Annapolis Book of Seamanship,* focuses on the technology of the boat and the thousands of special techniques used by masterful seamen to sail her, here we're dealing with the human factor. We'll see how to dress right for warmth and dryness, how to eat simply but well, how to cruise graciously and enjoyably, and how to get along with shipmates. Along the way, we'll also look at essential skills for safe and enjoyable sailing in both normal and wild conditions and summarize the fundamentals of coastal navigation, collision avoidance, sail trimming, and steering. As when writing *Annapolis,* I have tried to make the prose as lively and nontechnical as possible for the sake of readers who are new to this pastime's dense theory and arcane terminology. A glossary in the back of the book includes the most important terms. (To entertain trivia buffs, I've also included the fascinating etymologies of thirty key terms.)

Because flexible routines are all-important on a boat, I've included plenty of lists and succinct guidelines to take you step by step through all the important ones. I've tried to cover most of the challenges you can expect to face—whether buying foul-weather gear, tacking and jibing, lighting the stove, anchoring, cooking a fish stew, piloting, rigging a flying trapeze for your kids, or treating seasickness. The epilogue in *The Annapolis Book of Seamanship* applies to below-deck comfort just as much as to on-deck safety:

> Throughout this book we've suggested a truth that some might think ironical: to enjoy sailing, the most individualistic of all sports, you must try to standardize your techniques and your equipment and do every job the same way, time after time.

. . . With repetition come good habits, with good habits comes good seamanship, with good seamanship comes security, and with security comes enjoyment. And after all, isn't that what we're looking for in the first place?

Have fun.

John Rousmaniere

PART I

What to Wear
and
Where to Put It

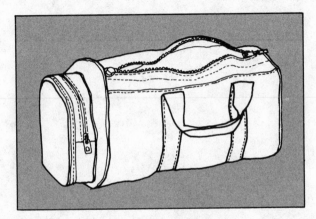

CHAPTER 1

Dry, Warm, and Ventilated: Sailing Clothes and Shoes

It seems simple enough: sailing clothes should keep you dry, warm, and functioning. Actually, those three words say pretty much the same thing. To quote Doug Daniels of North Sports, a major marketer of sailing clothes, "Dry skin is warm skin." A dry, warm body is a comfortable, strong, and alert body. Common sense tells us that much, and medical science reinforces common sense with some information about how the body sustains its vital functions when it gets cold.

Here's what happens. When its temperature is lowered even one or two degrees, the body must work harder to keep blood circulating in the vital organs in the trunk unless it can find a way to decrease its work in less critical parts elsewhere. In the interest of greater efficiency, then, it automatically begins to slow blood circulation in the extremities—the hands, feet, and head. If the body temperature is allowed to drop into the hypothermic ranges of the low 90s and high 80s, blood flow all but shuts down in the arms, legs, and head. The bad news about this remarkable feat of self-preservation is that when the blood flow slows in your fingers, toes, and brain, your movements become awkward and your thinking becomes lethargic. In other words, the more uncomfortable you get, the more inefficiently you behave. On a sailing boat, whose own welfare depends on her crew's, this can lead to problems, emergencies, and even disaster, as we'll see in Chapter 18.

All this happens when you get cold, and the quickest way to get cold is to get wet. Later on, in Chapter 2, we'll look carefully at waterproof foul-weather gear—how it works to keep you dry and what you should look for when you buy it. Here we're concerned with the nonwaterproof clothes that you wear alone on fine days and underneath foul-weather gear on wet days.

Unfortunately, the problem of staying dry is not as simple as it sounds. Dampness (leading to cold and loss of agility and strength) comes from two directions: from the outside in, from rain and spray; and from the inside out, from perspiration and condensation. To close off the first source of moisture we can seal off our bodies with waterproof fabrics, but to minimize the second kind we must allow our bodies to be ventilated. Absolute waterproofness and breathability are contradictions in clothing; to achieve the best of one we must sacrifice some part of the other. That is the paradox of sailing clothing, whether simple shorts and T-shirt for a hot, steamy summer day or heavy foul-weather gear for a cold gale. Every clothing choice must balance those two factors against each other in selecting from a wide variety of fabrics, fit, detailing, and style.

Which Fabrics Work Best When

Most of the time on a boat, you're going to risk getting at least a little wet. How can you best prepare for it? The answer is complicated, but it begins with fabrics. Each of the natural and synthetic fabrics used in the clothes you wear, alone or under foul-weather gear, offers its own trade-offs between comfort and resistance to wet and cold. The best way to exploit their advantages and minimize their disadvantages is to layer relatively light garments made of one or the other so there are several thin, insulating buffers between the body and the cold, cruel climate outside. We'll have much more to say about layering in Chapter 3; here's a survey of the fabrics you may be using in the garments you'll be piling on and peeling off.

Natural Fabrics

Cotton, when dry, is wonderfully soft against the skin and quite windproof, and it quickly ventilates perspiration without picking up odor. It's the most popular fabric for T-shirts and shorts and long-sleeved shirts, jeans, and corduroys. No comfort matches the feel of a soft cotton "chamois" shirt or rugby jersey against sun-baked skin as a hot, dry afternoon fades into a warm evening. Yet cotton absorbs moisture quickly, and when wet adheres to the body and so does not provide an insulating baffle of warm air. Wet cotton

Tough fabrics, double seaming, and a loose fit are the hallmarks of good sailing clothing. High collars on shirts and jackets are especially desirable for keeping out sun, wind, and spray.

also dries slowly (even if the water is fresh), mildews, and bunches up in a soggy, uncomfortable wad.

Wool warms well whether dry or wet because its long, scaly fibers trap dead air, which provides considerable insulation. For years, wool has been the material of choice for cold-weather garments like heavy sweaters, long underwear (often with an inner, nonscratchy cotton layer against the skin), and hats called watch caps. It also has a role on warm and cool days in socks and light shirts and sweaters. But wool doesn't block the wind very effectively, is relatively heavy and scratchy, and absorbs moisture like a sponge.

Work hard to keep your cotton and wool clothes from getting wet, especially around salt water, whose crystals will continue to absorb moisture well after the original dousing has evaporated. While staying dry is no easy trick, getting the moisture out of wet natural-fabric clothes can be even more difficult since, even in sunny weather, on-deck and below-deck humidity generally hovers around 90 percent. Fog or clouds can block off all solar drying power for days. To dry clothes when you're cruising, first shake or wring them out hard (on deck, please) to cast off all attached moisture; then hang them over an improvised clothesline near the warm galley stove. In a pinch, wear your wet underwear or other light clothes to bed in a sleeping bag; your body heat will bake the moisture out within a few hours. Just in case the sun does appear, take along a dozen clothespins so you can hang damp clothes on the lifelines. If you sail in salt water, shake out dried crystals and give your dried clothes an occasional fresh-water rinsing.

Synthetic Fabrics

Modern synthetics—polyester, nylon, acrylic, and polypropylene—wear well, hold their press, are nonabsorbant, and dry quickly. Small amounts of synthetics are often blended with wool to provide strength and with cotton to improve drying and insulation, but manufacturers have begun to use them on their own in a wide variety of practical clothing for active wear. In outer shells, synthetics provide excellent water repellency or, when coated with a waterproofing such as vinyl and polyurethane, even water resistance. In a sailor's clothing, synthetics are most important in warm, quick-drying garments used in place of wool in damp, cool weather.

Polyester-acrylic pile is the synthetic version of wool. Unlike wool, pile dries very quickly and doesn't smell bad when wet. Pile has a fairly hard, spray-repellent outer surface and, on the inside, thousands of long, soft fibers that trap dead air and provide a thick buffer of insulation around the body even when they are wet. Pile is commonly used in outer clothing—jackets, pullover pants, and cold-weather boot and glove liners. Like wool, pile is not very wind-resistant.

Polyester bunting, unlike pile, has short, trim, soft fibers on both sides; as a result, it provides less insulation than pile, so it may be the best material for very warm climates, where pile may be stifling. Bunting is used in top and bottom pullovers, socks, gloves, collars, and hand-warming pockets in foul-weather gear. It is also known by the trade name Polar Fleece.

Polypropylene underwear, developed originally for cross-country skiers, has gradually replaced wool and wool-blend long underwear. The polypropylene insulates just as well as wool when dry and perhaps even better when wet. More important, its absorbancy allows it to wick perspiration from the body. Sweat passes from the skin through the underwear to outer garments, leaving the skin dry (and warm) under a thin, insulating buffer (but also leaving the underwear somewhat malodorous after a couple of days). Poly-

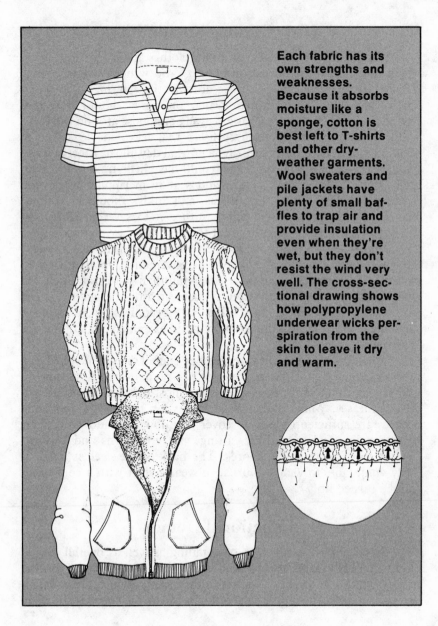

Each fabric has its own strengths and weaknesses. Because it absorbs moisture like a sponge, cotton is best left to T-shirts and other dry-weather garments. Wool sweaters and pile jackets have plenty of small baffles to trap air and provide insulation even when they're wet, but they don't resist the wind very well. The cross-sectional drawing shows how polypropylene underwear wicks perspiration from the skin to leave it dry and warm.

propylene long underwear is available in light, medium, and heavy weights for uses ranging from extremely active to relatively inactive and for bodies whose sensitivity to cold ranges from low to high. In hot, sticky weather, polypropylene long johns serve surprisingly well as outer garments or as your only clothing under foul-weather gear.

How Clothes Should Fit

"A sailor has a peculiar cut to his clothes and a way of wearing them that a green hand can never get." So wrote Richard Henry Dana 150 years ago in his classic account of seafaring, *Two Years Before the Mast*. According to Dana, the pants should be "tight round the hips, and thence hanging long and loose around the feet" —the traditional bell-bottom trousers that leave the legs free to make the pretzels required during a normal day afloat. Most activity on a boat is abrupt and quick, so you'll have little time to hitch up your pants to keep your crotch and seat from ripping when you stand up abruptly. The seat, knees, and ankles should be roomy, the waist and crotch fairly tight. Suffice it to say that skin-tight designer jeans may well blow apart the first day they go to sea.

Higher up, the shirt should be roomy around the chest, neck, elbows, and wrists to allow abrupt movement. On long-sleeved wrists, elastic wristlets are more forgiving than buttons (which can snag on fittings and lines, anyway). One reason "alligator" shirts and their preppy animal lookalikes have become so fashionable is that their fairly loose, almost boxy fit is extremely functional for active wear.

When trying on clothes, remember that all or part of your body will be exposed to intense sunlight for perhaps the first time in months and that sunburn is one of the most debilitating of all outdoor illnesses. Make sure, then, that your pants legs and shirt sleeves are sufficiently long to cover you down to, and even over, your tan lines when you are sitting with your arms and legs extended to perform ship's chores. The back of the neck is particularly vulnerable to vicious burns, so wear a shirt with a collar that can be turned up.

Functional Details

Practicality is a function of detailing as well as overall design and materials. Seams should be double-stitched and smooth on the inside next to your skin. Buttons and pockets, which are particularly vulnerable to ripping, should be sewn on strongly. Collars should be roomy so they can be buttoned up in cold weather without choking, and wool shirts should have a nylon or bunting neck liner to eliminate scratchiness.

Certain small added features can make your days aboard more pleasant or meet your special needs. For example, while you should choose clothes for active wear, anticipate that you'll be sitting down and inactive at least 75 percent of the time that you're on board. Perhaps your rear end will be cushioned by a small pillow, but don't count on it. The rough, nonslip surface on many decks will quickly wear through most unreinforced pants seats. For that reason, consider buying at least one pair of fairly heavy pants with double layers of fabric on the seat. At the least, take along a pair made of heavy cotton with large back pockets.

Seasoned sailors take seriously details that other people might consider trivial. Many seamen are careful to buy sailing shirts and pants with deep, wide, button-down pockets for knives, sunglasses, fittings, handkerchiefs, and the other small objects that always seem necessary on short notice. Others insist on having belt loops on which to hang knife lanyards. Since sailors are a prejudiced lot, it's not surprising that a whole different school of thought considers pockets to be dangerous protrusions just waiting to be snagged by fittings. Myself, I like to have a shirt pocket, at least two pants pockets, and belt loops. You may not. Either way, decide if you want these accessories before you make your purchase.

The Style of Sailing Clothes

The style of sailing clothes has hovered somewhere between preppy brightness and military practicality. On the one hand, an easily identified Establishment sailing look has hung on in the more exclusive yacht clubs and marinas for many years. For men, it consists of a monochromatic, usually navy blue, cotton T-shirt worn over baggy knee-length shorts or long pants made of khaki, madras, or Breton Red cotton. For women, the uniform includes a pink, lime, or navy T-shirt over the same type of pants or a skirt. On the other hand, self-consciously non-Establishment types have swung toward a much more informal look that includes faded long or cutoff nondesigner jeans, painter's pants, corduroys, army surplus khakis, white undershirts, and sweatshirts. This dichotomy in apparel, which has been around ever since I took up sailing thirty years ago, may be due to an exaggerated sense of social distinction borrowed from shore life.

Perhaps more important than status identification is the fact that the relatively small sailing community hasn't been given much choice by clothing manufacturers more interested in larger markets. If there has been a meeting ground, it is the practical, faded look typified by the ubiquitous khaki, whose color is light enough not to absorb heat on sunny days yet dark enough not to show sweat stains, and which is widely available in a variety of cotton and synthetic blends. As *Sail* magazine's Tina Sherman has pointed out, "we've essentially been wearing a navy and khaki cotton uniform for generations."

But all sorts of boating traditions are changing. For example, two generations ago most boats were painted either white or black and were named for women, ideals, or constellations. Now boats are orange with red stripes and their names are inspired by rock songs. Likewise with clothing. Both extremes—the Establishment and the semihippie—have swung toward a common style of handsome, colorful, and functional clothing that began to appear in the mid-seventies with the booming interest in the outdoors and fitness. Men and women who care about looking good can now buy colorful clothes that are appropriate both on and off the water. What you buy from outfits like Lands' End, Sears, or L. L. Bean for wear in any informal gathering can now be taken aboard a boat without fear of being thought too flashy by your conservative skipper-host or -hostess.

However, there is one trend that you should steer away from: if you want to impress your hosts with your eagerness to learn seamanship, *do not* come aboard wearing a shirt that advertises "A shipwreck can spoil your whole day," "Sailors do it in the sheets," or some other suggestive or ironic news. For people who spend so much time, energy, and money presumably enjoying themselves, sailors can be extremely serious—even pompous—characters. Though they may kid each other about their sport in the privacy of their own cabins, like all members of a beleaguered minority they will excoriate any outsider who dares to crack wise about their cherished values. The most sacred of those values is that going out on a boat, even for a two-hour sail on a calm August afternoon, is altogether too serious a matter for crude jokes.

Shore Clothes

Bathing suits and other skimpy, informal clothes may be all right on board, but when you go ashore to a town or village, be prepared to dress up a little to meet local standards. In many sailing areas, strangers who appear in stores and government offices barefoot or in swimsuits or shorts are treated rather coolly. A man should at least change into a pair of clean, pressed shorts and a shirt with a collar, and a woman probably should wear a sun dress or long pants and a shirt over a bikini top. At night, slightly fancier attire is usually required—perhaps even a blue blazer over a light shirt with a collar for men and long cotton pants and a blouse for women. In the past, ties and dresses were required after sunset at yacht club and other waterfront restaurants, and perhaps with the return of conservative fashions in other segments of our lives, they may be required once again. Understatement is everything here: a man's tie or lady's blouse or scarf covered with sailboats usually announces the wearer's status as a beginner. Fifty years ago, a Yachtsman with a capital *Y* was never seen without a formal white cap, but today such an affectation labels you a rock star, an airplane pilot, or—God forbid—a powerboat skipper.

Shoes for Sailing

In the old and not so good days, seamen often went barefoot, but only because suitable footwear did not exist. Today's average 30-foot cruising sailboat has more toe-stubbing deck fittings than the typical 150-foot square-rigger, and besides, few of us sail enough to toughen up our feet to the point where they can take the beating handed out by the sea. Sailing barefoot may seem salty, but unless you have run an occasional barefooted marathon, always wear shoes on deck. An exception to this rule is when sailing a small boat like a Laser or a sailboard—and even then shoes are a good idea if your feet are soft or if you must clamber across rocks or rough sand to get to and from the water.

In the last twenty years the shoe industry has developed a whole line of so-called deck shoes or boat shoes for the sailing market. While the uppers on these shoes look much like those on normal shore sneakers, moccasins, or oxfords, the soles are very different. That's because on a boat, unlike ashore, you must be able to keep your footing when the surface under you is tilting, rolling, and wet. One way to improve a sailor's footing is to make the deck itself less slippery. Wooden decks, particularly those with grainy teak, have a wonderful sole-grabbing surface, but since wooden decks are expensive, heavy, and difficult to maintain, boatbuilders usually cover the fiberglass deck with a nonskid coating. But even the best surface can turn into a skating rink in bad conditions. That's why the nonskid rubber sole found on modern deck shoes is so helpful. It is broken into thousands of tiny horizontal slits that stay closed when no weight is put on the shoe but open up when weight is applied. As they open, they do two things. First, the sole's surface area is greatly enlarged, and second, the slits work like squeegees to grip the deck. Most shoes and boots sold for boat use

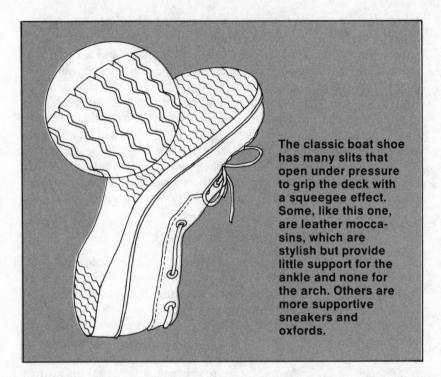

The classic boat shoe has many slits that open under pressure to grip the deck with a squeegee effect. Some, like this one, are leather moccasins, which are stylish but provide little support for the ankle and none for the arch. Others are more supportive sneakers and oxfords.

have this kind of nonskid sole. To identify it in the store, pull back hard on the toe and look for the opened slits.

Deck shoes come in a variety of styles of which the slip-on moccasin is widely considered the most fashionable—it became the ultimate preppy shoe a few years ago—as well as the most practical. With treated leather uppers, tongues, and thongs, with rubber soles, and with brass rust-resistant eyelets, a Top-Sider moccasin (a trademark of the Sperry Company) or one of its competitors should have a long life in the harsh saline atmosphere of the oceans. Unlike some other styles, the moccasin can be pulled on without untying the lace and can be worn barefoot with some comfort, though cotton, wool, or polypropylene socks provide insulation in cool weather and soak up perspiration, which may eat into the shoe's seams. The major drawback of moccasins is that they provide little foot support. They don't allow the use of arch supports—something that probably bothers more older sailors than younger ones—and when well broken-in are so flexible that they may fall off. Some brands of moccasin may bleed when wet, and thongs may be skinny, brittle, and hard to replace when broken. Even soft thongs will become untied under the slightest abrasion, so be sure to tie a double knot.

Besides the moccasin, deck shoes come in sneaker and oxford styles, most of which have good arch supports. Some sneakers have nylon uppers that dry out extremely rapidly, even after a soaking in salt water (unfortunately, they pick up foot odors just as quickly). The attractive lace-up oxford is more formal in appearance than the sneaker and, unlike the moccasin, provides excellent support for the ankle and arch. The oxford's one drawback is that it is relatively heavy and stiff.

In some Establishment yacht clubs and sailing circles, the oxford deck shoe is considered part of the uniform; in others, the moccasin is de rigueur. While you're probably not going to be snubbed just because of the shoes you have on, if you care about fashion, survey local customs before you shell out $60 for a pair of these shoes. More important than style when buying any deck or athletic shoe, be sure to check for double- or triple-stitching and for reinforcements at stress points, like the heel and toe.

Of course, there's no law requiring sailors to wear specialized deck shoes. Slit-soled running or basketball sneakers, or even work boots, may grip a wooden or nonskid deck as well as a real deck shoe. However, any footwear taken aboard must have white soles, since black soles will leave indelible marks all over the deck.

Experienced sailors wear their deck shoes (or sneakers) only when on board, since all those neat little slits pick up the gravel, tar, and dirt even more efficiently than they grip decks. If you must wear your boating shoes ashore, inspect and scrub off the soles on the pier before you climb aboard. Many owners leave a damp mop on deck as a not-so-subtle hint for their guests.

Now that we've inspected the normal clothes you'll wear aboard, let's take a look at the most expensive item in any non-boatowner's nautical inventory—the slick, functional, and (presumably) waterproof outer garment called foul-weather gear.

CHAPTER 2

How to Buy and Use Foul-Weather Gear

I f the key to comfortable, safe sailing is staying warm, then the key to staying warm is staying dry. According to Bill Riviere, in his informative chapter on clothing in *The L. L. Bean Guide to the Outdoors*, heat can be lost 240 times faster through wet clothing than through dry. The primary means of keeping dampness out is to wear the waterproof outer clothing that, more than any other object (except, perhaps, the lighthouse) symbolizes the sailor's life. It's usually called foul-weather gear. Sometimes going by other names (including slicker, oilskins, oilers, and wet gear), it is the sailor's armor against the damp slings and arrows of his outrageous environment. When worn over several light layers of insulating clothing, foul-weather gear is also the outer skin of a dry, warm cocoon that can sustain the sailor through just about any storm.

Today, most foul-weather gear is made by putting a waterproof —that is, leakproof—coating on one side of a water-repellent—or spray-proof—nylon shell. In the old days, when clothes were painted with linseed oil to make "oilskins," the end result was little better than a seaman's chances of being asked to dine with his captain, and until the 1960s most foul-weather gear wasn't a whole lot better than that improvised, leaky stuff. But as with dry-weather clothing, foul-weather gear fabrics, detailing, and even style have improved by leaps and bounds. We're now presented with a bewildering variety of materials, details, and styles that make a purchase of foul-weather gear much more difficult than it used to be. If you know a bit about what's available, and if you're rigorously honest about your own needs, you should end up with the best gear for you.

Waterproof and *Breathable:* What They Mean and Don't Mean

Before charging off to look at gear, let's reflect upon the meaning of two adjectives that appear so frequently in the literature of foul-weather gear that they may mislead many people into expecting miracles. These words are *waterproof* and *breathable*.

Waterproof means "keeping out water completely." Water-repellent, on the other hand, means "repelling water but not thoroughly waterproof." (There's also *water-resistant:* "repelling water for a short time.")

Now, just because a bolt of treated fabric is waterproof—that is, won't leak if a hose is turned on it—nobody should expect a garment stitched together from that fabric to be equally effective at keeping out moisture. "Making a high-quality garment is not very hard," says Mark Mordecai of Atlantis Weathergear, one of the most prominent manufacturers of foul-weather gear, "but making a high-quality garment that's waterproof *is* hard." Good suits are available (later on in this chapter we'll find out how to pick one), but even gear assembled carefully, with double-stitched and taped-over seams, may let in water around its edges, through cuffs and collars. As another foul-weather gear manufacturer, Bob Kettenhofen, points out, "It's almost impossible to keep some water that's hitting you directly in the face from going down your neck"—a comment that should echo the experience of anybody who's been out in a raw gale blowing horizontal rain. The best way to block off your neck is to plug the hole. You can make your own stopper out of a length of bunting or a small bath towel, cutting a slit near one end through which to stick the other end to form a bulky necktie. Or you can buy a neck cloth from a foul-weather gear manufacturer who, far from trying to cover up some defect in his product, is simply being honest about its natural limits.

Breathable is the other buzz word that bears examination. It suggests that the garment inhales dry air and exhales fetid body moisture so you don't stew in your own juices (to paraphrase Bill Riviere). The idea is attractive in concept, but given the enormous forces and strains of the sea, wind, and human body, it is less than

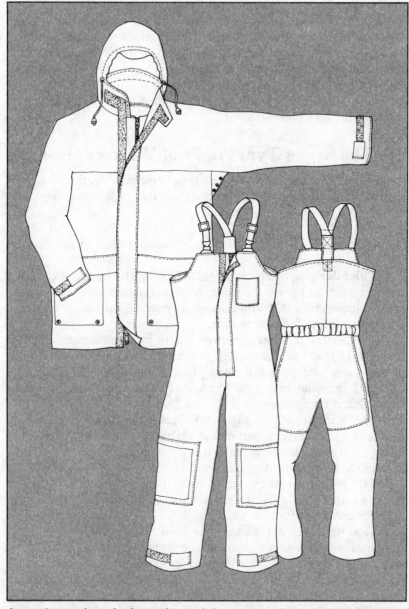

A good two-piece foul-weather suit has many of the details shown here: tight-fitting hood, high collar, top- and bottom-opening jacket zipper, Velcro zipper flaps and cuff closures, pocket and armpit drain and vent holes, chest-high pants, adjustable suspenders, several pockets, elastic pants waist, reinforced knees and seat, and an absence of seams in the shoulders, seat, and other vulnerable areas.

perfectly realized in execution. A suit may be so breathable that it is anything but waterproof, inhaling not air but rather spray or rain. Later on we'll see how the marine clothing industry has attempted to deal with the paradoxical relationship between waterproofness and breathability. For now it's enough to say that when you go shopping, don't expect any gear to be both dry and air-conditioned in very wet weather, regardless of the claims made by the salesperson and the sales literature.

The Seven Types of Foul-Weather Gear

Manufacturers provide seven types and combinations of foul-weather gear, each of which meets a relatively broad need.

The Jacket

Often called a slicker, the foul-weather jacket to protect the upper body comes in four styles.

Thigh-length, the most popular, covers the upper body from wrist to wrist and from the neck to several inches below the waist, thereby protecting the whole torso. It may be insulated with corduroy or bunting for cold weather.

The floatcoat is like the thigh-length jacket in general appearance except that foam is sewn in to keep the wearer warm when out of the water and buoyant when in it. Some floatcoats qualify as Type III Personal Flotation Devices (PFDs) under United States Coast Guard regulations.

The waist-length bomber-style jacket, usually seen in water-repellent windbreakers but also available in waterproof materials, offers no protection below the belt line but is easier to move around in than the thigh-length models.

The pullover smock, which extends to the knees, is worn in warm weather and water to protect most of the body without the need for confining foul-weather pants.

Most foul-weather jackets are sold with zip-up or snap-up fronts. Water may creep through the zipper or between the snaps (even when they are covered with a Velcro flap), but most sailors are willing to accept that minor loss of waterproofing in exchange for the assurance that they can easily put the jacket on in a bouncy boat and—more important—quickly pull it off should they ever fall into the water. A soaking wet jacket can restrict a swimmer's movements or even pull him under. Hoods (either retractable or removable) are standard accessories on good jackets. So, too, are at least one deep pocket with a waterproof flap and drain, elastic wristlets or Velcro straps to seal off cuffs, a high collar to keep wind and spray off the lower half of the head, and a liner to separate the wearer from any condensation that accumulates inside the jacket shell. Other options include a built-in safety harness, whose tether is clipped to the boat in heavy weather when there's a chance of falling over.

A thigh-length or smock jacket may be all the foul-weather gear you'll need if the worst weather you can expect is a warm, light afternoon shower, or if the cockpit or cabin always protects your legs from spray. In fact, the jacket needn't even be waterproof if the weather is consistently warm and the wind is light; a nylon, water-repellent windbreaker might do quite nicely. But if you anticipate cool, damp weather, pay the extra price for a good jacket or perhaps even a floatcoat.

The Pants

Foul-weather pants are either waist-high and held up with a drawstring, or chest-high with suspenders. Chest-high pants are sometimes called bib pants. Foul-weather pants may not be necessary on daysailers with cockpits, but you'll need them if it's raining and if you must sit on the deck when spray is flying; a surprising amount of water can creep from the rail up your back and down inside to your rear end. The higher the spray, the higher the pants should be. Good pants have a pocket for a knife or handkerchief, anklets or Velcro straps to seal off the ankle cuffs, reinforced knees and seat, a liner, and strong elastic suspenders with reinforced anchors.

The Two-Piece Suit

The most common foul-weather gear on boats sailing in moderately rough (and worse) weather is a two-piece combination consisting of the thigh-length jacket and chest-high pants. The suit offers excellent protection as well as the most versatility. The large overlap between thigh and armpits provides a double seal, and water must work hard to make its way up inside the jacket and down the trousers. Since each piece individually covers more than half the body, the wearer has good protection when taking either the jacket or pants off on a hot day to improve ventilation.

The Jump Suit

This is a one-piece version of the combination jacket and pants suit, offering more protection (since there is no opening near the waist) at a sacrifice of some flexibility (since the jacket and pants cannot be separated). Moving around the boat in a jump suit is easier than in a two-piece combination. People who sail in consistently rough, cool weather generally prefer this outfit. Accessories available include pockets, liners, reinforcements, and cuff closures.

The Dry Suit

If staying absolutely dry is a must—say when sailing dinghies or sailboards in cool or cold water—the dry suit may be the answer. Most dry suits are one-piece jump suits made of very light fabric with strong waterproof seals at the cuffs and collar. At least one brand has a separate top and bottom connected with a rubber seal at the waist. The wearer climbs in and out of the suit somewhat awkwardly through a back access hole, which is a disadvantage for people, like cruising sailors, who must put the suit on and pull it off frequently.

The Survival Suit

A kind of super dry suit with buoyancy, the specialized survival suit offers all-body protection for fishermen and navy personnel exposed to arctic conditions. While heavy and awkward, survival suits have saved the lives of many mariners who have gone overboard or abandoned ship into life rafts in frigid weather. A yacht heading off on a long cruise in cold water should carry a survival suit for everybody on board.

The Wet Suit

While as the name suggests it does not keep the wearer dry, the wet suit does provide warmth by trapping a layer of water between the skin and its flexible rubberized surface. The body heats the water, which provides a thin barrier of insulation. Difficult to put on and take off, wet suits are usually worn by boardsailors and dinghy racers sailing in cool water. They come in a variety of styles —top, bottom, full-length, and short.

Waterproofing Materials

The effectiveness and cost of foul-weather gear are determined by the materials and the amount and kind of detailing built into it. The most simple and least expensive type of wet gear is made of water-repellent (not waterproof) bare nylon. Though not suited for extended use in even moderate spray or rain, nylon pants and jackets are lightweight, wind-resistant, and breathable and may well provide all the protection you need.

However, most people who get serious about sailing eventually buy a top and pants suit of waterproof gear made of a nylon or cotton shell coated with one of four types of waterproofings. Each coating has its own advantages and disadvantages. In the chandlery (marine hardware store), you can determine which waterproofing is used on a suit by rubbing the shell between your thumb and fingers, reaching under the nylon liner if there is one. If the shell has a shiny exterior and textured fabric interior, it's waterproofed on the outside with PVC. If the shell exterior is textured and the interior smooth, the coating is on the inside and is either neoprene, PTFE, or urethane.

PVC Coating

Polyvinyl chloride—vinyl—is the slick stuff in many slickers. PVC is a rather heavy, glossy outside coating applied in one layer or, on the more expensive suits, two layers. It's the oldest type of waterproofing and, because it is the waterproofing applied to the most familiar gear, the inexpensive hardware store suits, it's the most readily recognized, too.

PVC has two major advantages over the other waterproofings: relatively low cost and welded seams. The seams in a PVC garment can be heated and stuck together in a welded joint that can be as waterproof as the fabric itself. (Since the other coatings are not heat-sealable, their seams must be sealed with tape.) In the better PVC gear, the seams are first sewn and then welded over. PVC tears can be easily repaired using kits provided by manufacturers. When PVC loses its integrity and begins to leak—an inevitable fate of all foul-weather gear—it frankly announces its demise by cracking on the outside. Inside coatings, on the other hand, fall apart out of sight, and the first a wearer finds out about their failure is a vague sense of dampness.

However, PVC has two disadvantages, one stylistic and the other functional. The first is that with its crisp surface and protruding seams, it looks more like a uniform for one of Darth Vader's storm troopers than like normal clothing. Manufacturers seem to be trying to turn this detriment into a benefit by making gear with stripes and unusual colors like green and white (an unsafe combination, since it cannot be seen in whitecapped waves). The other disadvantage is that while a well-made PVC suit is satisfactorily waterproof against rain and spray, it can be stifling. It may get even wetter inside than outside. The first problem, its plastic appearance, seems not to bother the thousands of people who like PVC's waterproofness, but the second, its heavy feel, is less easy to live with for many sailors in warm climates.

In 1985 prices, a PVC two-piece suit can cost anywhere between about $100 (for the simple hardware-store kind) to about $230 (for a sophisticated offshore brand).

Neoprene Coating

While PVC is the only exterior waterproofing, there are three types of interior coatings. Probably the most nearly waterproof (and also the most expensive) is neoprene, used on several well-regarded suits made by a pair of British companies, Henri-Lloyd and Musto & Hyde. Like most sailing gear made in Britain, where conditions are rougher and colder than in most of North America, this is tough, heavy stuff. Sailors in temperate and semitropical areas may find it, like PVC gear, hot and confining.

At the top of the neoprene lines are $400 to $500 suits (1985 prices) for serious offshore work in extreme conditions—like sailing around Cape Horn in the Whitbread Round-the-World Race. This gear is so pricey partly because neoprene costs much more than PVC and partly because its thorough detailing includes heavy seam taping, built-in safety harnesses, strips of reflective tape to facilitate recovery should you fall overboard, neat waterproof cuffs that function like gaiters, and flaps and baffles over every conceivable water-catcher.

PTFE Coating

Less expensive than most neoprene suits, and more commonly seen in American chandleries, is gear whose insides are sprayed or laminated with either of two types of synthetic waterproofings. These coatings have a jungle of trade and technical names that, for simplicity's sake, we'll break down into two categories: PTFE (polytetrafluoroethylene) and urethane.

The most promising and, at the same time, most controversial is PTFE. When the PTFE Gore-Tex was introduced in foul-weather gear in the late seventies, it was said to provide the final solution to the old waterproof-breathability problem. Billions of tiny pores would allow water vapor to escape while keeping solid water out—or at least that was the idea. How the PTFEs have fared is suggested by the following warning found in February 1984 on a tag on a Gore-Tex jacket:

> After being used for some time, it is possible that some moisture may pass through the material when walking in heavy rain, wet snow, or through wet bushes. Moisture can come through the material occasionally when the user is sitting on a wet surface and warming the water through body heat.

The references are to general outdoors wear, and the syntax is weak, but the point is clear: this suit may leak in very wet weather and under hard use. The initial storm of optimistic promises about

PTFE was quickly followed by a drizzle of disappointing reports of weeping seams and seeping panels. Some manufacturers stopped using PTFE altogether; others doubled up on seam tapes and laminations and forged ahead. There's no question that PTFE has a great deal going for it. Foul-weather gear waterproofed with it is breathable, windproof, resistant to spray, soft, lightweight (a whole Gore-Tex suit weighs about as much as a PVC jacket), and as sexy as a ski instructor's outfit. PTFE also is expensive, with most two-piece suits costing over $250.

Urethane Coatings

That leaves the crowd of materials known by the catchall *urethane* that are used in most gear made today by American companies. In this group are urethane (polyurethane) and nitrile (acrylic-nitrile butadiene), which are applied to the nylon fabric as liquids, and a urethane-derived film, which is glued to the shell. Though a couple of urethanes are claimed to be breathable (L. L. Bean has used one of these, Entrant, in a parka), most are simply lightweight, waterproof, and good-looking—which is sufficent for most uses until, and if, the PTFEs are improved. Though slightly glossier and stiffer than PTFE, the urethanes also have a fabriclike textured appearance and feel.

Like the other inside coatings, urethane can leak along seams, especially at the rear end, the crotch, and other flexible places. All seams should be double-stitched and thoroughly taped on the inside; some manufacturers use a different color tape to facilitate inspection. Outside seat and knee patches should be heavier than the shell and securely glued onto it.

Jacket and Pants Liners

Waterproofing keeps outside water off your clothes and body, and breathable fabrics allow muggy air from your body to escape before it makes you damp and cold. For different reasons, both systems have proved to be less than perfect. But there is another stay-dry tactic: using a liner in the gear to isolate condensation on the inside of the outer garment. At first, liners were sewn only into jackets, but manufacturers began to put them in pants, too, since annoying condensation can develop at the rear end and crotch. Besides helping to keep inner clothes and the skin dry, a liner has three other advantages: it protects your skin from the clammy inside of the shell; it protects the shell's seams from chafe from your clothes; and its slippery surface facilitates pulling the suit on. The liner should be sewn in throughout the garment except at the bottom, where an opening or drain will allow water to pour out if the wearer is doused by a wave or falls overboard.

Styling: Almost Like Real Clothes

If you remember the shapeless yellow bags that used to fill the clothing racks at chandleries, a glance at a 1985-vintage display will tell you that something has happened to foul-weather gear design. Many fascinating and appealing developments have been inspired by the skiwear industry (graduates of which, not coincidentally, now run several marine clothing companies). Alongside traditional suits with the sharp-edged, functional look of an army field jacket, hang jackets and pants with sexy colors (some in two-tone schemes), tapered arms and waists, hidden drain holes, and slash pockets. On the more practical side are high, waterproof collars, retractable and zip-up hoods, firm cuff elastics, and warm, bunting-lined collars and pockets.

It's a wonderful development, for if people look good in protective clothing they're bound to wear it more often. But there is one stylistic trend that is not progressive: the use of cool colors like white and blue. They are almost invisible in the spray of breaking waves. Pray that you never fall overboard in a suit that is not orange, yellow, or red. A few manufacturers have attempted to deal with this safety issue by adding red hoods to blue suits—which is fine so long as the unlucky swimmer has the hood on. Others sew strips of reflective tape on hoods and shoulders, which certainly will help during a night search. But the best choice is highly visible, if slightly unfashionable, hot-hued gear.

What You Should Expect to Spend

Of course, all those fancy new materials, accessories, and styles cost money, but you needn't spend a fortune to stay dry. In 1985 the top-of-the-line British neoprene suits, with built-in safety harnesses and other good things, weigh in at over $400; if you sail an awful lot, say daily for six or more months a year, that is an excellent investment. However, most of us will be perfectly happy in a suit costing much less. At the bottom of the list in price and detailing is the simple, unlined, $100 PVC suit sold in hardware stores, which may be fine in mild rain and protected water but is not sufficient in rougher weather. For about $160 you can buy a good all-round, partially lined PVC or urethane suit. For $200 to $260, you can get a deluxe, fully lined, thoroughly detailed urethane outfit that should keep you dry in just about all conditions. PTFE suits cost near the top of that price range. (To keep things in perspective, in 1985 $260 could buy an excellent marine radio.)

Budgeting the difference between a "better" $160 suit and a "deluxe" $260 outfit over a five-year suit life gives you an extra cost of $20 a year. You may not need the $260 suit. But if you plan to do a lot of sailing, please remember how uncomfortable you were —and how poorly you sailed—the last time you were cold and wet. As foul-weather gear designer and manufacturer Bob Kettenhofen puts it, "The next time you find yourself out there soaking wet and freezing cold in your cheap gear, ask yourself how much you'd spend to be comfortable. Ten dollars an hour? Twenty dollars?" A boatowner should be able to justify that marginal added expense quite easily, since good foul-weather protection might make the difference between loving or hating a $50,000-plus yacht.

How Foul-Weather Gear Should Fit

When trying on foul-weather gear in the chandlery, wear exactly the same clothes and boots you'll have on when the going is wet. As with all sailing and other outdoors clothing, the fit should be on the baggy side with the important exception that the pants' crotch should conform to your own so that you can spring into action without having to hitch up the legs. Give the gear a good tryout. Throw yourself down on your knees and grind away furiously on an imaginary winch handle. Leap up and reach high for a broken lower batten and low for the mooring buoy. Quickly pull the suit off and on. For a man, an important consideration may be the relative ease of opening the zipper one-handed while meeting a call of nature in rough weather, with the other hand providing secure anchorage, either to a grabrail in the head or to a lifeline along the leeward rail. (I once heard a shipmate punctuate a long period of fumbling with a recalcitrant zipper and undergarments, "Come out, you little coward, I know you're in there somewhere!") If your jacket zipper opens from the bottom, you won't need to remove the top during this exercise. As you go through these gymnastics, check if there is sufficient material in the back and elasticity in the suspenders to allow the gear to move smoothly with your body.

A Checklist for Buying Foul-Weather Gear

Before making your final selection, get it clear in your mind exactly how you will use the gear you're shopping for. This will help you purchase no more or less than you need. I can't tell you what your requirements are, but I can tell you mine as I listed them before making my own recent purchase. They may well be representative of other people who sail in temperate waters in a variety of climates.

✓ **Use.** The suit should be versatile. I usually sail on thirty-foot-plus cruising boats and ocean racers, generally in relatively warm, easy conditions but sometimes in cold, rough stuff. I can be found anywhere between the helm, in light spray, and the bow, hip-deep in water while wrestling with a recalcitrant jib. Since I usually wear only boots, chest-high pants, and a T-shirt in warm spray, a one-piece jump or dry suit is not suitable.

✓ **Accessibility.** I'll often be hastily putting the gear on and removing it in a crowded, damp, on-edge cabin rather than on a stable deck. The jacket and pants should pull on easily, so I'll want a smooth liner, plus zippers, snaps, and Velcro sealers that open and close with one hand (no buttons, please). Someday I may have to take the jacket off *very* hastily if I fall overboard, so pullovers are out of consideration.

✓ **Color.** Orange, red, and yellow are the *only* sensible choices.

✓ **Detailing.** There should be at least one waterproof pocket each in the jacket and pants for my knife and paper towels (to wipe my glasses). Since the boats I generally sail on are equipped with good safety harnesses, I won't need a built-in harness. Pulled up, the hood should not be too loose or restrict my hearing and peripheral vision. Since I use a hood very rarely—they tend to funnel warm air up from my body to fog up my glasses—it should be removable or thoroughly retractable into the collar. The cuffs should be closed off outside with Velcro straps and inside with elastic liner wristlets. (The elastic should not be so tight that it cuts off circulation.)

✓ **Construction.** I remember these past failings when inspecting gear in the chandlery: suspender elastics lose their spring and their anchors pull out of the pants; unreinforced knees wear out; a cleat or rough, nonskid surface tears off a thin, poorly glued seat patch; seams, cuff elastics, and zippers leak; a stiff jacket collar doesn't mold to my neck and water drips in.

✓ **Phobias.** I hate getting wet even in warm weather: damp feet and the sadistic drip-drip-drip of a leaky neck stimulate dark humors. Also, I don't enjoy lurching and creaking like the Tin Man before Dorothy oiled him; better no clothes at all than stiff, bulky ones. A tight collar makes me gag. Claustrophobia sets in when I get hot and can't ventilate by opening the cuffs and neck or quickly peeling off the jacket.

✓ **Cost.** No more than $300.

All that left me with a simple shopping list: a traditional two-piece suit consisting of a zip-up jacket and chest-high bib trousers, strongly built of medium-weight, flexible materials and with a modicum of functional detailing. Add a pair of shin-high seaboots and I'm ready for sea.

Obviously, my list of requirements reflects my special needs and circumstances. If instead of southern New England I lived in chilly San Francisco or were planning to sail across the cold north Atlantic, I'd seriously consider buying a well-insulated, one-piece jump suit or warm floatcoat. For dinghy racing in anything except the hottest weather and for dayracing in larger boats, I might buy a dry suit or a simple jump suit. For easy summer daysailing on Long Island Sound or Chesapeake Bay, a water-repellent nylon suit or smock jacket would be sufficient to keep out spray and wind.

After compiling that checklist and identifying my needs, I shopped around at several local chandleries and eventually decided on a brilliant orange Sea Gear Pro Suit. It had almost everything I needed—even a zip-off hood. All it lacked were internal wristlets, for which long, strong Velcro straps are a good substitute. After trying it on I first decided to get a medium jacket and large pants, but the salesclerk convinced me to go a size larger on the jacket. As I found out later, during my first cold April sail, I did indeed require all that shoulder room for layers of warm clothes.

Accessories: Seaboots, Hats, and Gloves

Since heat pours off the extremities, anybody going out in cool weather and water should have a pair of rubber seaboots, a hat, and perhaps a pair of gloves.

Seaboots

Many sailors—me among them—can almost tolerate being wet anywhere but in their feet and pull boots on long before they would even think of donning their foul-weather pants and jacket. Of course, seaboots should have nonskid soles. Most boots are shin- or calf-high, but some, used by people who regularly sail in very rough or cold weather, are almost knee-high. The shorter ones are less bulky and, in warm weather, less stifling, but they also offer little protection against water surging high up inside your foul-weather pants and then pouring down onto your socks as you wrestle with a jib on a foredeck plunging into steep waves. Knee-high boots are laceless and so are fairly loose on your foot, providing an insulating air barrier (and a sloppy fit). Most low models have laces so that they can be tightened to fit snugly for small-boat and dinghy racing.

Foul-weather pants cuffs are worn outside the boots and should be kept tight around them to cut off water flow up the leg. If the pants don't have cuff closures, you can make your own by leaving a heavy rubber band or a loop of elastic shock cord over the boot top and pulling it up over the cuff whenever you put the pants and boot on. The 1985 retail price of a pair of good seaboots is about $40.

Hats

Sailors are an individualistic lot, and one place where that's most obvious is in the choice of headgear. Some wear old-fashioned PVC sou'westers, whose long front and back brims protect the face and neck—at some sacrifice to good vision. Others like hoods, which keep the hair and ears dry but make it difficult to communicate and gauge wind direction when steering. (Hoods also funnel warm body heat, which fogs up eyeglasses.) A few sailors, myself among them, try to get by with wool watch caps, which continue to insulate long after they're soggy. No hat is perfect, as you can discover through endless experimentation. Fortunately, no hat costs much more than about $10 either, so experimentation won't break your budget.

Gloves

It used to be that the only gloves sufficiently waterproof to keep sailors' hands dry and warm were rubber gardeners' gloves, but the development of the outdoors clothing industry has, among other benefits, spawned whole lines of waterproof and water-repellent gloves lined with pile or bunting. These gloves cost $15 to $25 at good sporting goods stores.

How to Take Care of Foul-Weather Gear

With a little bit of care, a urethane suit may enjoy a lifetime of four or five years of moderate to heavy use, thirty to fifty days a year. PVC and neoprene suits should stay waterproof even longer. Maintaining gear is quite simple. After a saltwater wetting, hose it down (inside and out) to eliminate all those crystals that, when dry, will only absorb more moisture. Wash off accumulated dirt according to the manufacturer's instructions, using soap flakes. To keep dark nylon liners and shells from bleeding onto lighter-colored fabrics, thoroughly dry the gear before hanging it in a crowded locker.

If we are to believe the astonishing stories that manufacturers tell, consumers apparently understand the word *waterproof* to have talismanic value. Every year warranty claims come in from people who think that suits should resist all leaking even after being ripped, dry-cleaned, or doused with harsh chemicals, such as acetone. Read labels carefully, not only before buying your gear but also before cleaning; some fabrics require special care. The manufacturer can fix rips and leaky seams, which you can locate by tying off the cuffs and filling the garment with water. PVC is the easiest material to patch up; PVC repair kits are often sold in chandleries.

Like your foul-weather suit, seaboots, hats, and gloves should be rinsed out occasionally with fresh water and then thoroughly dried. Most boot rips and holes can be repaired temporarily with heavy tape or more permanently with tire-patching material or even silicone sealer.

All right, now you know something about the variety of inner and outer clothes that sailors can wear. What should *you*, sailor, take aboard, and where should you put it?

CHAPTER 3

What Clothes
to
Take Aboard

When choosing clothes to carry with you, either to take aboard a cruising boat or to leave in the car while you're boardsailing or daysailing in a small boat, think about the needs and functions they must satisfy. In particular, try to anticipate the range of temperature and dampness, and plan accordingly. In this chapter, we'll survey different types of containers for carrying clothes aboard, then go on to look at some questions you should ask yourself when packing. We'll discuss "layering"—a way of dressing for cool, wet weather. Finally, we'll end with some sample packing lists for different types of sailing.

The Ubiquitous, Essential Seabag

Pack your gear in a flexible container that (1) can be folded up and stuck out of the way once you've put your clothes in a locker (boats aren't equipped with suitcase closets) and (2) provides quick access to all your clothes if, as sometimes happens, there are no lockers on board and you must live out of your bag. As in so many other aspects of sailing, you'll need some specialized equipment here, since for a variety of reasons normal shoreside luggage just won't work. A hard-sided suitcase meets the second requirement—easy access—but not the first—collapsibility. A camp or army duf-

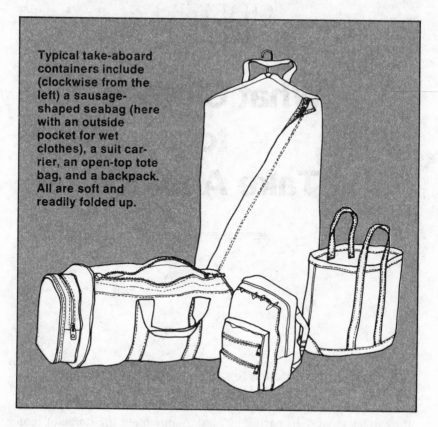

Typical take-aboard containers include (clockwise from the left) a sausage-shaped seabag (here with an outside pocket for wet clothes), a suit carrier, an open-top tote bag, and a backpack. All are soft and readily folded up.

fle bag with a drawstring or snap opening at one end meets the first but not the second. And an open-ended canvas tote bag satisfies both needs, but because it can't be closed your stuff may spill out when the boat heels.

The only container that meets both requirements is the mariner's old standby, the sausage-shaped seabag. Modern versions may be square or rectangular, but regardless of their shape all seabags have a long opening secured by buttons, snaps, or a zipper that provides quick access to the contents. A seabag's nonrigid construction permits it to be folded up out of the way.

With the rediscovery of simple, traditional outdoors gear, seabags are now available in synthetic fabrics from a variety of stores and mail-order firms. When selecting one, don't skimp on size; you'll always want to be able to take a lot of clothes. Look for a large, waterproof, recessed container for wet clothes and some inside pockets for valuables. For best security, the handles, which take a big load, should be extensions of heavy straps that extend all the way around the bag. The zipper should be heavy plastic or coated steel. Seabags designed for offshore use may have a Velcro flap over the zipper to forestall leaks.

A single medium-sized seabag, 9 by 26 inches, should suffice for all the sailing clothes you need for a short cruise in warm weather. Take two for longer cruises or cool or wet weather, when you'll have bulky sweaters or pile clothing and plenty of underwear, socks, shorts, and shirts. Being a bit of a fanatic about both warmth and efficient gear stowage, I have accumulated several seabags and duffles that I pack to within an inch of explosion with plenty of back-up clothes. A medium-sized sausage bag is big enough for an afternoon daysail or a warm-weather weekend cruise. For longer or cooler trips, I use a big PVC-coated 15-by-19-inch bag. On cruises, each of my sons carries his own color-coded, medium-sized seabag and an open-ended canvas tote bag, 13 by 21 inches, for snacks, books, games, the cassette player, tapes, and other odds and ends that he'll need in a hurry.

Stowing Shore and Foul-Weather Gear

Since seabags and duffles aren't rigid enough to keep nice clothes wrinkle-free, carry jackets, ties, pressed pants, skirts, and shirts in a flexible suit-carrier, which you can hang in the ship's main hanging locker. If you're worried about leaks or moisture (which will cause natural fabrics to mildew and some synthetics to run), stick the carrier's hanger hook through the bottom of a large plastic garbage bag and pull the bag down around the clothes. Leather shore shoes, if stowed in the bottom of a locker, are too easily forgotten and left to mildew; wrap them in a heavy garbage bag with the throat tightly sealed.

Foul-weather gear should not be carried around with the other clothes in the seabag both because it takes up too much room and because it may be carrying salt crystals, those breeders of dampness and mildew. Instead, roll the jacket and pants up tightly and stick each in a seaboot, then tie the two boots together with a two-foot length of light line (I use my knife lanyard) and drape the bundle over a free shoulder as you walk to the boat so that both hands are left free for other luggage. On board, unpack and hang up the gear in a designated hanging locker. Because foul-weather gear is prone to dampness, this locker should not be (but unfortunately often is) the same one reserved for shore clothes.

What Clothes Do You Need?

The first answer to this question always is, "More than you think." But exactly what kind of "more" you take along depends on the weather (which you can only guess at) and your own physical capabilities (which you probably know fairly well). So as you sit in your bedroom contemplating the open seabag lying there ready to be filled, ask yourself the following questions.

✓ **"How wet will I get?"** Always assuming that there will be spray, carry along a windbreaker, a water-repellent jacket, or, better yet, a waterproof foul-weather jacket. Take at least one extra set of dry socks for each day you'll be out there. If there's *any* chance of getting soggy, take foul-weather pants, seaboots, and a full set of back-up dry clothing.

✓ **"How cold will I get?"** Remember that the water temperature is almost always lower than the air temperature. Air that is sweltering on shore may be barely tolerable out on the lake or sound. Remember, too, the wind-chill factor. Each knot of apparent wind (the wind felt on the moving boat) lowers the temperature a sailor on board feels by about one degree. Therefore, when the air temperature is 80 degrees and the true wind (the wind felt on a stationary object) is 12 knots, the felt temperature is 68 degrees when the boat is standing still, and even lower when she's sailing into the wind. Since sailboats are rarely standing still, the apparent wind (the wind created jointly by the true wind and the boat's speed) can considerably affect the temperature felt by people on board. When a boat sails into or across the wind (on a close-hauled or reaching course), the apparent wind is greater than the true wind by a little less than her own speed. But when she is sailing with the wind (on a run), the apparent wind is less. For example, on an 80-degree day with a 12-knot true wind, a boat sailing close-hauled into the wind at a speed of 5 knots has an apparent wind of just under 17 knots, and her crew feels a temperature of about 63 degrees. On the same day, a boat running with the 12-knot true wind at 5 knots has an apparent wind of only 7 knots, and the temperature felt on board is 73 degrees, ten degrees warmer than the close-hauled temperature.

Obviously, then, the air temperature you feel on deck varies enormously when you're sailing. While packing, try to anticipate those fluctuations. In an air temperature of 63 degrees, most people would feel chilly without a medium-weight sweater or pullover.

✓ **"How much sun will there be?"** No matter how warm the air temperature is, if there's a good chance of burning—especially hazy—sunlight, take at least one long cotton shirt, such as an old dress shirt or a rugby jersey, and a pair of long pants, like lightweight jeans or sweatpants, to protect your arms and legs. Also pack some sort of head protection, such as a sun hat or a baseball cap. The glare on your eyes may be intolerable without sunglasses. For years I clipped Polaroids onto my prescription glasses; recently I bought and have been very happy with a pair of prescription photosensitive glasses that automatically darken in the sun. However, they do not absorb glare off the water as well as Polaroids do.

✓ **"How long will I be out there?"** Add up the number of days and nights and take a pair of socks and a pair of underwear for each day, plus one dry-weather outfit (depending on the temperature, shorts and T-shirt or long pants and long-sleeved shirt) for every two days. Unless you're sailing in a relentlessly damp, windy place like Seattle, southern Massachusetts, or San Francisco, follow this rule of thumb: for every three days of warm, dry sailing there will be one day of damp or cool weather. Be conservative; fill every nook and cranny in your seabag.

✓ **"How much privacy will there be?"** Except on large boats, cruising in mixed company is not an activity for prudes. Many ocean-racing boats as long as fifty feet have only one big cabin and a tiny head, where you can barely sit down much less comfortably change your clothes. Even if everybody observes a few common-sense customs aimed at allowing some privacy when dressing or washing, you'll inevitably learn more than you ever wanted to know about your shipmates' personal habits and private anatomies. For both your and your friends' comfort, then, think carefully about how revealing or skimpy your swimsuit and pajamas should be. The guiding word is *appropriate.*

Layering for Warmth and Dryness

For a long time sailors dressed for cool, damp weather quite simply: they pulled thick pants and a heavy wool sweater over their normal clothes, suited up in their foul-weather gear, and headed out there aware that their gear would be about 75 percent successful, at best. They knew that water would inevitably leak in from the outside through cuffs and collars, that their perspiration would soak their underwear, and that once wet, they would stay wet until salt sores began to appear. And they knew that there wasn't any alternative.

Since the late 1970s a whole new approach to outdoors clothing, borrowed from such land activities as cross-country skiing and
mountain climbing, has led sailors to expect better performance in
wet- and cold-weather clothes. Instead of pulling on a couple of
heavy natural-fiber layers under the shells, sailors now wear several
relatively light ones, made mostly from synthetics. This practice,
called layering, provides a number of thin, insulating barriers that
can either be increased as the weather gets colder or the wearer
becomes inactive or be decreased as his body warms up.

The classic layering garment is cotton fishnet underwear,
which, on first viewing, looks irrelevant, but whose honeycomb
structure provides hundreds of insulating air pockets between the
skin and the next layer out. Wool shirts and sweaters are woven
more tightly than fishnet, but not so tightly that all the air barriers
are eliminated. The problem with both natural fibers is that they

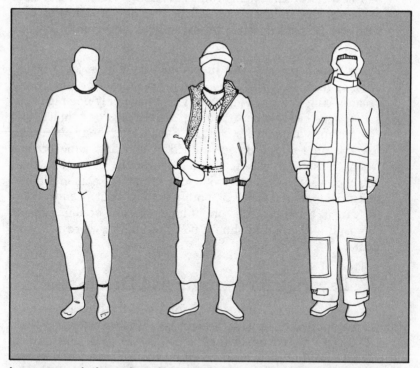

**Layer your clothes when dressing for cool, wet weather. (left to
right) Start at the skin with polypropylene long underwear and
socks, then add a wool sweater, pile or bunting top and pants, wool
socks, a wool watch cap, and bunting-lined waterproof gloves. To
keep water out, top everything off with foul-weather gear and seaboots.**

lose some utility when they get wet—cotton more than wool, but wool still functions best when dry.

As we saw in Chapter 1, compared with cotton and wool, the new synthetic materials—pile, bunting, and polypropylene—insulate better when they are wet, dry more quickly, and are better able to wick dampness from the skin and up through adjacent layers. Instead of a big bag of wool long johns, shirts, and sweaters, an ocean-going sailor now carries along one or two pairs of polypropylene long johns (one light and the other medium or heavy) and bunting and pile jackets and pants, all of which he or she will wear in a variety of layering combinations, depending on the weather. From underwear out, here's how the clothes may be layered:

Layer 1. Warm, mildly damp weather. Synthetic-cotton blend shorts and T-shirt worn under foul-weather gear.

Layer 2. Warm, very wet weather. Thin polypropylene long johns and socks, which wick sweat from the skin, worn alone (or under layer 1) under foul-weather gear. People who are especially sensitive to cold and not very active on deck may prefer medium-weight polypropylene if the wind-chill factor is great. Fishnet underwear is a natural-fiber alternative to the long johns, providing an air barrier through which perspiration can flow to the shirt and pants.

Layer 3. Cool weather. Bunting shirt and pants worn over layers 1 and 2 and, if spray or rain is flying on deck, under foul-weather gear. Bunting also wicks perspiration away from the body and dries quickly. A natural-fiber alternative is cotton fishnet underwear under a wool shirt or wool-cotton blend long underwear. Add bunting-lined gloves and a wool watch cap to keep warm air from pouring off hands and head.

Layer 4. Cold weather. A pile jacket, pants, and boot liners for added insulation worn over layers 1 and 2 and, if it is wet, under foul-weather gear. Add a balaclava (knit cap for head and neck) made of polypropylene (warm) or pile (warmest) to forestall heat loss through the neck and head, and wear polypropylene- or pile-lined gloves. Or, wear layers of cotton fishnet underwear and light wool shirts or sweaters, plus rubber gardeners' gloves over wool inserts.

A Checklist for Packing

As a guide, here's a list of clothing and accessories that I usually carry aboard for four days of cruising in an area where the days are hot and windy, the nights are cool, the seas may be rough, and the air may be damp.

✓ 2 pair cotton socks
✓ 2 pair wool socks
✓ 1 pair polypropylene socklets
✓ 3 pair underwear
✓ 1 pair polypropylene long underwear
✓ 2 pair short pants
✓ 2 pair jeans or corduroys
✓ 3 T-shirts
✓ 2 long-sleeved shirts
✓ 1 pile jacket
✓ 1 light wool or cotton sweater
✓ 1 heavy wool sweater
✓ 1 wool watch cap
✓ swimsuit
✓ deck shoes
✓ sunglasses
✓ a light line to secure eyeglasses

✓ toilet kit: sun lotion, toothbrush and paste, hairbrush, adhesive bandages, laxative, aspirin, seasickness pills, nail clippers
✓ 1 towel
✓ reading material
✓ eyeshades (for sleeping in daylight)
✓ rigging knife
✓ foul-weather gear and seaboots
✓ wallet with credit cards and $50 cash
✓ a small flashlight
✓ a plastic garbage bag for dirty and wet clothes

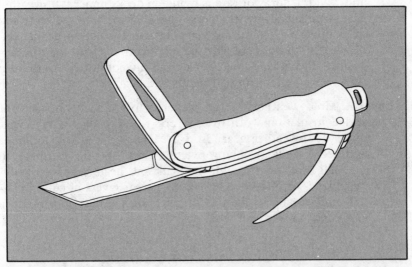

The best sailor's rigging knife has a sharp blade, a spike for loosening knots, a slotted extension for tightening and loosening shackles, and a short tip that can be used as a screwdriver.

Items that might also be included in the seabag are: sailing gloves to protect soft hands, a notebook, and a present for the boat, such as a bottle of wine, some beer, a chunk of good cheese, or fruit.

We've now spent three chapters just talking about getting ready for sailing—chapters that I wish I'd read when I first went to sea. Now let's get out there.

PART II

Welcome
Aboard

———

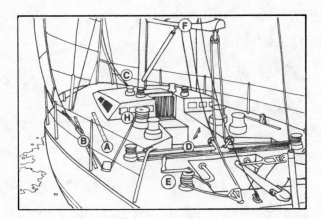

CHAPTER 4

How to
Learn How to
Learn How
to Sail

T he toughest part of going aboard a boat for the first time is dealing with lack of confidence, which naturally arises whenever we try something new. This uneasiness can affect experienced sailors crewing on a new boat just as much as it does neophytes going out for their first sail. It is always much preferable to a cavalier overconfidence, which could lead to crew disharmony, mistakes, and even more serious problems, yet it can be blown all out of proportion. The healthiest way to approach sailing on a new boat is to take for granted the assumptions described in this chapter.

Sailing Is Meant to Be Fun

Even sailboat racing is meant to be fun. And pleasure on a boat means enjoying the marine environment, the company of one's shipmates, physical exercise, and the mastering and performing of some challenging skills both alone and as a team. Sometimes accomplishing a difficult task—especially one that concerns the boat's safety—may require a decisiveness that can hurt your shipmates' feelings. A talented helmsman, for instance, may brusquely take the wheel from a novice in order to steer the boat around a dangerous shoal area. Remembering that enjoyment is the paramount goal should help all parties smooth over any hurts later on.

Sailing Well Demands Alertness

Go sailing to go sailing—not to get drunk. The United States Coast Guard estimates that drinking is a factor in between one-half and three-quarters of boating accidents leading to fatalities. According to the Coast Guard, a blood alcohol level as low as .035 percent —about one-third the .10 percent level generally considered on the boundary of safety for driving an automobile—may severely impair the judgment of a skipper or crew on a boat under way. A 150-pounder can attain that .035 percent limit just by imbibing a couple of beers or a shot of whiskey in an hour.

Long ago I learned that drinking even a can of beer will throw judgment and equilibrium off even on a relatively calm day. I was sailing in my first long-distance race, from Stamford, Connecticut, down Long Island Sound, around a light tower off Martha's Vineyard, and back. As we approached the tower at about 6 P.M., I joined my shipmates in a happy-hour beer, and then went forward on deck to prepare to lower the spinnaker and set the jib for the long beat back to Stamford. The rolling deck, which had been as firm as the Rock of Gibraltar, suddenly became very unsteady under my legs. Instead of walking I had to crawl on my knees. Every job seemed to take twice as long as it once did, and still my mind could not focus entirely. It was an eerie feeling. For a while I blamed it on my relative youth and inexperience with both alcohol and boats, but it has since come upon me again when cockiness led me to toss down a couple of beers while on watch.

It might be reassuring to hear that how much somebody drinks while the boat is under way is a matter best left to personal judgment. Personal judgment, however, is usually booze's first victim. It's better for the skipper to make firm rules before heading out. There will be plenty of time for cocktails once the boat has been safely anchored or docked.

You'll Never Learn It All, but Keep Trying

This is one of the very few sports whose techniques never quite match the demands. Throughout a sailing career we never stop finding new skills to master and problems to solve. This lifelong learning curve is a reason why many sailors stay active well into old age, long after they have given up golf, tennis, and other pastimes. You're a learner, but so is everyone else. Try to learn from your mistakes and from new situations, be tolerant of your (and your shipmates') minor errors, and do your best not to make them again.

Sailing Demands a Routine

Of all the paradoxes and ironies in this extraordinarily complex pastime, the most important is that to enjoy sailing—the most individualistic of all sports—you must standardize your techniques and your equipment and do every job the same way, time after time. The famous military doctrine of KISS ("Keep It Simple, Stupid") is an extremely helpful guideline on a boat. One way to keep jobs simple is to do them the same way every time. Standardization permits predictability: every time you do a job, you and your shipmates will know how to undo it. Standardization also leads to good habits of seamanship.

Now, there is often more than one right way to do most jobs on a boat. For example, of the four essential knots described in Chapter 5, two are used to make loops: the bowline and the double half-hitch. For one reason or another, every skipper and experienced sailor has a strong prejudice in favor of one of those knots for certain jobs, like tying the dinghy's line to the boat. That prejudice may be based on personal experience ("I remember once when a bowline let go in that gale in '73 . . ."), on hearsay ("My dad once told me, never depend on a double half-hitch . . ."), or on authority ("At sailing school, the instructor said . . ."). However it starts, once a conviction or prejudice has sunk its foundations into a sailor's memory, it's likely to stay there no matter how many tornadoes try to lift it out. Therefore, "We always use the bowline on this boat" is not a statement to be contradicted unless you, the new crewmember, are an authority in your own right.

So when going aboard a new boat, expect your skipper, no matter how casual he or she may be ashore, to have a fairly firm routine. (More, *hope* that there is a routine.) And don't be surprised if that routine differs from the ones used on other boats you have sailed on. At first, your desire to relax and leave problems and routines on shore may lead you to be somewhat rebellious when you are told exactly how and when you should do a job. You may feel that you have unwittingly stumbled into a slave ship run by a descendent of Captain Bligh rather than a pleasure boat owned by a man or woman who is (or used to be) your best friend. Some of the expectations that you encounter may strike you as unduly militaristic—until you have a frightening experience in which a firm routine makes the difference between order and chaos, ease and disaster. People who make up and impose routines are generally people who, through hair-raising experience, understand how dangerous the sea can be.

On the other hand, you may be right. Maybe the skipper *is* overly rigid and insufficiently self-confident and allows no room for relaxation. If so, do your best to keep calm or (if the skipper's a good friend) to suggest tactfully that he or she may be pushing a little too hard. If those tactics don't work, try to distract yourself by getting to know one of your fellow sufferers, reading a book on navigation, or projecting your frustrations on a flight of nasty, scavenging sea gulls—and then turn down the next invitation to sail aboard this *Bounty*.

But then again, allow yourself a moment of reflection. Perhaps you're merely oversensitive. People don't like to think they're being bossed around, especially when they are insecure about their competence. Remember what it was like the time you had to teach a subject you knew well to a raw novice. Orders that appear abrupt to you may simply sound matter-of-fact to the skipper. Give the skipper the benefit of the doubt, and you may soon see him or her coming around. By respecting the boat's routine, you're showing your skipper (and yourself) that you respect the traditional, necessary caution of seafaring.

What Kind of Boat Is the Best Teacher?

To learn how to sail with skill and sensitivity takes a long time and many talents, among them good hand-eye coordination and depth perception and a well developed feel for the wind's changing direction and strength. Some people work at it for years but never really master it; most learn just enough to get by safely in easy conditions and become harried and insecure whenever the wind strengthens and the waves build.

The best way to learn sailing is to do a lot of it in many different types of boats and in many different wind and wave conditions, where the need to "change gears" in order to adapt to new stimuli will blow away whatever bad habits and false assumptions you may have picked up in one boat or a single type of weather. The variety of boats available is so wide that new sailors are often confused. To clear things up, here is a quick profile of modern sailing, with some concluding comments about which kind of boat is best to learn in.

Daysailers

These are the simplest boats, ones not equipped with bunks (beds), galleys (kitchens), heads (toilets), and other accommodations for living aboard. But saying what a daysailer is not is much easier than describing what it is. Some daysailers are eleven-foot-long sailboards on which the sailor stands and holds up the sail. Others are boats between eight feet and sixty feet long (an America's Cup twelve-meter is a daysailer) in which the sailor or sailors sit. If it's light enough to be pulled out of the water by a couple of people and carried on the roof of a car, it's called a dinghy, but if it has a heavy keel as a counterweight to keep it from tipping over, it's called a keel daysailer.

Daysailers may be raced against each other with or without time handicaps, and some daysailer classes (or boats of the same specifications) have extremely large racing fleets. But most daysailers (for that matter, most sailboats) are, literally, *day-sailed*—casually sailed around on pleasant afternoons with little concern for speed.

Cruising Boats

These are live-aboard boats with all the bunks, galleys, and so on that allow people to stay on board for an extended period of time. If you live aboard and sail from harbor to harbor during the day, you're *cruising*. *Weekend cruising* takes place over short periods of time like a weekend; *long-distance* or *offshore cruising* means taking long, nonstop trips, or passages, from one harbor to another over a large body of water (like a big lake or an ocean). You can own a cruising boat, or you can charter (rent) one in wonderful vacation areas such as the Caribbean and Maine. Despite their moniker, cruising boats may also be raced for a few hours, overnight, or for weeks across oceans.

Some cruising boats are only twenty feet long, but you need at least twenty-eight or thirty feet to achieve the volume needed for decent comfort for a crew of three or more people. People who enjoy their privacy prefer not to cruise with more than three other people in a boat smaller than thirty-five feet, or with more than five others in one smaller than forty feet. Bill Robinson, my former boss at the old *Yachting* magazine, strongly recommends that if two or more couples are aboard, the boat should have two heads to allow the greatest flexibility for the most private of all functions.

Most of this book is about cruising, on the assumption that cruising is what most sailors want to do.

How to Become a Better Sailor

So what's the best way to learn? You can take all the classroom courses you want, but the lessons really won't begin to sink in until you get out on the water with a standard to measure yourself against. One good standard is an instructor's watchful eye. You can go to one of the many excellent sailing schools in cities and resort areas. They are advertised in the brokerage section of *Cruising World, Sail, Yachting,* and other magazines and are listed by the American Sailing Association (13922 Marquesas Way, Marina del Rey, CA 90292) and the National Association of Sailing Instructors and Sailing Schools (15 Renier Court, Middletown, NJ 07748). At a sailing school, you'll most likely go out in a fast, sensitive keel daysailer with two or three shipmates and a trained instructor, but dinghies or sailboards may also be used. Many sailing schools offer advanced courses in cruising boats to people who have passed the basic sailing requirement.

People who have mastered basic boat handling can either move on to big, heavy boats and cruising (in which case their skills probably won't improve very rapidly) or find another set of standards to measure themselves against. One of these standards is the challenge of dinghy or sailboard sailing. Capsizable dinghies are even more unforgiving of mistakes than a tough instructor; trim the sheet a bit too far, push the helm a few degrees the wrong way, and you're no longer in the boat but swimming next to her. Although they don't have sheets and rudders, sailboards, such as Windsurfers, also make excellent teachers because to sail them you must understand the all-important principle of balance (and I don't mean the balance required to stay standing on the board), which we'll explain in Chapter 6. Those small, wet boats will sharpen your wits and techniques and make you a much better all-round sailor.

Finally, you can hone your skills on the race course in any kind of boat. There, a mistake in sail trimming, steering, or wind reading will be noticed immediately when a competitor moves out ahead. As with any competitive sport, there are limits to racing's benefits. You can push yourself to a frenzy and forget completely that this is supposed to be enjoyable, and there's always the chance of excessive risk taking, such as carrying too much sail in fresh winds. But if you can resist the temptation to push yourself, your boat, and your crew to insane limits, you'll see your technique and feel for the boat and wind improve in huge steps. In almost every area there are enough different types of racing to allow it to be pursued with varying degrees of intensity. Some classes are very intense, others relatively relaxed; you may quickly find the level at which you're most comfortable. Many sailing schools and clubs have racing programs that allow their graduates to charter boats. For more information about racing, contact the United States Yacht Racing Union (Box 209, Newport, RI 02840).

As we've seen in this chapter, getting started (or getting better) in sailing takes a little time, energy, and attentiveness—not to speak of a good sense of humor. Enough on basic assumptions; let's begin learning how the experts do it.

CHAPTER 5

Six Things You Should Know Within Thirty Minutes of Coming Aboard

The special demands your skipper will put on you, and you on your skipper, will depend on the people involved, but on every boat there are six things the crew should know about within a half-hour or so of coming aboard. Three of these concern the cabin and its equipment: where to stow your personal gear; how to work the plumbing and stove; and how to keep the cabin tidy. The rest apply on deck: how the sail-handling gear is laid out; how the crew will be organized; and what to do in an emergency. Experienced sailors usually pick up these routines and gear arrangements on their own, taking a few minutes for a self-guided tour of an unfamiliar boat. Less knowledgeable people, on the other hand, should be given a tour during which the skipper outlines the boat's normal routines.

Whether seasoned or just starting out, if you're new on board and aren't familiar with any of these areas, be sure to ask questions. This is also a good time for new crewmembers to give the skipper an honest account of their sailing knowledge and experience, as well as a brief description of their special abilities (say, with electronics) and physical limitations (for example, a partial hearing loss).

A note to skippers: As we mentioned a few pages ago, it's easy to overemphasize on-board routines to the point of spoiling everybody else's fun. While the good habits that we'll describe are important (and in the case of lighting the stove, downright vital), the points will usually get across much more smoothly and effectively if they are made in a low-keyed, positive, yet decisive way. In situations like this, experts are always tempted to show off by overemphasizing dangers, but an encouraging welcome does not have to include a declaration that the boat will immediately sink if a guest doesn't flush the toilet properly. Some of these routines can be established very easily and quickly by setting an example or with an offhand comment—for example, "You can put your seabag over there on that bunk." Others may require an item-by-item demonstration or—if the directions (such as those for flushing the toilet) are especially important or complicated—written instructions.

Where to Stow Your Personal Gear

As soon as you go below after coming aboard, securely stow your clothing and other personal gear. By securely I don't mean in a safe (presumably, theft is not a worry), but rather in a place where, when the boat heels and pitches, your stuff won't spill out all over everybody else's gear and common territory like the cabin sole (floor). There is so little room in a boat that sailors must follow the advice given by the neighbor in Robert Frost's poem "Mending Wall": "Good fences make good neighbors." Relations in such tight quarters, at best the size of a small kitchen or large closet, must be governed by an unwritten constitution, the first and most important clause of which is, "I'll take care of mine if you'll take care of yours." The second clause is, "Then we'll both take care of ours."

Presumably, you've brought your goods in a collapsible seabag, duffle bag, or open tote bag. If you're aboard just for a day's sail, you may find that a bunk (also called a berth) has been set aside for it and other crewmembers' bags. The bunk should have built-in or cloth restraints called bunkboards or leecloths to keep seabags and, at night, sleepers from rolling out when the boat heels. There are several different types of bunks. Quarter berths are tunnels set into the boat's back part (or quarter) on either side of the engine compartment, whose walls provide a restraint. In the main part of the cabin, a pilot berth is high up on the side, above the cabin seats, which can be converted at night to make settee berths. (The pilot berth apparently derived its name from the fact that professional pilots, who helped navigate ships into port, needed an out-of-the-way bunk for taking naps.) In the forward cabin, there may be a V-berth, which is a V-shaped combination of two bunks joined at their feet.

Before a short sail, the whole crew usually put their bags in a free bunk. But if you're staying on board overnight, the skipper should either assign you a bunk or simply tell you to choose one for yourself, most likely making it clear which is his or her own berth. Unless you brought your own bedroll, you'll be given a sleeping bag or sheets and a blanket. If there's a shortage of lockers for stowing

This sketch of the interior of a Beneteau racer-cruiser shows a typical cabin arrangement. In the foreground to port is the galley. The gimballed (self-leveling) stove has an oven, fiddle rails to hold pots, and a strong restraining bar to keep the cook off the burners. The icebox—its lid has a finger hole—is under the bowl. The deep single sink has two faucets: one operated by the foot pump for salt water, the other operated by a pressure system for fresh. Note the high fiddles around the counter, and the corner hole that facilitates cleaning. In the foreground to starboard is the chart table. The circular handhold in the low bulkhead and the two grabrails suspended from the ceiling provide support for people walking fore and aft. The two vertical bars in the foreground support the deck, and the mast is visible beyond the table. The main cabin table is gimballed so the leaves (which fold down to provide walking space) remain horizontal when the boat heels. On either side are settees that can be easily converted to single berths, and whose backrests cover lockers for clothes and gear. Behind the port settee is a pilot berth; behind the starboard one are more lockers. Long windows and a skylight let in plenty of light. Beyond the far bulkhead are the enclosed head and a hanging locker (closet), and beyond them is the forward cabin with a V-berth over lockers.

clothes, you may be asked to "live out of your seabag," which means that you'll keep your full seabag in your bunk (it can be a good pillow). Otherwise, you'll be assigned a locker—a small cabinet with a locking door, usually built into the side of a bunk.

You can store your gear in a locker in one of two ways. The most thorough is to unload your clothes and then carefully stack them in the locker. It's a good idea to first cover the bottom of the locker with the empty seabag or a plastic garbage bag, just in case water seeps up from the bilge when the boat heels. This is a problem common to modern boats with very shallow bilges; there's nowhere else for the water to go except into your underwear. The simpler way to pack the locker is simply to squeeze the full bag into it, leaving the zipper open on top for ready access. Either way, put clothes that you anticipate needing first near the top, and bunch types of clothes together—say, socks in the righthand corner and T-shirts in the left. Some night you may find yourself dressing hurriedly in the dark, and you won't have much time to search for the clothes you want.

Foul-weather gear and seaboots should be left in a hanging locker, or closet, with your name or initials clearly visible so nobody else takes your gear. On larger boats, there's usually a special hanging locker called a wet locker reserved solely for foul-weather gear, so that semiformal and shore clothes can be hung in their own, dry space. If there is only one hanging locker, protect your good clothes with clothing bags or large plastic garbage bags.

Toilet kits belong in the head, or bathroom, so that all moist objects are isolated in one place. A decent head has several shelves or hooks for these little bags and your towel. Clearly mark your stuff on the outside using an indelible marking pen.

The Biggest Stowage Problem, and How to Solve It

Theft shouldn't be a problem, since you presumably can turn your back on your shipmates (and since you probably didn't bring many valuables along anyway). But don't trust the boat with your valuables any farther than you can carry her; just about every small, slippery object you bring aboard is a prime candidate to slide into some inaccessible corner of the bilge.

Some people have problems keeping money where they put it, so they secrete their wallet or small purse deep in the toe of a shore shoe far at the end of the locker or seabag. As for loose change, my friend Harvey Loomis suggests putting coins in a match box secured to the wallet or purse with a rubber band. Eyeglasses can also be a problem, since they'll bounce off a shelf. You can hang them by the string used to hold them on your head over the reading light in your bunk. Better yet, put them in a case between the bunk mattress and the side of the boat or in the toe of a hard leather dress shoe.

Although money and eyeglasses have been the source of many woes over the years, my own big stowage hassle on a sailboat involves another slippery valuable, keys. They can disappear (and have disappeared) as soon as I take my eyes off them. I can't sleep if I don't know where they are. You'd think that sticking them into a corner of the seabag would be sufficient, but keys (at least *my* keys) simply won't stay in one place until they have settled to a rusty grave in the bilge. My most wrenching experience with boats and keys involved an antique Mercedes that I once borrowed. The Mercedes was in Los Angeles, the boat on which its keys were last seen was in San Francisco, and I didn't discover the loss until I had reached my home in Connecticut. The scenario wasn't pieced together until after I made frantic phone calls to people all up and down the West Coast. The seventh call was to the owner of the boat, who was happy to finally learn who owned those keys he had found while cleaning out the bilge.

Here's my solution to the great key problem: on one of the seabag's handles I keep a fairly large stainless steel screw shackle—the kind you must turn to open and close. After locking my car at the marina or yacht club where I meet the boat for the day's sail, I tightly shackle my key ring to the seabag's handle. There it hangs in rattling security ready for me to inspect at any time of day or night. To lose the keys I must lose the seabag, and while I've known of wallets, foul-weather gear, boots, books, clothes, toothbrushes, and, of course, keys disappearing in boats, not once have I suffered the loss of a blue seabag the size of a large dog.

Lands' End, that superb mail-order outfit, offers a simpler solution to this problem in its canvas Square-Rigger attaché case, which includes a sturdy snaphook for keys and plenty of little pouches and holders for eyeglasses, wallet, datebooks, pens, and other easily lost items. The Lands' End catalog, which is full of other goodies for sailors, is available from the company at Lands' End Lane, Dodgeville, WI 53595.

Getting Acquainted with the Head and Galley

A cruising sailboat has many of the amenities of a house—a kitchen (called a galley), a bathroom (called a head), and so on—but you can't take them for granted the way you do the fixtures in your own home. In many ways, to live aboard a boat requires much the same attention to mechanics, resources, and details needed to live on a farm in the days before electricity and running water. Not only must the cruising sailor adjust to limited supplies of power; he or she must contend with an inhospitable environment and be extremely conscientious about safety.

The head is a marine bathroom, with a toilet and, usually, a sink. Federal and state antipollution laws require that the toilet either pump into a holding tank (which can be exhausted at a pump-out station in a boatyard or marina) or through a small treatment system. These laws are extremely controversial: sailors point out that the pump-out stations often dump a boat's tiny heap of waste right back into the water along with tons of urban and industrial pollution that, in quantity and filth, beggar what a fleet of pleasure boats expel. Some boatowners have been known to ignore the law altogether and pump untreated waste directly into the water. They usually get away with it, since the Coast Guard (preoccupied with more important matters like drug-running, illegal immigration, and boating safety) has indicated that it will not search for illegal toilets. Whether legal or illegal, holding-tank or secondary treatment, the normal marine toilet has one feature that makes it potentially dangerous: a water intake (and sometimes an outlet, too) that can get clogged. With improper use, seawater may back up through the system, flood, and even sink the boat. In addition, the marine toilet's small valves and pipes can get blocked so badly that they must be taken apart and cleaned out by hand—not the sort of chore that most of us relish on or off the water.

So before you use the toilet, make sure the skipper has told and showed you how to use it. In particular, know: (1) how to turn on and off the seacock that closes the water intake valve at the through-hull fitting, where the pipe passes through the boat's skin; (2) what objects may and may not be flushed (sanitary napkins, human hair, matches, and cigarettes are normally outlawed); and (3) how many times to pump the manual flush handle up and down (usually twenty or more swings are needed to clear the pipes completely). Find out, too, how to operate the head's ventilation system —a simple cowl vent or an electric fan—and where the scrub brush, sponge, and cleanser are located so that you can clean up after yourself.

The head's sink and shower use fresh water from the boat's own tanks. The total water capacity varies from boat to boat, and so does the water demand. Since we need only about half a gallon a day, usually there's a large safety factor, but you never know for certain how long it will be before you have a chance to top off the tanks again. If there is a shower, ask how it works and how often you may use it. No matter how liberal the policy is, you won't be allowed to take as many showers as you're used to, so master the art of taking a sponge bath and learn how to live with a sticky body. When taking a shower, keep the water running only to wet yourself down and rinse off. Long hair may have to be washed on deck in "outdoors" (sea or lake) water and then rinsed below in fresh (be sure to clean hair out of the drain). Don't despair: you'll eventually stop at marinas and fuel docks, where real showers are usually available for a small charge.

The galley is the boat's kitchen. It has a sink, a stove, a refrigerator, and storage cabinets. Despite its compact size it works much like your home kitchen. The sink may be dual, with two deep recesses for washing and rinsing. There may also be two water faucets. One leads from the fresh-water system and so should be used as sparingly as the head's faucet. The other leads from the sea or lake. As long as it is not polluted, sea or lake water serves perfectly well when steaming vegetables or washing hands and dishes (do the final rinse in the ship's water). As in the head, these water intakes can malfunction; they should be closed off with seacocks when the crew goes ashore.

The galley stove can be the most temperamental piece of equipment on board—and the most dangerous. In the chapter on the galley we'll have a lot to say about stoves and how to light them without starting a fire or blowing the boat up. Don't even think about trying to use the stove until you are told *exactly* what to do.

While showing you the stove, the skipper should point out the fire extinguishers, the number and type of which, by Coast Guard regulation, depend on the size of the boat. Do not assume from looking at it that you know how to turn on and aim the extinguisher. Take it down from its mounting and read the directions. Check the pressure gauge; if it reads low or empty, tell the skipper so that the extinguisher can be recharged before the cruise begins.

Housekeeping Goals and Hints

The boat's housekeeping routines will be governed largely by common sense, but a good skipper will probably assign certain jobs in order to minimize chances of misunderstandings and hurt feelings. Typically, chores that require specialized skills and experience should be left to people who know them and the boat well; cooking and stowing food are two of these. But old-fashioned janitorial work like washing dishes, wiping puddles off the cabin sole, swabbing the deck, dumping garbage, and cleaning the toilet should be shared by everybody, much as they would be in a well-run home.

The skipper's style of command will determine how this work

is accomplished. Some people prefer to post assignments and job rotations, perhaps after consulting with guests. While that tactic may strike some as unduly militaristic, it has the advantage of forthrightness and clarity. Other skippers choose a less formal arrangement and make verbal assignments.

The third, most usual, and most counterproductive way to get chores done is to wait for volunteers. In the short run it may be the easiest way (since most of us don't like bossing our friends or being bossed by them), yet overall it is less effective than making direct assignments. For a variety of reasons, the same people always seem to volunteer for the grubby jobs, at first cheerfully, later fatalistically, and finally resentfully. They soon begin to feel like martyrs, while nonvolunteers (for whatever reason) become typecast as shirkers. Hard feelings result and, if the cruise is long enough, may eventually surface in passive-aggressive behavior and arguments touching on just about everything except the real matter at hand, which is who's going to do the dishes or clean out the toilet bowl. A skipper who does not enjoy giving orders should, if at all possible, be tactfully pinned down on crew assignments before his laid-back style creates an anything but laid-back atmosphere. If you encourage a little decisiveness, you will, at worst, be subject to that old criticism reserved for reformers: "You did the right thing but in the wrong way." Yet before the day is up you will probably find your efforts somehow rewarded. At the least, you won't get stuck with the dirty dishes at every meal.

Four Housekeeping Hints

1. Keep your mess to yourself. (You've heard that before, haven't you?) There is so little storage space in the typical cruising sailboat that you must live as compactly and self-sufficiently as possible. "Living out of your bag" is the rule of thumb. For weekend and longer cruises, I always take along the largest seabag I own, leaving extra room inside so I can stuff clothes in loosely. For books, games, a bottle of rum, and various loose items, and also for quick stuffing of clothes that I find lying around, I also take along an all-purpose canvas satchel, 8 by 17 by 16 inches, that the L. L. Bean catalog calls a Boat and Tote Bag. (When I was a kid, Boat and Totes were called "ice bags" because they were used to lug ice from the shore to the boat.) And I also carry one or two large, heavy-duty plastic garbage bags for use as dirty and wet clothes hampers.

Your shipmates are no more keen to live with your socks and underwear than you are to live with theirs, so try to keep track of your own clothes in your own area. Leave the satchel in your bunk behind a restraint with its mouth toward the side of the hull so when the boat heels your stuff won't pour out. When you find some of your gear loose, just stick it into the bag. Most bunks are long enough, and most sailors are short enough, that the seabag and satchel can be stuck down at the end of the berth at your feet when you're sleeping. One of my sometime shipmates decisively reminds people of their wandering clothes and shoes by hiding them either in the bilge or in the forepeak, with the anchor. A long search for the last pair of socks should remind a careless sailor to keep them properly stowed.

If your clothes get dirty or damp, store them in a plastic garbage bag that you bring along or, if there is one, in your seabag's waterproof compartment. If your clothes get soaking wet (at least your socks eventually will), instead of draping them around the cabin, rinse any salt water out and either leave them to dry with clothespins on the lifelines on deck or hang them over the door handle of the warm oven. Remember where you have stowed wet clothes; if left too long they will mildew and rot.

2. Never leave an object unrestrained on a flat, high surface. Unlike houses, boats roll, pitch, and heel—and with amazing quickness and force even when lying at anchor. Somebody who was once caught in a storm reported later that even cartons of cottage cheese were potentially harmful as they flew around the cabin. Never put anything down unless you're sure of its stability. Be especially alert about cups of liquids, heavy tools, knives, and glass bottles (glass does not belong on a boat unless it surrounds alcoholic beverages).

Set objects as low as possible, nearest the boat's center of gravity. The safest, most secure place to put items that you're about to use is the bottom of the galley sink. Experienced sea cooks will put cups into the sink before pouring coffee or hot water into them. If the sink is crowded, either hold onto the object or place it low in the boat. Tool drawers should be low in order to minimize the force of their trajectory should they get loose; knives must be stowed carefully so they won't fly loose.

3. Offer to help out, but don't get in the way. You may not be the most qualified person available to deal with the stove's eccentricities, and somebody else may know where the food is squirreled away in the myriad of small cabinets. In any case, as a quick glance at the galley will indicate, there probably is room for only one person, so don't feel offended if the cook turns down your offer to help. Perhaps you can scrape vegetables on deck or—most helpful of all—wash dishes when the meal's finished. But don't put them away until told where they belong.

4. Keep an eye out for the vessel's cleanliness and welfare. The ancient seaman's rule "one hand for yourself, one hand for the ship" applies here: look out for the boat, your shipmates, and yourself with equal attentiveness. This of course means keeping track of your clothes and gear, but it also means that you leave the head as clean as you found it, conserve water and cooking fuel, wash any dishes that you use between meals, shut cabinet doors before the goods inside pour all over the cabin sole, don't use the last dollop of peanut butter. In general, be attentive to your shipmates' standards and needs. This rule especially applies to smokers, who, even more than on land, must be especially alert to the fallout of their habit. They should keep track of the mounds of ashes that form on deck, particularly along the drain ridges in the cockpit seats. And they should not automatically assume that they may smoke anywhere they please. The responsible skipper of a boat with a gasoline engine may set severe limits on smoking, but so may somebody who just doesn't like inhaling another person's exhaust in a cabin on a hot, windless day.

Besides these four rules, the courtesies of common decency will warn people away from obnoxious behavior such as interminable whistling or humming, irritatingly idle and endless chatter, repetitions of the same crude ethnic joke, and other rudenesses that you wouldn't tolerate in your own home.

How the Sail-Handling Gear Is Laid Out

You can always spot a seasoned sailor as the person who, after stowing personal gear below, takes a thoughtful bow-to-stern tour (either alone or escorted by the skipper), and, without being asked, helps get the sheets and sails ready for sailing. More often than not, the novices lounge around in the cockpit drinking beer, totally oblivious to the boat and the work that's going on around them. Even if you're not an expert, you might be able to fool everybody else and win a modicum of respect by finding out as much as you can as soon as you can about how the boat is worked—how the sail-handling and anchor gear is organized, where the emergency equipment is located, and which crewmembers are responsible for what jobs.

Don't assume that you will handle only gear in the aft (rear) part of the boat, in the cockpit. You may well be asked to go forward on deck to raise or lower a sail or the anchor. So walk to

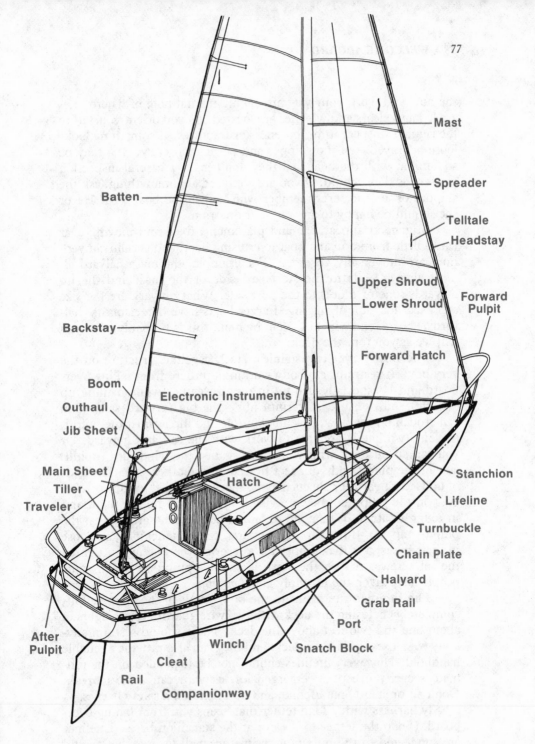

- Mast
- Spreader
- Telltale
- Headstay
- Upper Shroud
- Lower Shroud
- Forward Pulpit
- Forward Hatch
- Stanchion
- Lifeline
- Turnbuckle
- Chain Plate
- Halyard
- Grab Rail
- Port
- Snatch Block
- Winch
- Companionway
- Cleat
- Rail
- After Pulpit
- Traveler
- Tiller
- Main Sheet
- Jib Sheet
- Outhaul
- Boom
- Backstay
- Batten
- Electronic Instruments
- Hatch

The deck layout on a typical racer-cruiser sloop. Variations include a steering wheel, tracks on deck for the jib lead blocks, halyard winches on or near the mast, and a headstay groove for the jib luff in place of hanks.

the bow and work your way aft, taking mental note of where lines are led and cleats and winches are located. As you orient yourself to the rigging, inspect it for looseness or fractures. If something looks loose or frayed, tell the skipper and permanent crew, who may be so familiar with the boat that they don't make a careful inspection as often as they should. If you are confused about anything, ask the skipper or another crewmember who knows the boat well. He or she should be happy to answer your questions.

In general appearance and placement, fixed and moving gear varies little from cruising boat to cruising boat, and certain conventions are universally observed. For example, the main halyard almost always leads to the starboard side of the mast and the jib halyards (one or more) to the port side. What do vary are the size and exact location of rigging. Larger boats have bigger masts, halyards, sheets, and winches. Item by item, this is probably what you will see as you tour the deck:

The bow pulpit is a stainless steel, cagelike structure on the very bow. It restrains anybody working up there from falling overboard and is especially helpful in rough weather while hauling up (raising) and dousing (lowering) jibs—the big forward sails. You can crouch on the bow, bracing your leg and hip against the pulpit, so your two hands are free to work with the sail and halyard. Or you can sit on deck with your back against the windward (uphill) side of the pulpit and your feet braced on the other side. The ends of unused halyards or sheets may be shackled or tied to rope or steel eyes on the pulpit so they are visible and easy to find at night and in rough weather. While you're on the bow, push hard against the pulpit's top rail. If the vertical supports, called stanchions, are loose in their bases, ask the skipper for a screwdriver so you can tighten the set screws. Aft on the stern is another pulpit to which some people have given the ungainly name *pushpit*.

The lifelines run aft from the bow pulpit to the stern pulpit, completely enclosing the deck with two wire guardrails at heights of about one and two feet above the deck. These should restrain anybody who loses balance on deck, and they can also provide a reliable handhold. However, lifelines should not be depended on for ultimate security except in emergencies, as wire can always break. Don't sit or stand on a lifeline, and don't clip on a safety harness— a body harness with a long tether that keeps you from falling overboard. (Snap the tether to the eye at the stanchion base.) Lifelines are connected to the pulpits with line or small fittings that should be tight and taped over. Near the cockpit, a section of the lifelines may be detachable to form an open boarding gate; the hooks there sometimes fall open unless they are tightened and taped. Like the pulpit stanchions, the lifeline stanchions must be securely anchored in their bases with set screws.

On some boats, sail stops or ties (long lengths of webbing) are looped through the stanchion bases forward of the mast before getting under way; they're used to tie down the jib when it's doused (lowered) and lying on deck. Sometimes light line is also woven between the foredeck and the lifelines to make a net that restrains doused jibs from falling overboard. The line should be replaced when frayed, broken, or rotten.

The anchor may be stowed on deck in a small locker or special brackets, or it may simply be tied to the mast or a small fitting. If not on deck, it may be below in a special locker or other container (such as a plastic laundry basket). In any case, the anchor rode (the combination of line and chain that keeps it connected to the boat when it's on the bottom) should already be secured to the anchor with a sturdy shackle. While you're looking at the anchor, twist the shackle pin; it should be so tight that it can be unscrewed only with the leverage of pliers, a wrench, or a spike, and it should be tied to the shackle with a wire or line mousing (several wraps of light wire or nylon line). The rode should be coiled in large loops, preferably with lashings (tape or rope ties) to keep the coil from falling apart.

The forward hatch, granting access to the forward cabin, has two or more latches whose operation you should understand. Some hatches can be unlocked and opened only from below, in the cabin, but others have top- and bottom-operating latches. If it has a good rubber gasket seal to keep water from dripping below, the hatch will lock only when you push or pull down hard on it. Make sure you know the difference between partly and wholly closed; a slightly open hatch will take in water and its lip may snag a flying jib sheet.

The standing rigging includes the mast, boom, and wire stays that support the mast. Stays are made of very low-stretch extruded stainless steel rod or stiff stainless steel 1×19 wire—one strand with nineteen individual wires. Turnbuckles at the bottom of the stays, on deck, can be adjusted to lengthen or shorten the stays in order to keep the mast straight or bend it to improve sail shape. Look closely at the turnbuckles to check for cotter pins that keep the barrels from unwinding and the stays from disconnecting. Two or three layers of tape should cover the cotter pins so that they don't rip sails or ankles. A hydraulic adjuster may replace a turnbuckle on the backstay, which runs from the top of the mast back to the stern. Also inspect the gooseneck, the large fitting that connects the boom and the mast. Sometimes the pin or bolt that is the main component comes loose or undone.

The halyards, on the mast, pull and hold the sails up. With the sheets, they are the main type of *running rigging*. To cut down on windage, the halyards may run down through the mast, out holes near the bottom, to geared winches. The typical cruising boat has only three halyards—main, jib, and spinnaker. To speed up sail changes as the wind increases or decreases, many racer-cruisers (cruising boats that may race) are equipped with three combination jib and spinnaker halyards and the main halyard.

So that sails keep their designed shape, most halyards are made of low-stretch, flexible stainless or galvanized steel 7 × 19 wire rope, which has seven large strands each consisting of nineteen small wires. Wire is hard on hands, so Dacron fiber rope is spliced onto the wire as halyard tails (ends). Lightweight, low-stretch rope fibers such as Kevlar have come into use in place of wire halyards in an increasing number of racing boats and may soon be standard on cruising boats, too. On the outside, Kevlar looks like Dacron rope, but its inside core is yellow while Dacron's is white.

Obviously, it's important to be able to identify and keep track of all these wires running aloft so that you don't tangle them up. Once the halyards are twisted aloft, they will saw away on each other (eventually leading to a break) or jam in the sheave (pulley) at the top of the mast so that they can't be lowered or raised. Halyards should be color-coded using plastic tape in the traditional sequence of green for starboard, red for port. The bitter end (very end) of each halyard must be secured in some way or it will accidentally get pulled up and lost inside the mast. Many sailors tie it to a fitting on the base of the mast, such as a cleat or padeye. The only problem is that the bitter end doesn't rotate as the rest of the halyard twists under torque. Eventually the halyard will develop kinks. By untying the bitter end, you can allow the rope to spin the kinks out. Better yet, besides securing the end, tie a knot in it. The figure eight knot is fairly easy to tie but may come loose if it is allowed to flog about; the simple overhand knot is more permanent. Whichever knot you use, tie it several inches in from the bitter end so if it slips it won't open up.

The halyards should be marked against a reference point with an indelible marker, a piece of tape, or a length of light wire to show when they are hoisted all the way. Otherwise, an overeager crew may pull the shackle into the sheave at the top of the mast and jam it there.

Shackles are small, metal linking devices. The quick-opening ones used on halyards and sheets are called snap shackles; short trip lines make it easier to open the spring-loaded pins. Slower-working but more secure fittings are called screw shackles; they should be tightened more than hand-taut using pliers or a spike.

Blocks are pulleys, either fixed (permanently closed) or snatch (quickly opened). If it sticks, give it a squirt of oil.

Cleats secure halyards, sheets, and other lines. The best are horn cleats—simple metal or wooden bars around which the line is wrapped once, followed by a loop over the top and a locking jam loop. Quick-action cleats, rigged where lines must be freed in a hurry, are the Clamcleat (an open tube with ridges that grip the line) and the cam cleat (with geared locking arms).

Winches are geared drums used to pull heavy loads, such as the last few feet of a halyard or sheet. While one person tails (pulls on the line) the other grinds (turns) the winch handle, spinning the drum. A special type called a self-tailing winch has a built-in cleat eliminating the need for a tailer.

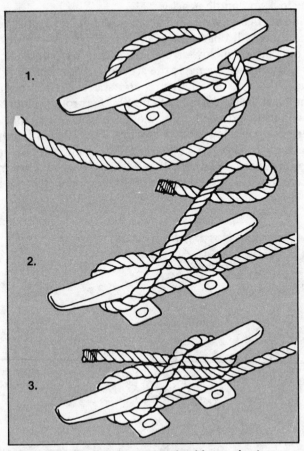

How to cleat a line on a standard horn cleat.

Winch handles are all too often forgotten until they are needed to grind in a halyard or sheet. At least one winch handle must be left near the halyard winches, and at least two should be aft in the cockpit near the sheet winches. They should be stowed in special slots or fabric sacks, into which the halyard tails may also be shoved when the sail is hoisted. You can also put the handles in the cowls (scoops) of ventilators when they're not being used. There are two types of winch handles: lock-in and non-lock-in. A small metal tab on lock-in handles automatically snaps into a recess in the winch when the handle is inserted, and unless you activate a lever the handle will not come out. This provides a great safety advantage over a non-lock-in handle; if a handle slips out while you are turning it, it may well whack you in the face, body, or wrist—and winch handles are both heavy and sharp. If any winch is located in such a way that the handle is likely to fall or slip out, there should be at least one lock-in handle nearby.

The sheets are, with the halyards, the main part of the running rigging. Almost all boats use Dacron rope sheets to pull their sails in and out, although low-stretch Kevlar is becoming increasingly popular. (By the way, *rope* is the stuff on drums before it is cut up and made into *lines* like halyards and sheets.) The jib sheets lead from the clew (back corner) of the jib aft through blocks on deck and to winches and cleats. On most cruising boats, the jib sheets are secured to the clew with a bowline knot, which is both secure and relatively hard to shake loose. When tying the bowline, make the loop through the clew small and leave about 4 inches in the tail, since there may be some slippage before the knot tightens up under load.

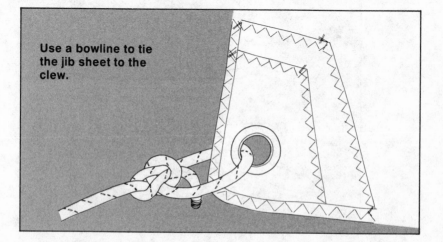

Use a bowline to tie the jib sheet to the clew.

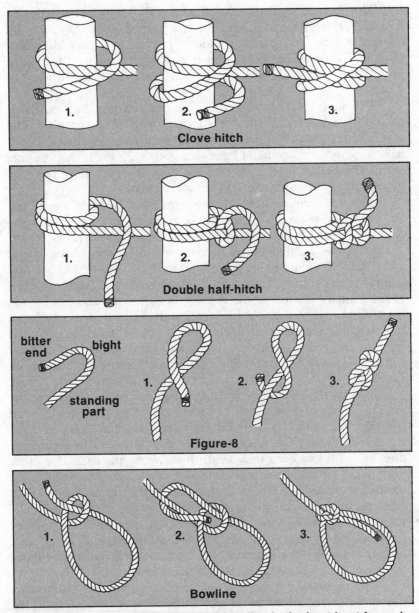

Clove hitch

Double half-hitch

bitter end
bight
standing part

Figure-8

Bowline

How to tie four essential knots. The bowline is the best knot for making loops; the figure-8 keeps line from running out through a block; the clove hitch secures a docking line to a post or a fender line to a lifeline; and the double half-hitch (tied here with an extra turn to absorb some of the load) makes a loop when a line is under load. Leave a long tail on each knot. Other helpful knots are the square knot, the sheet bend, the fisherman's bend, and the rolling hitch.

The jib sheet deck blocks (called leads) usually can be adjusted fore and aft on a track. Each jib has a proper lead for every wind condition. The correct leads should be marked on deck with a piece of tape or an indelible pen, or written down somewhere (for example, "Large genoa jib lead—seven track holes showing forward of block").

The main sheet controls the main boom and the spinnaker sheets the spinnaker. They're attached with snap shackles. The other, bitter ends of all sheets except the spinnaker sheets should have a figure-8 or overhand knot tied in to keep them from pulling out of the blocks when they're slack. (In an emergency, you may have to let the spinnaker sheets out all the way.)

The sail-shaping controls are lines other than the sheets and halyards that affect the shape of the mainsail and jib. One is the outhaul, which tensions the foot (bottom edge) of the mainsail. The outhaul is eased in light wind to make the sail more full, or baggy, and trimmed (tightened) in fresh wind to make it more flat. Another control is the cunningham, which tensions the luff (forward edge) of the mainsail and jib. It too is eased in light wind and trimmed in fresh wind, not to increase or decrease the sail's draft (or fullness) but to move the point of deepest draft aft (when it's eased) and forward (when it's trimmed). The boom vang is the third of these controls—a tackle or hydraulic adjuster that keeps the boom from rising.

Also on the boom is a set of reefing lines used to decrease the mainsail's area in fresh wind. The reefing lines are often led forward from the end of the boom and down to winches and cleats on deck; sometimes there may be cam cleats called jammers to secure the lines after they've been tensioned, thus freeing the winch for other duty. Another important sail control is the mainsail traveler, a car under the mainsheet blocks that slides athwartships (from side to side). Sailing upwind (about forty degrees to the wind) in light air, the car is adjusted so that the boom is over the center of the boat. As the wind increases, the car is let down to leeward to decrease heeling (tipping). We'll have much more to say about reefing lines, the traveler, and sail shaping in later chapters.

The mainsail has three or four plastic or wooden battens that should be inspected when the sail is unfurled (unfolded) from the boom before hoisting. If they're missing, the sail will have a terrible shape; if broken, the sail may rip.

The helm is the last stop on the deck familiarization tour. Learn how the tiller or steering wheel works and where the helmsman sits. (If you show an interest in steering, you'll probably get a chance to do it.)

The instruments include the compass, speedometer, wind direction indicator, and other performance-related devices on deck as well as radios and electronic navigation devices below. Most have digital read-outs; some may be interfaced with each other by computer.

The sail and gear lockers may be on deck or below. They are bins and lockers where sails, sail-handling gear, and tools are kept. Sheets, blocks, and other removable items are often stowed below in the locked cabin when nobody's on board; the crew will have to take them on deck and rig them. Since particular gear probably fits and works best in particular places, a newcomer should ask a crew-member who knows the boat well for advice on what to rig and where to rig it. All on board should know where to find spare line and blocks, a can of oil, a roll of tape, and basic tools, especially pliers, a crescent wrench, and a screwdriver.

How to Work the Emergency Equipment

By emergency equipment we mean any gear that will help you get out of potential disaster: the engine, the bilge pump, the anchor, man-overboard equipment, safety harnesses, life jackets, the life raft, flares, and fire extinguishers. While the engine and anchor mainly serve nonemergency functions, you'll someday have an emergency if you must quickly start the engine or drop the anchor in order to avoid running aground and you don't know what to do. Unlike sail-handling gear, this equipment is arranged differently on every boat, and sometimes it may require special handling.

Although a newcomer might find out about this equipment on his or her own, the best way is to have the skipper explain it during a briefing both in the cockpit and down below. The skipper should take each piece of gear in hand and demonstrate how it works— starting the engine, pumping the bilge, simulating working the flares, and so on. He or she should show where safety harnesses and life jackets are stowed and how to put them on. This is the best time, too, to explain emergency procedures, for example, how to pick up somebody who has fallen overboard (described later in Chapter 17).

It's important that everybody come out of the meeting not only with a familiarity with the boat but also with a sense of community and mutual trust. The briefing should be presented with authority but without intimidation; much of this equipment, after all, may never be used. Crewmembers must be allowed to feel that they can ask any question, no matter how naive it may seem. One of the worst sailing disasters in recent years—a sinking that led to the

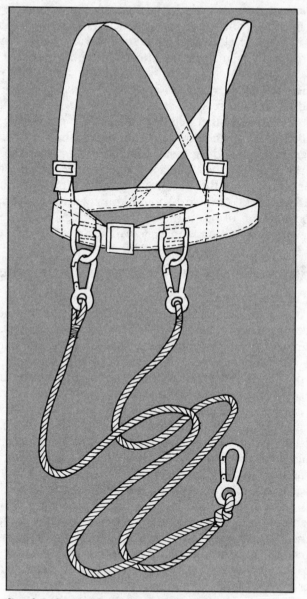

A safety harness provides that "one hand for
yourself" that's so important when working on
deck (or just sitting in the cockpit) in rough
weather. Hook the tether to a secure deck fitting
—not the lifelines, stanchions, or stays—as far
to windward (or uphill) as possible, and keep it
as short as you can so that any fall is not a long
one.

deaths of three sailors—was probably due partly to an unwillingness on the part of the skipper and the first mate to accept their shipmates as partners and to respond seriously to their questions about emergency procedures.

Who Does What

Crew assignments should be discussed during the same briefing. The complexity and seriousness of the table of organization depend on the length of the trip. For a short daysail, all the skipper need do is offhandedly but publicly appoint a second in command ("Bill's in charge if I'm taking a nap"). On the other hand, a cruise should be preceded by some careful planning of navigating, cooking, and cleanup duties, with primary responsibilities being clearly assigned. Of course, this doesn't mean that others can't use the chart table or galley (if they've been briefed about safety problems); it's only a way of clarifying what could turn into a frustratingly unclear situation.

Special skills, interests, and aptitudes can be identified and matched with the many jobs that have to be done. The computer and math whiz probably will learn piloting more quickly than the poet, the one claustrophobic person on board may not be the best nominee for cook, and a strong, agile college kid might be a better candidate for work on a pitching, heaving foredeck than an awkward sixty-year-old. At the same time, all should remember that this is *fun*—not survival training or warfare—and that all should be given a chance to try out whatever they feel like doing, so long as the boat's welfare is not endangered.

This is the time, too, for some straight talk about on-deck routines. If the skipper has strong opinions about some aspect of safety—for example, that all children should wear life jackets, that nobody should sit on lifelines, or that helmsmen should avoid alcoholic beverages—they should be voiced now, firmly but encouragingly. If you're not sure what's expected, ask.

Watch Bills

For overnight sailing—one of the most enjoyable ways to go out in a boat—watches should be assigned and scheduled and watch bills written out and posted. At all times there must be one experienced helmsman on deck and preferably two, since few people can steer well for more than a couple of hours. Besides steering, another concern is sail-handling competence. There must be enough people on deck to handle normal chores like trimming, tacking, and jibing, although somebody from an off-watch may be called to help reef or change sails. The leader of each watch is the *watch captain*.

Watch schedules take a variety of forms. The major consideration is allowing the off-watch sufficient time to fall into a deep sleep
(at least 3 hours) while not leaving the on-watch out on deck so long
that *they* go to sleep (no longer than 6 hours in good weather, but 5
hours in extremely rough, cold, or hot weather).

Using a six-person crew as an example, here are five ways to
organize the watches.

✓ Two three-person watches, each on for 4 hours. Once a day,
the watches run only 2 hours (this is called "dogging the
watch") so that the schedule reverses every day. The same
watch does not stand the murky "mid-watch" of midnight to 4
A.M. every day. (Advantage: simplicity.)

✓ Two three-person watches standing 3-hour watches between 8
P.M. and 8 A.M. and 4-hour watches between 8 A.M. and 8 P.M.
(Advantages: short night watches, when people lose their alert-
ness quickly; self-dogging.)

✓ Three two-person watches each on for 2 or 3 hours, giving the
off-watches 4 to 6 hours of sleep. (Advantages: long sleep periods and a short time on deck; self-dogging.)

✓ Two three-person watches standing 4-hour watches between 8
P.M. and 8 A.M. and 6-hour watches between 8 A.M. and 8 P.M.,
with a dogged watch once a day. (Advantage: allows one long
rest period daily.)

✓ The so-called Swedish system. Two three-person watches on a
5–4–4–5–6 schedule: 7 P.M.–midnight, midnight–4 A.M., 4
A.M.–8 A.M., 8 A.M.–1 P.M., 1 P.M.–7 P.M. (Advantages: variety; short watches after midnight, when people are sleepiest;
self-dogging.)

On some boats, the cook and navigator stand watches, but if
they're especially busy they'll need all the sleep they can get, so
should be counted on only for back-up calls.

Having used each of these five watch schedules, I have found
none to be perfect all the time in all conditions and situations. For
a relatively short overnight sail, the first three work best. For voyages running two or three nights or longer, the last two allow both
extended time for reading and privacy and a lengthy period of sack
time for catching up on the sleep that is always lost during the first
day of adapting to a new environment. Try them all, or create your
own system.

When I began sailing, I quickly noticed that the shipmates who had the most fun as well as the greatest responsibility were the ones who immediately familiarized themselves with the boat and her gear when they first came aboard and who were never afraid to ask questions. This chapter has been about that familiarization tour; the next one is about some of those questions.

CHAPTER 6

"Will This Thing Tip Over?" and Other Reasonable Questions to Ask about How Boats Work

Sailing a boat well is one of the most satisfying of all experiences because it harnesses both natural and man-made elements in a harmony and balance determined as much by the boat as by the way you handle her. The laws of buoyancy and gravity provide a performance envelope—a limit of possibilities—and within her built-in limitations every boat, whether a 50-pound sailboard or a 40,000-pound cruising boat, can tip only so far, cut only so close to the wind, steer only so well, and sail only so fast.

Although many highly skilled sailors can no more explain sailing theory than they can the principles of meteorology, during years on the water they have developed an intuition for how boats work just as they have picked up a feel for weather. Taught that way, those lessons come slowly; new sailors don't enjoy the luxury of so much time. While the details of sailing theory are beyond the scope of this book, we can attempt some explanations in the form of answers to four reasonable and commonly asked questions about how boats work.

"Will This Thing Tip Over?"

At one time or another, everybody who steps aboard a boat of any size wonders if she's going to roll over and disappear beneath the surface, crew and all. For many people, that concern long out-lives the initial, normal queasiness felt when a heeling boat violently changes tacks or blasts over a wave and falls off its crest, like an elevator dropping on the bias. All new sailors start out in fear of capsize; because they never are convinced of the boat's built-in relative stability, many never graduate from it. Depending on the boat involved, the answer to our opening question is either no or maybe. The "no" boats (typical keel, monohull cruising sailboats) are in function and appearance a long way from the "maybe" ones (dinghies and multihulls), and the differences cover a lot more water than whether the boats can or cannot capsize easily.

Stability Through Ballast

Most of the force of the wind acting through the sails is to the side, at about a right angle to the sail's surface. The side force causes the sails and rig to tilt, pulling the hull over on its side, at an angle of heel. Stability is resistance to heeling and it is created by a com-bination of ballast and hull shape.

Ballast serves as a counterweight to those side forces. It consists of either a large quantity of lead or iron fixed in the keel and bilge, or the weight of the crew moving from side to side on deck, and often both. If the ballast balances out the side force, the boat's heel angle stops increasing; if it is greater than the side force, the heel angle may diminish and the boat may swing back upright. Think of a seesaw: heeling is like the effect of somebody sitting on one end; ballast is another person of the same weight who climbs on the other end.

Fixed ballast in a monohull (single-hull) sailboat's keel and bilge puts a boat in the "no capsize" category. Granted, she'll heel fairly quickly—in fact there are few times when she won't be heel-ing—but that doesn't mean she'll tip over. The angle of heel will gradually stop increasing when it's approximately 25 degrees off the vertical, which is usually when water begins to lap up at the leeward (downhill) rail. At that point the fixed ballast deep down in the keel begins to exert maximum leverage on the sails. At a heel angle of about 35 or 40 degrees, which usually is short of capsize, most keel boats will reach the point of ultimate stability. They simply won't heel much farther except in hurricane winds and forty-foot seas (which I assume you'll try to avoid).

To be effective, fixed ballast must make up at least 35 percent or more of the boat's total weight and have a center of gravity low enough to work as an effective counterweight once the boat has heeled about 15 degrees. The heavier and lower it is, the better. Most cruising boats meet these requirements with ease and, while they may at first seem tippy and bouncy, are sufficiently well ballasted to be stable even in very strong winds of forty knots and over, assuming they are being handled with caution and skill.

As we'll see in Chapter 16, limiting heel is not difficult. But if she is being sailed very carelessly, a boat may reach a 30-degree heel angle. With that much heel, an open boat with a large cockpit may swamp (fill with water), yet her built-in buoyancy will still keep her afloat. To keep water from accumulating dangerously on keel cruising boats, the cockpits drain overboard automatically and the interiors can be quickly sealed off with hatches and doors. At a 30-degree heel angle, water will come on deck but not pour into the cabin unless the hatches are left wide open. However, if enough water gets below to more than half fill the cabin, a keel cruising boat may sink. Don't hold your breath, though; it takes an enormous wave to accomplish that disaster.

Movable ballast, as the name suggests, is shifted to keep the

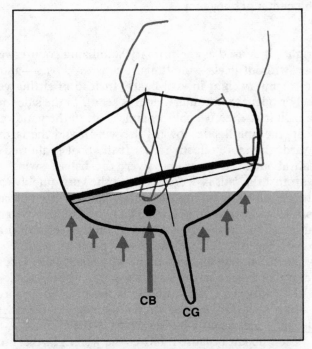

In a keel boat, the center of gravity (CG) created by the heavy lead or iron ballast acts like a lever around the center of buoyancy (CB), which is the locus of all forces keeping the boat afloat. As long as the CG is to windward of the CB, the boat won't capsize.

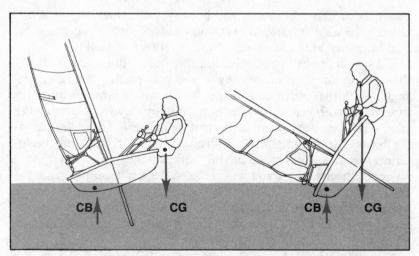

A boat without fixed ballast, like this centerboard dinghy, relies on the movable ballast of her crew to keep the center of gravity to the side of the center of buoyancy.

boat upright. It is used as the primary stabilizing counterweight in light boats without keels—the "might capsize" boats—and as the secondary counterweight in keel boats. Instead of sitting very low in the keel or bilge, the counterweight is set off to the side, on deck. Movable ballast is effective only when it is off to the windward side of the boat (the uphill side, toward the wind), and the farther it is to windward, the more effective it is. If the boat is allowed to heel more than about 20 degrees, however, the ballast swings up, its leverage against the sails is decreased, and she very quickly capsizes. In the nineteenth century, this counterweight consisted of sandbags shoved out to windward on boards. Today it is human weight. The heavier it is and the farther it gets away from the leeward (downhill) rail, the more heeling force it can resist. Boats with large sails require a greater counterweight than one with small sails. One type of human movable ballast is the standing sailor leaning back against the pull of a sailboard's sail. Another is the crew in a more traditional boat "hiking out" as they stretch their bodies over the windward side, their feet held by hiking straps in the cockpit. A third—and the most efficient because it moves the weight farthest to windward—is the sailor suspended on a trapeze (a wire and harness hanging from the mast) with feet against the windward rail. Movable ballast is the major resistance to capsizing in the small centerboard boats called dinghies, which will stay upright while under sail in fresh winds only if the human ballast sits to windward. On some racing dinghies the crew actually outweighs the boat herself, and the ballast they can heave out to windward allows them to carry a lot of sail area in fresh winds at correspondingly high speeds. If crewmembers move downhill to the leeward rail, the boat will flip right over on them. Even though the fiberglass in their hulls is heavier than water, dinghies and daysailers with movable ballast will not sink after they capsize because they're kept afloat by tanks full of air or foam built under their decks; most dinghies may even be quickly righted and sailed away as the water sluices out through automatic drain holes. Obviously, sailing an unstable dinghy is much more of an athletic event than plugging along in a noncapsizable keel boat.

Stability Through Hull Shape

Stability, or resistance to heeling, is affected by the shape of the hull as well as by the amount and location of ballast. Up to a point, the most stable boats are multihulls—triple-hulled trimarans and twin-hulled catamarans—most of which have no ballast at all.

The trimaran carries no fixed ballast, but because she is so big and heavy it would take an enormous crew to provide enough movable ballast to keep her upright. Her stability comes from a three-hulled (actually, one hull and two float) configuration that may be twice as wide as the beam of a monohull the same length. When she sails, the leeward float acts as an antiheeling device, its own positive buoyancy counteracting the side force of the sails, like a lever under a weight. When the heeling force exceeds the float's buoyancy, the effect is the same as if a crew hanging out on a trapeze to windward suddenly lets go: the boat quickly rolls over.

The catamaran is another unballasted multihull that is extremely stable up to a point, at which she capsizes abruptly. Length for length, she's less beamy than the trimaran but still considerably wider than a monohull. As she sails, the leeward hull depresses in the water but the weight of the windward hull and the crew sitting on it pulls down against the side, heeling force; the greater the distance between the two hulls, the greater the leverage the windward one has against heeling. The stability of small catamarans, like Hobie Cats, is even greater because their crews hang out on trapezes, allowing them to carry clouds of sail and go extremely fast. Small cats (catamarans) have been timed at over 25 knots, or 28.75 mph, and a large one has gone 35 knots, or 40.25 mph. (A knot is 1 nautical mile, or 1.15 statute miles, per hour. Just say "knot." "Knots per hour" is like saying "miles per hour per hour.")

The monohull's stability is also affected by her width. If a wide beam helps keep a catamaran upright, it will work for a single-hulled boat, too. Not surprisingly, then, relatively light ballasted keel boats and centerboard dinghies are wider for their length than heavily ballasted keel boats. The cross-sectional shape of the hull is important, too. A boat's hull that is as wide near the water as it is on deck will resist the heeling force quite well until the wind is fresh. But if the beam near the water is very narrow, the boat will heel quickly even in light wind.

If stability were all that mattered, boats would be wide and boxy for light winds and have heavy keels to keep them upright in fresh winds. But boxy hulls also have more underwater surface area and make more water-resisting friction than narrow, slim ones. They are slow in light winds. The yacht designer is constantly struggling to find just the right balance between stability (for safety and good fresh-wind performance) and low wetted surface (for good light-wind performance).

The average, relatively beamy, keel cruising boat should not be allowed to heel more than about 25 degrees for two reasons: (1) an increase in heeling over that amount will make her slow and hard to steer; and (2) heeling causes the keel to tilt up, decreasing resistance to side forces under the water and allowing her to make leeway (slide sideways). For the same reasons plus a third—reducing the chances of capsizing—multihulls and centerboard dinghies should not heel more than about 15 degrees.

To bring any kind of boat back upright, you can decrease the heeling force by depowering the sails—a fancy way of saying, "make them pull less." The easiest way to depower is to ease the sheets way out and let the sails luff (flap), but you may also reduce the sail area by reefing the mainsail or shortening down (changing to a smaller jib). We'll have a great deal more to say about depowering in Chapter 16.

An Example: Why the Winged Keel Worked

The famous "winged keel" that more than any other factor helped *Australia II* win the 1983 America's Cup match is a perfect illustration of how relatively small changes in a boat's shape can have a large effect on performance. This curious appendage, a fairly small keel sprouting slightly drooping lead wings at its bottom, had these four advantages:

✓ The wings lowered the center of gravity of the lead ballast, which increased the keel's leverage over the side forces on the sails and made *Australia II* more stable than her competitors. By heeling less, she sailed faster and made less leeway (side-slippage).

✓ When *Australia II* eventually heeled and her keel tilted up, the leeward wing automatically dropped to vertical and added leeway-resisting area.

✓ The wings reduced speed-robbing turbulence at the bottom of the keel.

✓ With the ballast working more efficiently down low, the top part of the keel could be made smaller. This had the joint effect of decreasing friction and making the boat easier to turn sharply.

Leaving aside the controversy over the legality and national origins of the keel's design (which became so intense that it was called "Keelgate"), *Australia II*'s winged appendage was a remarkable technical achievement. Like most innovations, it was a new solution to a very old problem, solidly based on basic principles that had been well known for many years. Yacht designers had been experimenting with keel shapes for more than a century—adding bulbs of lead on the bottom, changing shapes, reducing or increasing area—but apparently nobody had been able to put so many different pieces together as well as Australian yacht designer Ben Lexcen did in 1983.

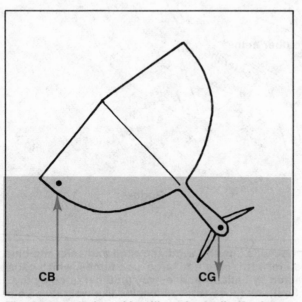

CB   CG

The famous "winged keel" on *Australia II*, winner of the 1983 America's Cup match, is an excellent example of how keels work.

Twelve-meters aren't the only boats that can benefit from a more efficient keel. One of the challenges of cruising-boat design is how to provide a keel that both performs well and is shallow enough for sailing in shoal-draft areas like Chesapeake Bay and the Bahamas. For a long time that combination seemed unlikely, since deep keels have almost always provided more resistance to heeling and leeway than shallow ones. A handful of winged-keel cruising boats appeared within a few months of *Australia II*'s victory and perhaps they'll prove to be successful. However, wings have been banned by many racing rules because of their expense.

"How Can a Boat Sail into the Wind?"

Square-riggers make perfect sense. Their sails are spread across the sky to catch wind from astern, and like hot air balloons, the sails slide through the air pulling everything attached along with

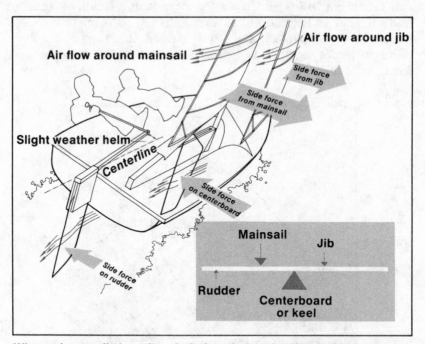

When a boat sails into the wind, the wind and sails combine to create a small forward force and large side forces, which cause heeling (counteracted by ballast) and leeway (counteracted by the centerboard or keel). All those forces combine like weights on a seesaw, and if the sails are trimmed properly and they're in balance over the hull, the tiller or wheel will be centered. In practice, however, it's best to carry a slight weather helm.

them. Likewise, the triangular, fore- and aft-rigged sail works logically when it catches a stern wind. But when it actually pulls or pushes the boat across and even into the wind, the modern sail at first seems to defy reason.

A boat can sail at an angle between 90 and about 40 degrees to the wind because the sails and hull work in partnership to convert the contrary wind into forward thrust. First, the sail, which looks kind of like an airplane wing, shapes the flow of the wind. Where a plain, flat board provides only abrupt resistance, a wing or sail smoothly redirects the wind to create two forces, one large and the other small. The larger of the two forces pushes sideways to leeward and the smaller pushes forward.

Speed + Appendages = Low Leeway

If there were no hull and appendages (keel or centerboard and rudder) in the water, these two forces would combine to capsize the boat or, at best, push her like a leaf mainly to leeward and slightly forward. As sailors put it, she would make about 70 degrees of leeway. For every mile she sailed ahead, she'd slide sideways about 1⅛ mile, and the course-made-good (the effective rather than the steered course) would be distinctly crablike. However, with well-designed, airfoil-shaped appendages resisting most of the side force, the boat would make only 3 to 15 degrees of leeway; her course-made-good would be very near the steered course. The amount of leeway depends on the type of boat and the conditions. All boats make less leeway when sailing relatively fast into the wind in moderate breezes and smooth seas, and more in very light and heavy winds and in rough seas, which slow them down. With her extremely efficient, relatively large appendages, a racing twelve-meter may make 3 to 5 degrees of leeway. On the other hand, the average cruising boat, designed more for comfort than for sailing performance, may slide sideways 5 to 10 degrees; for every mile she sails ahead, she slips between 500 and 1500 feet to leeward.

So, while the sails actually convert the wind's potential energy into a small, forward-driving force, the appendages almost neutralize the wasteful aspects of the wind's leeway-causing side thrust. If the wind is gasoline and the sails are the engine, the keel, centerboard, and rudder act like the wheels to keep the vehicle on track in the right direction. In the next chapter we'll see how the sail controls act like the transmission and throttle.

The size and shape of a keel or rudder has a lot to do with its efficiency at resisting leeway. That was one of the lessons of the winged keel. Appendages that are carefully shaped more or less like airplane wings, with fairly thick leading edges that taper to sharp trailing ones, will resist leeway more efficiently than a flat appendage with squared-off leading and trailing edges. A well-shaped keel or centerboard not only looks but also acts like an orange seed that squirts forward when you press down on it sideways.

"How Does She Stay on Course?"

A boat's balance is the relative symmetry between her hull and her sails. We've already seen two balancing acts—one in which ballast counterweighs heeling forces, the other in which well-shaped appendages resist side forces. Now we'll look at a third—the way the sails and hull are balanced so that the boat can be steered. A boat sails more or less in the direction you aim her partly because the appendages work to resist leeway but also because her sails and hull are balanced, allowing her to be steered on a fairly straight course without too much difficulty.

Balance, Heeling, and Helm

A boat is built symmetrically, the two sides of her hull having exactly the same shape. When she is sailing upright, the water should flow around each side at the same speed and with the same volume. If that's the case, the boat is well balanced and has no tendency to yaw, or steer to one side or the other. A balanced boat behaves like a car whose front end is aligned, whose tires are properly inflated, and whose weight is equally distributed. On a well-balanced boat or automobile, you turn the steering wheel until it's centered and go straight ahead.

Heeling destroys that symmetry on a boat as quickly as letting ten pounds of air out of a front tire does on a car. As one side is submerged and the other elevated, the hull's underwater shape becomes less and less symmetrical and the water flows at unequal speeds around the two sides. This imbalance tends to push the bow away from the downhill or leeward side. Heeling also tilts the mast and sails to one side, which creates a twisting force thrusting in the other direction. So when the boat heels to leeward, the two forces combine to push the bow to windward. (When she heels to windward, which is rare, the bow is pushed to leeward.) Just like the unbalanced car, the unbalanced boat tends to yaw (steer off to one side) and the steering wheel pulls in the opposite direction. To get both vehicles back on course, the steerer must counteract the wheel's pull.

Windward or weather helm is a pull on the tiller or wheel that shows that the boat is yawing to windward. It almost always occurs when the boat is heeled to leeward more than about five degrees,

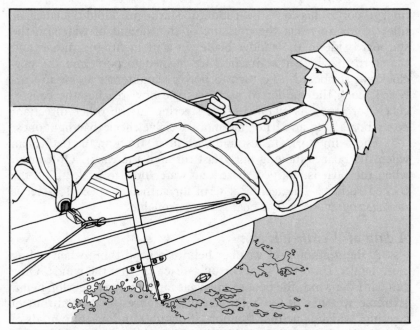

The girl hiked out on this dinghy should pinch or ease the sheet a little to decrease heel and weather helm.

but it may also occur if the mainsail is trimmed too much and the jib is eased out too far. To counteract it, the tiller must be pulled up to windward or the wheel turned down to leeward.

Leeward or lee helm is the opposite. The heel is to windward or the jib is trimmed in too far and the mainsail is eased out too far. The helmsman must counteract it by pushing the tiller to leeward or turning the wheel to windward.

How the Helm and Rudder Work

Adjusting the helm to turn the boat or to counteract weather or lee helm creates its own asymmetry. As the tiller or wheel changes angle, so does the rudder connected to it. Down below the surface, water packs up on one side of the cocked rudder and pushes it and the stern in the other direction. The stern is one end of a seesaw, the bow is the other end, and the fulcrum is about half-way between. So if the stern goes one way, the bow will go the other. Turn a steering wheel in the same direction you want to head, but push or pull a tiller in the contrary direction. Therefore, to turn the boat to starboard (the right) in order to counteract a yaw to port (the left), either rotate the steering wheel to starboard or push the tiller to port. This cocks the rudder to starboard. Hold the wheel or tiller firmly to resist the pressure of the mound of water on the starboard side of the rudder blade. In a moment, the rudder and the stern to which it's attached are pushed to port, and the bow clocks to starboard. (To turn to port or counteract a yaw to starboard, cock the rudder to port.) As the bow reaches the course, check (or stop) its swing by oversteering in the other direction; heavy boats need an earlier and more decisive check than light ones.

The helm works fastest and with least strain on the helmsman when the boat is moving fairly fast through the water. Obviously, when the boat is stopped there's no water flow to pack up on the cocked rudder. The technical term for sufficient speed to steer is *steerageway;* without it, a boat is uncontrollable.

A Tug of Weather Helm

A slight amount of weather helm is a good thing when sailing close-hauled (into the wind) or on a reach (across the wind). On a run with the wind, the boat rarely heels far enough to develop helm. Extreme weather or lee helm can make a wrestling match out of steering, which is neither fun nor safe; with hundreds of pounds of water packed up on the rudder, not only is steering exhausting but also the boat is sailing very slowly. What you want is just a bit of weather helm, with the rudder cocked only about three degrees to leeward. With this three degrees of weather helm, the rudder is working as efficiently as it can to steer the boat and resist leeway. A light tug of weather helm also provides a reference point so the helmsperson can steer without constantly looking at the compass or the sails. Don't worry too much about having the exact angle. What's more important than the numbers is the feel of the helm. If the helmsperson has to fight the tiller or wheel, there's too much helm, and that means four things:

✔ The rudder and sails are fighting rather than cooperating with each other and you're wasting considerable energy that could go into forward drive.

✔ The rudder is making too much resistance and slowing the boat down.

✔ The boat is probably heeling too far and making much more leeway than she has to.

✔ It's time to depower the sails to ease the helm and bring her back upright by changing the trim, reefing, or shortening sail. The greater the angle of heel, the greater the amount of weather helm—and the more the sail area must be reduced.

We said earlier that boats with wide beams resist heeling better than narrow boats. But like all advantages, this one has its price. Because their underwater shapes change very quickly when they heel even slight amounts, beamy boats tend to go out of balance more quickly than narrow ones. In sailor's parlance, they are not very forgiving. So their helmsmen and crews should be especially wary of setting too much sail and heeling too far.

"How Fast Can We Go?"

Speed is a relative thing. Compared with most other means of conveyance, a boat is ridiculously slow. The world sailing speed record is only about 40 miles per hour, and most boats that sailors call fast, like big trimarans, are lucky to break 20 knots, or about 23 mph. The average sailboat is a turtle even compared with humans; a good runner can do a 26-mile marathon in about three hours, but most sailors would be happy if their 35-foot cruising boats could cover the same distance in four.

Despite its relative modesty, a boat's speed is important, if not vital, in several ways: (1) Steering is more sure and rapid when water is moving quickly over the rudder than when the flow is languid. (2) Sailing fast is the best way to minimize the effects of contrary tidal currents. (3) A fast boat can make longer legs and cover more distance on a cruise. (4) A fast boat can beat a storm to port on shorter notice than a slow one. (5) And, being human, most sailors have more fun going fast than slow. Racing, for many, is what sailing is all about; besides the competition, it offers what many consider to be the best classroom for learning the skills of steering, sail trimming, and boat handling.

Planing and Hull Speed

The main limit on a boat's potential speed is the resistance of her hull against the water, resistance that is increased by waves that the hull stirs up. Most boats create waves until they seem to be riding in the trough between two crests, one at the bow and the other at the stern. In a wind of 12 knots or more, a light boat with a large sail area can accelerate up and over the bow wave, slipping across it with her bow flying free and only a bit of her stern digging into the water, like a carpenter's plane sliding across a board. This exhilarating experience is called planing. Dinghies, sailboards, and some lightweight keel boats plane. A few heavier boats have been known to plane briefly in strong winds, and they can also reach high speeds while surfing down the faces of big waves. Multihulls don't plane but rather owe their tremendous speeds to their slim, low-

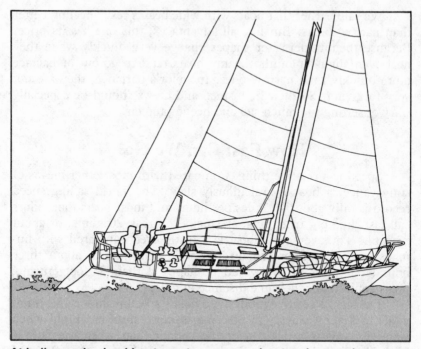

At hull speed, a keel boat creates a wave about as long as her waterline length. She can't climb up and over it unless boosted by a wave from astern.

resistance hulls, which create relatively small, nonlimiting waves.

The maximum speed of a nonplaning boat is a function of her length, and for that reason it's called her hull speed. A wave (and any object on it) can only go at a speed equal to the product of 1.34 and the square root of the distance between its crests. To use that formula when figuring hull speed, take the square root of the boat's waterline length—the distance between the forwardmost and aftermost points where the hull normally touches the water—and multiply it by 1.34. Granted, a heavy boat may exceed her hull speed when surfing or planing down a wave or when sailing in perfectly smooth water, but most of the time the best she can do is the result of the following formula:

$$\text{hull speed in knots} = 1.34\sqrt{\text{waterline length in feet}}$$

The waterline length (abbreviated LWL for *load waterline*) is one of the dimensions listed with a boat's plans in the design sections of many boating magazines. If it is 33 feet (which is about right for a boat with an overall, or on-deck, length of 40 feet), the square root of its LWL is 5.75 and the hull speed is 7.7 knots. If 25 feet (the LWL of a modern-day 30-footer), the hull speed is 6.7 knots.

The hull speed, remember, is the maximum theoretical speed of a nonplaning (or displacement) monohulled boat. It applies neither to a boat that is planing nor to a multihull, whose performance is limited by whether the crews can keep them from capsizing. When well sailed by expert crews in optimum conditions, both those types may sail faster than twice the square root of their overall length.

How to Predict Average Speeds

Because the typical cruising boat rarely sails in enough wind or is pushed sufficiently hard by her crew to achieve her hull speed, an estimated average speed is more indicative of her performance. In his exhaustive treatise on modern yacht design, *The Offshore Yacht*, A. T. Thornton figures that the average speed of a cruising or racing monohull or cruising multihull may be between 0.8 and 1.0 times the square root of the waterline length, or:

$$\text{average speed in knots} = 0.8 \text{ to } 1.0 \sqrt{\text{waterline length in feet}}$$

For a boat with a 33-foot waterline length, that's 4.6 to 5.8 knots; for one with a 25-foot LWL, it's 4 to 5 knots. For racing multihulls, Thornton estimates an average speed of between 1.2 and 1.5 times the square root of the waterline length of the longest hull.

Keeping in mind that the engine is powerful enough to push a cruising boat at about that speed in a calm, the lower ranges of Thornton's figures for cruising monohulls sound about right for cruising under power or sail (or both) in typical North American conditions, where the wind is usually very light in the morning and blowing 10 to 15 knots in the afternoon. If you're racing or doing a lot of sailing off the wind in fresh breezes, the higher figure may be more accurate.

So much for theory. Now let's trim the sails.

CHAPTER 7

The Willful Wind
and
How to Use It

A little theory goes a long way toward developing an understanding of how a sailboat works, but getting in the boat and actually going sailing is more fun. In this chapter we'll climb into the cockpit, get our hands on the sheets and the helm, and trim the sails and steer the boat. We'll see how the sail controls work and what to do with them to shape the sails properly for fast, controlled sailing in light, medium, and fresh winds. Using step-by-step instructions we'll tell how the helmsperson and crew handle the boat, sailing both into the wind and with it. First, though, we'll have to understand how to look at the wind and its effect on the sails—and the sails' effect on it.

The terminology may at first sound unfamiliar and arcane. I'll try to define terms as I go along, but if you get confused, stop for a moment and consult the glossary.

The Infuriatingly Variable, Absolutely Essential Apparent Wind

Many sailors, even experienced ones, never come to understand sail trim because it is so maddeningly variable in its demands. The wind (to quote Scripture) "blows where it wills," the boat's course is rarely steady, and the interrelationship between the sails and their spider's web of lines is complex. All in all, the wind is much less reliable than, say, the numbers shown on the magnetic compass, which mirror the almost immutable relationship between the globe and the earth's magnetic field. From year to year, the compass direction from any point on earth to the locus of the magnetic field, which is called magnetic north, varies by less than one degree, or 0.2 percent of the 360-degree dial. On the other hand, the angle between boat and wind is rarely stable from second to second; it can and frequently does change 180 degrees (one-half the 360-degree sweep of the compass dial) in a matter of moments, leaving the sail-trimmer to try to pick up the pieces. Coping with this variability is often frustrating, but it lies so close to the soul of sailing that we must try to come to terms with it and identify what few constants are hidden deep within it.

True Wind + Course + Boat Speed = Apparent Wind

The main ingredients of the unstable sail-wind relationship are the true wind and the boat's course and speed, which combine to create the all-important apparent wind.

The true wind is the one blowing across the earth and sea. It is indicated by stationary flags and seagulls, which always stand and take off into the wind. This is the wind direction and strength reported by meteorologists, the wind you feel when you first go aboard the anchored or docked boat in the morning.

The boat's course is the direction in which she's moving, under power or under sail, either into, across, or away from the true wind.

The boat's speed is just that—how fast she's moving.

The apparent wind is the marriage of all three in the wind felt on the moving boat.

Moving vehicles like cars, bicycles, and boats make their own wind. Obviously, this created wind doesn't disappear when a true wind is blowing. Depending on whether the boat is headed into or away from it, the boat's speed augments or decreases the force of the true wind as it is felt on board, and may even change its direction. For example, the crew on a boat doing 5 knots under power feels a different apparent wind depending on the strength and direction of the true wind:

> In a flat calm (when there's no true wind), they feel a 5-knot apparent wind from dead ahead (head wind).

> In a 5-knot true wind from dead ahead, they feel a 10-knot apparent head wind.

In a 5-knot true wind from dead astern, they feel no apparent wind at all.

In a 5-knot true wind from abeam (at a 90-degree angle), they feel a 7.5-knot apparent wind from 45 degrees off the bow.

The Five Points of Sail

Besides being the wind that the sailor feels on the face, the apparent wind is the one that fills the sails and creates the side and forward forces that make the boat move. It's the breeze that we trim our sails by. When a sailor says "wind," almost all the time he or she means "apparent wind." Conceivably, there are 360 different apparent wind directions in constant flux as each of the variables—true wind, boat speed, course—alters. Yet over the years mariners have, with typical practicality, reduced these directions to five points of sail—each a family of angles between the apparent wind and the sails. There are many terms in the sailor's glossary that you can forget, but these five are part of the essential vocabulary of sail trimming and steering.

Head to wind (also dead into the wind)—with the bow aimed into the eye of the wind.

Forereaching—with the apparent wind just either side (10–30 degrees) of the bow.

Close-hauled (also beating, sailing to windward) —the closest angle to the apparent wind at which the sails are full and not luffing (flapping), 30–50 degrees either side of the bow.

Reaching—across the wind; either a close reach (apparent wind 50–80 degrees either side of the bow), a beam reach (80–100 degrees), or a broad reach (100–170 degrees).

Running—with the wind on the stern or 10 degrees on either side of the stern.

The five points of sail break down into two families—*upwind* (also *into the wind*) and *downwind* (also *off the wind*). The first family includes head to wind, forereaching, close-hauled, and close reaching; the second, beam reaching, broad reaching, and running.

Eight Ways the Apparent Wind Works

The apparent wind's effect on the boat's performance varies predictably with the point of sail and the wind strength according

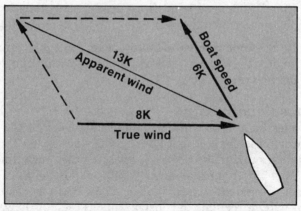

The apparent wind is created by the true wind and the boat's speed. Close-hauled or on reaches, it is further forward and stronger than the true wind.

to these eight rules of thumb:

✔ The apparent wind is the felt wind on the moving boat, but the true wind makes the waves. Often the two will differ and the waves will come at an acute angle to the apparent wind.

✔ When she is sailing upwind (close-hauled or close reaching) or on a beam reach, a boat's apparent wind is greater and further forward than the true wind. As she accelerates, the apparent wind increases in speed and draws forward (or "heads" her). As she decelerates, the apparent wind decreases and draws aft (or "lifts" her).

✔ When she is sailing downwind (broad reaching or running), a boat's apparent wind is less than, but from the same direction as, the true wind. When she accelerates, the apparent wind decreases in speed; when she decelerates, it increases.

✔ If the difference between the boat's speed and the true wind speed is small, the apparent wind will vary greatly from the true wind in speed and/or direction. If the difference is great, the variation will be small. Therefore, relatively fast boats change light true winds dramatically and fresh true winds slightly. Relatively slow boats change light true winds less dramatically and fresh true winds hardly at all.

✔ In light winds (1–8 knots true), most boats will sail fastest on a close reach.

✓ In moderate winds (9–15 knots true), the fastest point of sail usually is a beam reach.

✓ In fresh winds (16–22 knots), a boat usually sails fastest, and under the most control, on a beam to broad reach.

✓ In strong and gale-force winds (23–40 knots true), the fastest and most controllable point of sail usually is a broad reach.

As you sail, keep asking yourself, "Where's the true wind? What is the boat's effect on apparent wind? How does the apparent wind change as I head up or bear off? How could I be sailing faster or more comfortably?" Experiment with different courses and note your impressions of their effects. If you keep these guidelines in mind and stay alert, you'll soon find yourself developing a sixth sense for the boat and wind that will make sailing even more pleasurable and safe.

How to Trim Sails

The sails must be shaped properly to use the apparent wind well. They have a shape built in by the sailmaker as panels of Dacron, Mylar, Kevlar, and nylon cloth are sewn together, but since changing wind strengths and points of sail require different sail shapes, and since sailcloth stretches, several ingenious but simple adjusting devices called sail controls have been devised to help the crew make the sails work most effectively. Back in Chapter 5 we took a tour on deck and looked at the maze of lines and other equipment used to hoist and trim sails. Now let's see how they affect sail shape. Line by line, here are the sail controls and how they can be adjusted on each point of sail in light, medium, and fresh winds:

Mainsail Controls

The main sheet is a line that runs from the boom to the cockpit through several blocks, which decrease the load and facilitate adjustment. The sheet pulls both sideways and down on the boom. Trimming the sheet pulls the boom to windward until it is over the main sheet blocks on deck; then, further trimming pulls down on and flattens the sail. Easing the sheet lets the boom out to leeward and makes the sail more full, or round. These rules of thumb usually apply in light to moderate winds (1 to 15 knots true):

✓ **Running and reaching.** Ease the sheet until the luff (forward edge) of the sail luffs (flaps or bubbles), then trim it back until the flap or bubble is barely eliminated.

✓ **Close-hauled.** Trim the sheet until the leech (aft edge) twists (curves to leeward) about 5 degrees. The twist is right if the top batten is about parallel to the boom. The luff of the sail may be just bubbling.

The traveler is an athwartships (sideways) running deck track in which the main sheet blocks slide back and forth on a car. Adjusting the car changes the angle the boom and sail make to the wind when sailing close-hauled or on a close or beam reach, and provides the quickest way to decrease heel and weather helm and so bring the boat back into balance. The traveler has no effect on the other points of sail when the boom is eased well out to leeward.

✓ **Beam and close reaching.** Keep the traveler car under the boom as the sheet is eased in order to keep the boom from lifting.

✓ **Close-hauled.** In light and moderate apparent winds, pull the traveler car up to windward so the boom is over the centerline

(left to right) Close-hauled sail trim for light, medium, and strong winds. As the wind builds, the sails are trimmed farther outboard with more twist.

(the imaginary line running fore and aft between the center of the transom and the headstay). But ease the car to leeward if the boat slows or if weather helm increases beyond about 3 degrees; in fresh to strong apparent winds, adjust the car until the helm is right, trimming the main sheet slightly as you ease the traveler car down.

The boom vang is a tackle or adjustable rod that controls the rise and fall of the boom. Close-hauled, it should be slack so that the main sheet can pull the boom down or ease it up. Otherwise, it should be tight enough so that the leech twists off about 5 degrees —slightly more in light wind and slightly less in fresh wind.

The outhaul is a line running from the aft end of the boom to the clew (aft lower corner) of the sail; it's used to adjust the shape of the foot (bottom one-third) of the mainsail. When tightened, it flattens the sail and decreases side and forward forces. When loosened, it makes the sail fuller and increases side and forward forces. For best performance, the sail should look as follows:

✓ **Running.** Moderately full with the outhaul eased some of the way (the foot should have shallow wrinkles).

✓ **Broad reaching.** Very full with the outhaul eased almost all the way (the foot should be wrinkled).

✓ **Beam and close reaching.** In light and moderate apparent winds, moderately full; in fresh apparent wind, slightly full with the outhaul eased a little (the foot should not be wrinkled).

✓ **Close-hauled.** In light apparent wind, moderately full; in moderate apparent wind, slightly full; in fresh apparent wind, flat with the outhaul pulled out all the way (tension lines should appear along the foot when the sail is luffing).

The cunningham is a line used to increase or decrease tension along the luff of the sail. Unlike the outhaul, the cunningham does not control the amount of draft, but rather affects the fore and aft position of the point of deepest draft. The mainsail is built with this point about half-way between the luff and the leech (its forward and aft edges), but a high apparent wind—the kind that occurs when a boat is close-hauled in moderate to strong winds—causes stretch in the sail, which blows the draft too far aft. Tightening the cunningham pulls the draft back forward again. Two guides to use are the wrinkles in the luff and the angle of the battens: tighten the cunningham until the luff is just free of wrinkles and the cloth curves smoothly from luff to leech without a knuckle at the forward edge of the battens.

Reefs decrease the sail area in fresh and strong apparent winds, when the angle of heel and weather helm are extreme. A reef is taken in by lowering the halyard several feet, tying the bottom part of the sail to the boom with reef lines led through cringles (steel-reinforced holes in the luff and leech), and pulling the sail up tight again. Most cruising boats carry two or three sets of reef cringles, allowing the sail area to be decreased by almost one-half in a matter of minutes.

The topping lift (which holds up the boom), while not a sail-shaping control, should be loose after the sail is set. If it's tight, the main sheet cannot be trimmed far enough.

Jib Controls

The jib sheet is a draft-adjusting line that works like a combined outhaul and main sheet. It pulls the jib's clew (aft corner) aft and the leech (aft edge) down to flatten the sail.

✓ **Running and reaching.** Ease the sheet until the luff starts to bubble, then trim it back in until the bubble just disappears.

✓ **Close-hauled.** Trim the sheet so that there is about 5 degrees of twist (curve) along the leech and so that the sail is very full (light apparent wind) to quite flat (fresh apparent wind). An overlapping genoa jib should not be trimmed closer than about 2 inches off from the tips of the spreaders. If the mainsail is properly trimmed but luffing over its forward one-third, the genoa sheet is probably trimmed too tight and the sail is back-winding the mainsail (directing the wind into its leeward side and making it luff badly). Ease the jib sheet slightly.

The jib sheet leads are adjustable blocks through which the sheets pass. They determine the relative amount of aft and downward pull by the sheet and its athwartships angle. When the jib lead is adjusted properly, the jib should luff (flap) at the same time all along its luff as the boat heads up into the wind or the jib sheet is eased. If the top of the sail luffs first, slide the jib sheet lead slightly forward. If the bottom luffs first, slide the lead slightly aft. On reaches and runs, move the jib lead outboard to the rail and forward. Upwind in light wind, move the jib lead as far inboard as possible; as the wind increases, move it outboard toward the rail to decrease heeling forces.

The jib halyard, besides hauling and keeping up the jib, can be used like the mainsail's cunningham control. Tighten the halyard to move the point of deepest draft forward and ease it to allow the draft to go aft. The jib's point of deepest draft should be just forward of halfway between the luff and leech, and there should be tiny wrinkles all along the luff.

Reefs decrease the area of some specially-designed jibs, either by bunching up the bottom part of the sail or by rolling up some of the luff area.

Steering and Boat Handling on the Points of Sail

The points of sail make many demands on crews. Here is some advice on the advantages and challenges of each point.

Head to Wind and Forereaching: The Utility Headings

These two points of sail don't provide speed. Rather, they are utility headings that either stop a boat or slow her down so that the crew can set and douse sails, anchor, pick up a mooring, or rest.

Head to wind, as the name suggests, leaves the bow pointed directly into the eye of the wind with the sails luffing (flapping); the boat has no way on (is stopped dead in the water). Heading into the wind is the best way to stop a boat quickly in order to anchor, dock,

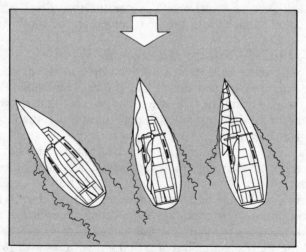

Dousing the jib (left to right). The best way to raise or douse the jib is to head up from a close-hauled course until the boat is forereaching. However, drop the mainsail when heading into the wind.

or pick up a mooring. It's also the point of sail to be on when hoisting and lowering the mainsail. Watch out, though: the sails can bang around quite violently, and somebody may be whacked by the flying boom, sliding traveler car, or flailing jib sheet.

Once she's stopped dead into the wind with mainsail and jib hoisted, getting her moving again with steerageway (enough speed to steer) requires getting the bow to swing about 40 degrees either side of the true wind's eye so the jib can fill. A full jib will create some steerageway. When getting going under sail from a mooring, back the jib (pull its clew to one side to catch wind and push the bow off the other way). Gathering steerageway with only the mainsail hoisted may be difficult. Try to back the mainsail by pushing the boom to one side. Once she's sailing backwards, steer the bow either side of the wind's eye by adjusting the helm *opposite* to the way you'd push or pull it when sailing forward (think of turning a car steering wheel when backing into a parking space).

Forereaching is the point of sail just either side of head to wind. This is when the bow has fallen off 10 to 30 degrees from the true wind and the boat is jogging along slowly on port or starboard tack with her sails partially filled, partially luffing. Forereaching is the best point of sail to be on when hoisting and lowering the jib, since the sail will bang around the mast violently if you're head to wind. This is also the best point of sail for slowing the boat down without absolutely stopping her: just head up from a close-hauled course until the sails luff a bit. Be careful not to tack accidentally and be caught aback (with the jib trimmed on the windward side).

Close-Hauled Sailing: Hard on the Wind

When you're sailing at a narrow angle to the apparent wind and the sails are trimmed almost flat, you're close-hauled. Your own speed is augmenting the true wind, and with all that apparent wind whistling through the rigging you may think this is the fastest point of sail. But because the sails' forward force is very small compared with the side forces, and because the boat must climb not only into the wind but also through waves coming at her, sailing close-hauled is almost always slower than reaching and running (except when sailing in light wind and smooth water). Other terms for close-hauled sailing—*on the wind, upwind, beating to windward,* and *working to windward*—tell how a close-hauled boat is not only sailing toward the wind's source but also doing it with some effort.

Close-hauled means "with sheets and sails trimmed tight." The sails have to be pulled in pretty far and set quite flat because the angle of attack to the wind is narrow (generally speaking, the farther off the wind the boat is sailing, the farther out the sheets are eased and the fuller the sails are set). The optimum angle of attack varies from boat to boat and condition to condition. Relatively fast boats, such as racing dinghies and catamarans, sail well at fairly wide angles of attack—about 40 degrees to the apparent wind. Nonplaning boats, like the average racer-cruiser or cruising boat, sail narrower—about 35 degrees. And boats with extremely efficient rigs and appendages, like twelve-meters and ocean racers, can sail closer still.

When sailing close-hauled in a moderate to fresh apparent wind, don't become so obsessed about optimizing sail shape that you forget about balance. If it's trimmed too flat or if the traveler is pulled too far to windward, a sail—no matter how terrific it looks—may cause excessive heel and, consequently, unmanageable weather helm. A good way to guard against overtrimming is to remember that tug of weather helm on the tiller or wheel that we talked about in Chapter 6. Keep it slight. The helmsperson can report how the helm feels, or a crewmember can watch it. If the tiller's up under the helmsperson's chin, there's too much weather helm and something should be eased.

With the sails trimmed correctly, the sheets are cleated (except in fresh winds in dinghies, which might capsize if sheets are not quickly let out) and the helmsperson steers by the jib, not by the compass or any other indicator. The challenge is not simply to sail as close as possible to the apparent wind but also to keep the boat sailing fast. It's an endlessly fascinating problem demanding patience, concentration, and alertness. Steerers on racing boats get some help from sophisticated electronic instruments that calculate and display the apparent wind angle and boat speed, and from microcomputers that factor the two against each other to indicate sailing efficiency relative to a theoretical optimum. The average boat, however, may have only a boat-speed indicator, leaving the helmsperson to steer more by feel than by the numbers.

How to Steer Upwind with Jib Telltales

Whether or not he or she has electronic assistance, the helmsperson's best guide is the luff (forward edge) of the jib, which he or she steers by (uses as a steering reference point). The steerer wants to sail at an angle of attack where the sail is completely full but just on the edge of luffing (flapping and spilling wind). By sitting or standing on the windward side, a steerer will be able to watch the approaching waves and steer around the bad ones.

In the days of cotton and early Dacron sails, the soft cloth bubbled visibly just as it began to luff. Today's hard-finished, stiff, low-stretch sailcloth is less sensitive and harder to read, so sailmak-

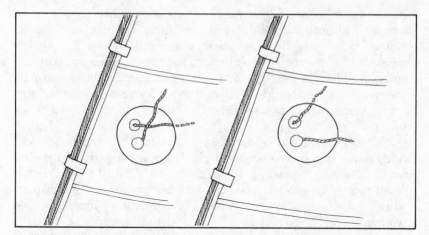

(left) If the jib telltales look like this, with the windward one lifting about half of the time and the leeward one streaming, on a close-hauled course you're sailing about right and on a reach the sails are trimmed correctly. (right) But if they look like this, either you're sailing too far off the wind or the sails are trimmed too tight. Use green yarn on the starboard telltale and red on the port one in order to eliminate confusion.

ers and sailors attach simple wind-flow indicators called telltales near the luff on either side of the sail. There should be three pairs of telltales distributed at equal intervals up and down the luff. Telltales may be made of yarn or ribbon (ideally, green on the starboard side and red on port) taped to or sewn through the sail cloth on both sides 6 to 12 inches aft of the luff. They should be short enough not to wrap around the stay but long enough to be visible from the helm. Sometimes a plastic window is sewn into the sail's luff to facilitate reading the telltales.

This is the story the telltales recount:

✓   If the leeward telltale is streaming straight aft and the windward one is streaming half of the time and just lifting half of the time, you're sailing perfectly—neither *footing* (sailing too wide) nor *pinching* (sailing too close).

✓   If the windward telltale is lifting straight up and the leeward one is streaming aft, either the jib is eased too far or you're pinching (sailing too close to the wind). To make the jib work at optimum again, trim the sheet a couple of inches. But if it's already trimmed hard, bear off a couple of degrees until both telltales are streaming. Pinching is not all bad, since it can be a quick way to make the sails less efficient and spill wind when a sudden gust hits. (For some reason, pinching through a gust is called *feathering*.)

✓ If the leeward telltale is lifting more than about 20 degrees and the windward one is still streaming, the angle of attack is too broad. This is called "sailing stalled" because the air flow is stalling on (or stagnating and separating from) the sail. To get the air flowing properly again, head up. Or ease the jib sheet until both telltales are streaming and foot (sail a little broader than close-hauled).

The goal, remember, is to sail as close to the wind as is efficiently possible. Although footing takes the boat through the water faster, in most conditions most boats lose too much ground to leeward to make footing pay off. The major exception is when sailing in a rough sea, where you want to be moving fast in order to slice through waves without being stopped by them.

The steerer should never become complacent. Like a fly fisherman teasing a line across a stream's surface, he or she keeps testing the angle of attack, constantly edging the boat closer to the wind until the windward telltale lifts about 20 degrees, then nudging the bow off a bit. The course may waggle, but the sails will always be trimmed at or near peak efficiency.

Reaching: Sailing Fast

On a reach, the helmsperson usually doesn't use the jib luff telltales as the steering guide. Rather he or she steers either by the compass (keeping its forward mark, called the lubber's line, over a specified degree mark) or by a buoy, star, harbor, or landmark on shore, keeping the bow aimed at the object. Meanwhile, whoever is in charge of trimming the sails adjusts the jib sheet until both the windward and leeward telltales are streaming aft. If the windward one lifts, the sheet is trimmed until they both stream; if the leeward one, the sheet is eased. After the jib is trimmed correctly, the main sheet is trimmed or eased to keep the mainsail from luffing. Tighten the boom vang until the boom is about horizontal to the deck with the mainsail leech twisted off about 5 degrees.

When reaching in fresh and even moderate winds, as when sailing close-hauled, it's easy to forget about heel angles and weather helm as you trim the sheets to optimize sail shape. Sure, keep the sails pulling as hard as possible, but if this means sailing way over on the boat's ear with her leeward rail under water, ease out the main sheet (and even the jib sheet, too) and let the sail luff a little to bring the boat back up to a heel angle of under 20 degrees (10 degrees for a centerboarder). Already sailing fast, the boat will seem to take off as soon as her decks are dry.

Running: Easy Street, Mostly

When the wind comes over the stern and the mainsail is eased out until the boom is almost at a right angle, the boat is on a *run* (sometimes called *running free,* a *square run*, or a *dead run*). The jib will be blanketed by the mainsail; to make it fill with wind, pull it around to windward and set it wing-and-wing to windward either with or without the spinnaker pole. Set the pole about perpendicular to the apparent wind, and trim the sheet so there's a constant but small curl in the windward leech.

If you have a spinnaker and the crew is sufficiently large and talented and the wind not too strong, set it to increase your speed. Hoist it behind the jib, which blankets it, pull the guy (windward sheet) around through the spinnaker pole, let the sail fill, and lower the jib. If the big sail threatens to take charge of the boat, release the sheet and either let the sail luff or pull it around to leeward of the rehoisted jib before dropping it. A special cruising spinnaker is not set on a spinnaker pole but hoisted like a jib, only it is not hooked to the headstay.

Sails don't produce much forward drive on a run; they are simply pushed by the wind, and as they are pushed they pull the hull along. In light and moderate winds, therefore, a run may be even slower than sailing close-hauled. To speed up, head up to a beam reach and, as the speed of both the boat and the apparent wind increases, gradually head off, keeping on a slightly broad reach with the wind at about 110 degrees off the bow, or at about 4 or 9 o'clock. "Head off in the puffs and up in the lulls" is a time-honored, proven rule of thumb for keeping the sails working well when sailing downwind. As the wind freshens (strengthens), it will kick up waves down which the boat may surf at high speeds. Yet the same waves may also cause her to roll violently. To stop the boat from rolling, head up to a broad reach and trim the main sheet; the side force on the sail will steady her.

On a run, the helmsperson may steer by the compass or by an object off the boat, simply aiming the bow at the destination. But he or she must keep track of the wind to avoid sailing by the lee (with the wind shifting to the leeward side of the stern). If that happens, there will be an accidental jibe, and the mainsail may be slammed across the boat unexpectedly, possibly injuring crew members or breaking gear. A good way to avoid sailing by the lee is to sit or stand facing forward and keep the wind pressure equal on the backs of both ears, with your hood or hat off. Another way, when running under jib and mainsail, is to keep the jib hanging across the center of the foredeck. If it blows to windward, you're by the lee; to leeward, you're safely broad reaching. With the spinnaker up on a run, steer the bow under its center like a seal keeping its nose under a ball. If the spinnaker sways to windward of the bow, you're by the lee and must head up; to leeward, you're broad reaching and may bear off (head off).

Changing Tacks the Right and Wrong Way

By heading up or bearing off, the steerer can alter course through about 150 degrees, from a run to close-hauled. Sometimes, however, a more drastic course change is called for, and he or she changes tacks by steering the boat through the eye of the wind so that the sails must be trimmed on the other side. The windward side becomes the leeward and the leeward side the windward. The two tack-changing maneuvers are tacking and jibing. Tacking is a turn made into the wind; jibing is done facing away from the wind.

Tacking

To tack, head up to dead into the wind from a close-hauled course, and then bear off on the other tack until close-hauled again. It may help to preselect a reference point on the compass for the new tack before you start the maneuver. Say, for example, that on starboard tack the compass course is 150 degrees. The true wind is 195 degrees, which indicates you're sailing 45 degrees off the true wind. Therefore, when close-hauled on the *port* tack (after you change tacks), you will be steering 240 degrees—or 45 degrees the other side of the wind direction. Keep the helm over through the tack until you're near that course and then check her swing.

Tacking is often called "coming about," and the skipper's warning is "ready about." When that command is given, one crew-member uncleats the jib sheet and checks to see that the sheets and sail are clear; he or she then answers "ready." Next, the steerer heads up by sharply pushing the tiller to leeward or turning the wheel to windward, and says "hard alee" (meaning, "the helm's going far to leeward"). When the jib begins to luff, the crew lets go the jib sheet, making sure it isn't tangled or kinked. As the bow swings through the wind's eye, a shipmate trims the jib sheet on the other side, starting with one or two clockwise turns on the winch and adding more as the strain builds. When the trimmer can pull no more, somebody grinds the sheet in with the winch, watching the sail to make sure it isn't trimmed too flat (a common occurrence with today's big, powerful winches). The jib should be trimmed

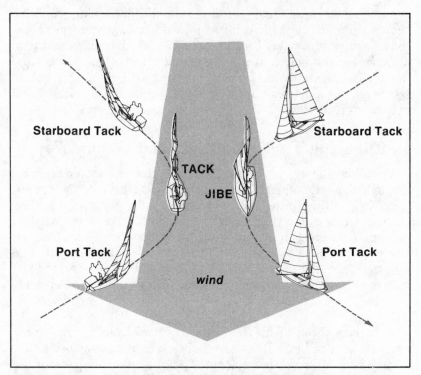

(left) To tack, or come about, head up into the wind and off on the other tack, easing and trimming the jib sheet. (right) To jibe, bear off and ease sheets. When the wind is astern or just beyond it, quickly trim the main sheet and throw the boom across as the jib sheet is eased and trimmed.

almost as far as it was before the boat changed tacks and then pulled in to where it was as she gains speed.

Before the tack, the mainsail traveler car should be put in the center of its track with its two control lines tight to keep it from banging around as the sail luffs. Otherwise, the mainsail tends itself during the maneuver.

Most bungled tacks are due to one or more of the following mistakes:

✓ The steerer stops turning the boat too soon and the boat is left hanging dead in the water head to wind.

✓ The steerer turns her too far and ends up on a beam reach with the sails trimmed for a close-hauled course—a sure invitation to an unpleasant knockdown (sudden heeling) in a gust of wind.

✓ The helmsperson allows the boat to be stopped and lose steerageway during the tack because she was turned too fast or because she was slammed by a wave. Adjust the helm firmly but smoothly, and choose a relatively flat spot of water between waves before beginning the maneuver.

✓ The old leeward-side jib sheet is let out too slowly, or it kinks and jams up in a block leaving the jib backed (trimmed to windward) on the new tack.

✓ The crewmember trims the jib much too far on the new tack, perhaps tearing it on a spreader, because he or she is not looking at it.

Jibing

Jibing is altering course away from the wind. A jibe usually is slower and takes up more water than a tack; since the mainsail must be trimmed most of the way, it may be more physically demanding, too.

Before jibing, get on a broad reach or run. The skipper warns "stand by to jibe." When the crew is ready—one or more on the jib sheets and another on the main sheet—they respond "ready." The steerer commands "jibe-o" and bears off in a smooth, gradual turn as the main sheet is trimmed rapidly to keep the boom from wildly banging across. The boom should be over the boat's centerline when the stern passes through the eye of the wind. To avoid an accident on deck, be sure the traveler is centered and its control lines are tight. Then the main sheet is eased out very rapidly. In a very light wind, the main boom may be allowed to swing across the boat on its own without trimming the sheet. The old leeward jib sheet is let go just as the stern swings into the wind's eye and the new leeward one is trimmed.

In any wind stronger than moderate air, the boat may broach (suddenly head up uncontrollably and heel violently) as she finishes the jibe. Here's a simple way to avoid this: just as the sails fill and the boat begins to heel on the new tack, the steerer sharply bears off about 5 degrees to check the spin of the bow; when the boat has leveled off, he or she heads up to the new course.

In fresh and strong winds, a poorly executed jibe can lead to serious trouble since (unlike on a tack, where the boat is luffing dead into the wind) her sails are always full and there's no way to spill wind. Here are the typical causes of a bad jibe:

✓ The steerer loses track of the wind direction and heads up too rapidly on the new tack. Before the jibe, find a couple of reference points that will help locate the wind—its feel on the back of your neck or your ears, a telltale on a stay, a masthead fly (wind indicator at the top of the mast)—and refer to them as you bear off, jibe, and head up on the new tack.

✓ The steerer does not adjust quickly to the boat's new orientation to the waves and loses control after the jibe. This is why the best and most experienced helmsperson should be steering during a jibe in rough seas and fresh winds. (Often the most qualified downwind helmsperson on board is a young dinghy sailor who has developed a good feel for the wind while avoiding capsizes in a tippy little boat.)

✓ The main sheet is not trimmed far enough before the jibe, so it bangs across violently, perhaps injuring a crewmember or filling so quickly that it causes a broach.

✓ After the jibe, on the new tack, the steerer tries to head up onto a reach before the main sheet is eased. With the sail trimmed tight, the boat will broach when she comes up.

✓ The jib sheet is eased too far before the jibe and the jib wraps itself around the headstay (wire running from bow to mast).

Jibing in light wind is easy, in moderate wind a handful, in fresh wind a real challenge, and in heavy wind a major risk. When in doubt about your ability to handle a jibe, swallow your pride and tack.

Those are the fundamentals of boat and sail handling—all easier to describe than accomplish. The very best way to learn and master them is to go out and practice them, preferably in a light, quick boat whose relatively small gear won't bruise you too badly when you make a mistake (and you will) and whose sensitivity sets a challenging standard. In *The Annapolis Book of Seamanship* I say a lot more about the subtleties of sail trim and helmsmanship; perhaps you'll want to do some reading there. In any case, the next chapter may answer some of your questions (and cries for help).

CHAPTER 8

Tricks of the Seaman's Trade for Better Steering, Easier Trimming, and Safer Sailing

Seasoned sailors have spent years accumulating a repertory of rules of thumb that make handling and living aboard a boat more efficient, safe, and enjoyable. Here we'll summarize the most important tricks of the trade, opening with ways to improve steering and sail trimming, moving on to hints for safe sail handling, and closing with some important advice on how to walk around on deck without losing your balance.

Five Hints for Alert Steering and Sail Trimming

As with all skills, sailing competently begins with alertness. Yet it's harder than, say, driving a car safely, because the indicators a sailor must be alert to are not part of modern everyday experience, which is far removed from the forces of nature. In order to evaluate those forces, we must consciously retrain our senses to feel and interpret subtle changes in the relationship between wind, water, sail, and helm.

First, always know where the wind is from. That advice may sound simpleminded, but it's amazing how many people need a weatherman or electronic instrument to tell which way the wind blows. Develop a feel for the wind on your body. Take off your hat or hood and face the wind; when the pressure is equal on your cheeks and ears, you're facing directly into it. Refer to wind indicators—the telltales on the jib luff and the stays, the masthead fly or flag at the top of the mast, and the luffs of the sails. Indicators off the boat can be helpful, too. Among them are smoke or flags on shore, other boats under sail, and the direction of waves, clouds, and bird flights. Whichever reference point you use, you should be able to point in the direction of the true and apparent winds, as well as sense when the velocity has increased or dropped.

Second, develop a feel for the boat's performance relying on the one indicator that mirrors all the boat's forces, the helm. If there is a lot of weather helm—more than a slight tug or about three degrees of rudder angle—the boat is heeling too far to leeward or the mainsail is trimmed too flat and the jib too loose. If there is lee helm, the boat is heeled to windward or the jib is trimmed too tight and the main sheet is eased too far. Correcting excessive helm *always* improves speed and comfort. Besides being attentive to the helm, the helmsperson and sail trimmers will do well to learn to estimate the boat's speed and angle of heel, using a speedometer

Reliable wind indicators include the wind arrow at the top of the mast called the masthead fly, a flag, smoke from a stack ashore, seagulls (which always stand facing the wind), and other boats.

and an inclinometer (a carpenter's level), if they're available.

Third, look at the sails. Too many people try to steer by the compass while the sails luff inefficiently. Regardless of the compass course, the sails are the boat's engine. You don't have to stare at them; just keep your eyes moving around the boat from sail to sail, then to the helm, then to the compass. The good sailor is the person who comes on deck and immediately looks up at the sails; who can have a pleasant conversation and still know if the trim is right because he or she is facing forward; who can tell whether the helmsperson is steering well simply by the feel of the boat.

Fourth, don't trim the sails too flat. "When in doubt, let it out" is an old sailor's dictum worth writing down and taping where everybody can see it. Flat sails don't provide much forward drive, while full ones (even if they are luffing a little) shape the wind so it can produce drive. If the speed is low and the helm feels wooden, ease the sheets a couple of inches and let the mainsail's traveler car down to leeward a bit. If you're close-hauled, bear off a couple of degrees. An experienced crew will know to ease the sheets by the feel of the boat's heel decreasing in a wind lull and to trim them again when the heel increases.

Fifth, realize that *the goal is not to sail the boat but rather to help the boat sail herself.* There is no way that a well-designed boat can sail fast and comfortably unless the crew takes advantage of, and is attentive to, her inherent seaworthiness, speed, and seakindliness. Granted, some boats are faster and more weatherly than others, and it's important that you not try to exceed built-in limitations. For instance, a heavy cruiser with a small sail area and shallow keel cannot be made to sail close-hauled in light wind as fast as a modern ocean racer. But you *can* help her sail up to her own potential if you are alert to all her indicators.

If you have to fight the helm, if the boat's heeling way over, if the sails are luffing wildly, if the speed is low, if she is bouncing up and down violently or wallowing in waves instead of sailing over or through them—in brief, if the boat is not moving comfortably where she is aimed—then something's wrong. In fresh wind (over 16 knots), the culprit almost always is bad balance brought on by too much heel. In light (0–8 knots) and moderate (9–15 knots) winds, it's usually trying to sail too close to the wind with sails trimmed too flat.

Even when the solution is unclear, simply identifying the problem is an important first step. This ability is what mariners call "a feel for the boat," and despite the common wisdom, it's something you can develop. Open your mind, use your eyes, and above all, stay alert.

What the Steerer and Trimmer Do

The helmsperson steers the boat and the sail trimmer—usually another crewmember but sometimes the steerer as well—adjusts the sheets to make the sails pull and the boat balance. The two sailors should keep up a running conversation about the boat's performance.

The Helmsperson

The person who is steering lets eyes and senses roam alertly around the sails, the compass, the water ahead, and the various wind and speed indicators, both natural and electronic. He or she should sit or stand in a position that provides a clear view of the luff of the jib and any obstructions or big waves to steer around, and has the right to ask shipmates to move out of the line of sight. Every experienced steerer has a favorite position. Most prefer to sit or stand up to windward, where the visibility is greatest, but sitting to leeward has its appeals—among them an enthralling sense of power and speed as the water races by just inches from your elbow.

When you steer, don't just grab the wheel or tiller in a lock clutch. Hold it gently with your fingers and move it smoothly but firmly with wrist action. As the wind builds, tighten your grasp but avoid getting into a wrestling match. Downwind in rough weather, you may have to make very abrupt helm changes, especially if the boat is light and unstable. Yet turning the rudder too sharply will cause it to stall out, which means that the water flow becomes detached from the blade. To get the flow attached again, pump the helm back and forth several times. Counter a roll to the side by steering slightly into the roll, heading up as the boat rolls to windward and bearing off as she rolls to leeward.

Good steering depends on quick reactions, mental alertness, and good hand-eye coordination—all of which alcohol consumption impairs. Almost as harmful as excessive drinking are exhaustion, overconfidence, and an inflated, euphoric feeling of heroism. Whenever I have got into trouble on the water, it was because I either pushed myself beyond my physical limits or overevaluated my abilities. If you begin to get weary or bored at the helm—and most people do after an hour or so—ask somebody else to take it. Before a long sail, the most experienced, skilled helmspersons should be identified and assigned to tricks (turns) at the helm at regular one-hour intervals. Perhaps the conditions will be easy enough to allow everybody to steer, but at least the crew will have a routine to fall back on if conditions get rough.

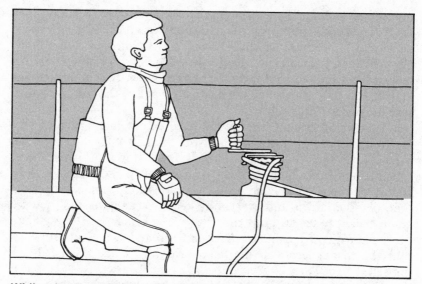

While trimming the jib, sit facing forward near the sheet winch. As shown here, the sheet must lead up to the winch so it does not foul around itself on the drum. This trimmer is wearing leather sailing gloves to protect his hands.

The Sail Trimmer

It may seem at first that the person trimming the sails is playing second fiddle to the steerer, but he or she has an important role in making the boat sail fast and comfortably. Like the helmsperson, the trimmer should be alert to every part of the boat and, especially, to changes in wind velocity that might require adjustments to the sheets. He or she should sit to leeward when trimming the jib and to windward when trimming the mainsail, in each case watching the sail's luff while adjusting the sheet. Because the helm generally is the best indicator, whoever is steering should have last say on sail trim. However, a good sail trimmer glances at the helm occasionally to see if the boat is balanced. Being tuned in to the helm also allows the trimmer to see when the steerer is getting careless. The speedometer, if available, is a helpful auxiliary guide that both sailors can refer to, but with practice they should be able to judge the boat's speed with reasonable accuracy by the rush and gurgle of the passing water.

Coordination and Teamwork on the Points of Sail

On a reach or run, when sailing a compass course, the best procedure is for the steerer to get the boat on that course, shouting "mark" or "course" when the forward lubber's line (vertical post) on the compass is right over the designated number. Next, the crew trims the jib properly for that heading so its windward luff telltale lifts when the helmsperson steers a few degrees too close. Then the mainsail is trimmed so it luffs at the same time that the jib telltale lifts. If this trim causes too much weather helm, the trimmer must ease the main sheet slightly.

Using this system, the sailors have complementary guides—the compass and the luff of the sails. If the sails luff when the boat is on course, they should be trimmed; if they don't luff when she is a couple of degrees high of course (upwind of course heading), they should be eased. On racing boats, a couple of crewmembers watch the sails like hawks and everybody keeps exchanging information about balance, speed, and trim. But when cruising or daysailing, the steerer might be able to check on trim and, when adjustments must be made, let go of the helm briefly to make them her- or himself.

Close-hauled sailing, when steering by the sails rather than by the compass, is a bit more dependent on alert steering than reaching and running. When the wind direction changes (as it does every few minutes), the steerer simply heads up or bears off to keep the jib's luff telltales streaming. While the compass is not the primary guide, he or she should keep an eye on it. If a close-hauled boat is heading more than 45 degrees off the direct course to the destination, it usually pays to come about; the heading on the other tack will probably aim the boat closer to her destination and get her there faster.

When the wind changes in velocity rather than direction, or when the sea condition alters, the sail trimmer makes small alterations in the sheets and other sail controls. If the wind lightens or the waves get bigger and threaten to stop the boat, make the sail fuller by easing the sheets a couple of inches and slightly letting out the outhaul, cunningham, and jib halyard; don't try to point too close to the wind. Later, if the wind freshens or the sea gets smoother, flatten the sails by trimming the sheets and controls back and point a little higher. Of course, be attentive to the boat's balance through the helm.

On breezy days, you'll find that the quickest and easiest way to adjust heel and helm angles is to depower the mainsail by playing (constantly adjusting) the main sheet traveler car. Letting it down usually decreases heel and weather helm. Pulling it up increases both heel and helm. On many boats the traveler control lines are handy to the steerer so that he or she can make quick adjustments in gusts and lulls. We'll cover other ways to make fresh-air sailing more comfortable in Chapter 16.

Safety Guidelines for Sail Handling

Although there are occasional disasters—like the 1979 Fastnet Race in England, in which I sailed and about which I wrote a book —remarkably few serious accidents occur on sailboats. In almost thirty years of aggressive sailing I have yet to suffer an injury worse than a cracked thumb bone (caused by a fall) and I've seen only one accident that put a sailor in the hospital (he let go of a handle on a reel-halyard winch, a winch with a take-up like a fishing reel, which spun, broke his wrist, and inflicted a concussion). But minor and semiserious accidents occur all the time. These include badly rope-burned hands, deep welts, huge bruises, minor concussions, wrenched shoulders, broken teeth, and other mishaps that may leave you or a shipmate in pain and the crew shorthanded.

You can avoid these accidents if you follow some simple guidelines for safe sail handling, a few of which I was lucky to learn in my mid-teens from a couple of experienced seamen who, no doubt

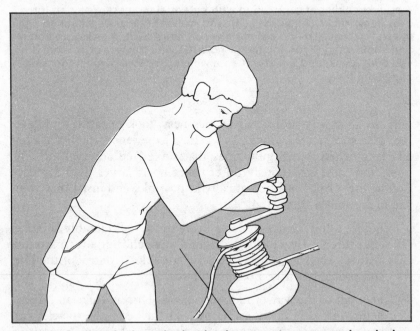

**To control a line that's under load, take some turns around a winch.
When grinding, lean over the winch and use your back muscles.**

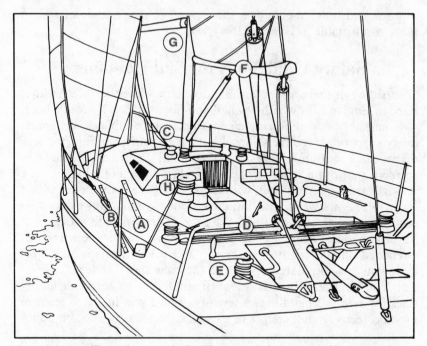

A cruising sailboat is crowded with potential dangers. You can trip over deck tracks (A), sheets (B), and lifelines (C), or be whacked by the traveler car (D) or a spinning winch handle (E). A swinging boom and boom vang (F) or spinnaker pole (G) may fracture your skull if you don't duck, and the sheet on a winch (H) could pinch fingers or snag long hair.

nervous about my adolescent recklessness, took me aside and gave me some succinct warnings. As I gained experience, the list gradually lengthened to ten guidelines that should be observed on any boat, and most assiduously on cruising boats larger than 35 feet. Follow these rules as automatically as possible, and insist that your shipmates follow them, too.

✓ Before a line comes under a load, snub it. Preferably, take at least three turns clockwise around a winch, but a turn around a sturdy cleat may do. Otherwise you'll lose control of the line and probably suffer a bad rope burn.

✓ Stay out of the way of moving objects. During tacks and jibes, dodge the main boom swinging over the deck, the traveler car banging across the cockpit, the jib clew whipping across the foredeck, and the winch handle whirling around a winch. Sailors have lost eyes to flying bowlines tied into jib clews.

✓ Don't step or sit on a loaded line or in the V formed by a line running to and from a block. If the line or block breaks, you will be lashed overboard or into the rigging.

✓ Remove a winch handle not in use. It may fall out, trip a passerby, or snag a line. And always remove the handle before letting go of the brake on a reel-halyard winch.

✓ Don't be a hero by trying to do difficult tasks singlehanded. Two-person jobs like lifting a heavy spinnaker pole or jibing the main boom in fresh air are just that—two-person jobs.

✓ Keep all lines coiled and under control in pouches or corners of the cockpit. Neaten up after every maneuver by recoiling any line that's been used. To avoid kinking, always coil line properly: braided line is coiled in loose figure-8's; laid three-stranded line is coiled with a slight clockwise twist of the wrist at the end of each loop so that it ends up hanging in a loose oval.

✓ Keep kinks out of sheets and halyards. Braided line twists up like a cold noodle, and the resulting kinks will constipate and

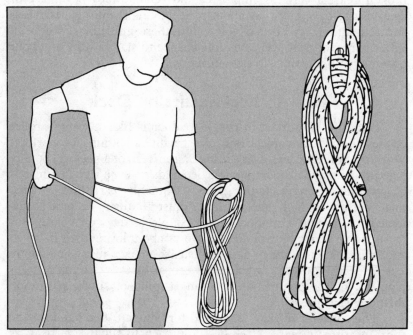

Here's how to coil braided line, which is generally used everywhere but in the anchor rode. It should hang in loose figure-8's.

stop it as it tries to run out through a block. Either milk (ease) the line through your hands to clear it of kinks, or cleat one end and heave the rest overboard (unless the propeller is turning!) to spin them out quickly.

✓ Look at the sail you're adjusting when trimming or hauling on a sheet, halyard, or other line.

✓ Don't take anything for granted. Just because shipmates say they're performing a job, don't automatically assume that they are actually doing it. Double-check cleated and coiled lines. Triple-check for lines dragging overboard before putting the engine in gear (or you'll need a hacksaw to cut away the tangle around the propeller).

✓ "One hand for yourself, one hand for the ship." This means that you give equal attention to your own safety and that of the vessel and your shipmates. If you're secure and doing your job well, the odds are that the vessel is safe.

There's no way to guarantee that following these rules will keep you free of injury; if perfect security were all we wanted out of life, we'd never leave the house. Bad luck, sudden weather changes, broken gear, a careless shipmate, and other forces beyond your control may have more say about your fate than your own alertness and self-sufficiency. But if you follow these guidelines, you're at least giving yourself every possible chance to stay healthy and your boat every opportunity to sail efficiently.

How to Feel Secure on Deck

Handling a sailboat in rough weather is like steering a roller coaster through a tropical rain forest while standing on one foot. Working, walking, and even sitting on the deck of a heeling, bouncing sailboat make near-impossible demands on even a good athlete's balance and strength. Some gymnasts quickly learn how to keep their feet under them; the rest of us must gradually become accustomed to the boat's motion over a couple of days on board. But most people at one time or another worry about losing their balance, and since that one time or another usually appears just when you're least expecting it—say, when a powerboat races by as you're stepping out of the companionway—an attitude of supreme caution should always prevail.

The constant refrain "one hand for yourself, one hand for the ship" neatly summarizes the best approach to staying vertical; as you move around the boat, give equal attention to your job and your own safety. Whenever possible, be within arm's reach of a lifeline or grabrail. Below, lean against cabin furniture and, if possible, swing from one grabrail to another like Tarzan moving through the jungle on vines. Only at anchor or in the marina—and then only in flat water—should people with doubtful balance walk across an open area like the foredeck without a hand on a support.

As you stand or walk, keep your weight low and well distributed in a boxer's wide crouch. Absorb the deck's rise and fall in your bent knees. If the boat is rolling violently from side to side, stand with your feet spread crosswise; but if she's pitching, with her bow and stern lifting and falling violently, turn and face to leeward. The safest thoroughfare from the stern to the bow is along the windward, uphill deck. Up there, you can walk with dry feet and with one or both hands firmly on the windward lifelines, in full view of the rest of the crew. Always stay inside the lifelines. Few things frighten a responsible skipper more in rough weather than losing sight of somebody who was "just there a moment ago" and who may have fallen overboard. It can be a long fall from the windward rail to the leeward one, so hang on tight if you're moving. If the weather's bad, put on a safety harness and clip its tether onto a deck fitting—not the lifelines themselves, which may break under a heavy, sudden load—and shorten the tether as much as possible to limit the length of a fall.

Sitting for Security

If you feel unsteady and aren't doing anything, *sit down*. Don't let false pride or an exaggerated eagerness to be involved keep you standing any longer than necessary. A standing crewmember obstructs the steerer's vision and is extremely vulnerable to toppling when the boat makes even small rolls and pitches. Sitting is also the most secure position on board for doing many jobs, among them pulling down a jib, trimming a sheet, and hauling up the anchor. Not only is your center of gravity lower when you're sitting, but with a three-point foundation you can wedge your feet against the leeward rail or some other object. In rough seas, you may find that the best way to get around is either to crawl on your hands and knees or to slide around on your butt.

It's remarkable how little time sailors spend actually doing anything. Mostly, we're just sitting there. The average cruising boat's cockpit can seat half a dozen people comfortably, half on one side and half on the other. When she's heeled far over, however, sitting on the leeward seat and facing to windward may inspire the less than pleasurable feeling that the boat will soon roll over on you. Then you can sit on the windward seat, facing to leeward and hunk-

When working on the foredeck, use the lifelines, pulpit, and rails for support. Sitting down is the most secure position, but be cautious about sitting (or walking) on slippery sails.

ered down behind the cabin to avoid flying spray. If the cockpit is full of your shipmates, find a perch on the windward deck with your back against the lifelines and feet braced against the cabin.

Now that we've seen how to get around on deck, let's look at getting the boat around on the lake or sound—the art of piloting.

CHAPTER 9

How to Find Your Way

In this chapter we'll lay out a quick and simple summary of the tools and skills of coastal navigation, or piloting. Piloting is the nautical art (and sometimes science) of knowing where you are, determining where you are going, and avoiding running into land. The pilot's guidemarks include the magnetic compass; electronic instruments like the depth sounder and various kinds of radio receivers; and navigational aids such as buoys and lighthouses. Data concerning these guides are printed in miniature on a nautical map called a chart, on which the pilot plots the boat's position and progress. This scale model of the vessel's surroundings and maneuvers is often supplemented by written entries in the logbook, a kind of diary. Between the two written histories of the journey, the pilot has enough information not only to determine present position and a safe course to the boat's destination but also to backtrack to a previous position should he or she get lost. Fascinated by these tools and the skills that go with them, many sailors find that piloting can be one of the most enjoyable and rewarding aspects of cruising.

The Pilot's Tools and Skills

The pilot relies on four simple tools to perform the basic skills of position finding and course planning. These are the magnetic compass, which is used to steer courses and take bearings on (determine directions of) objects; the chart; the plotter, which transfers bearings and courses to and from the chart; and dividers, which measure distances on the chart.

Compass Courses and Bearings

The heart of the magnetic compass is a circular dial showing the four cardinal compass directions (north, east, south, and west) as well as the 356 degrees that separate them. Magnets attached to the underside of the dial orient it to the earth's magnetic field so that no matter which way the boat is headed, the north arrow points to the locus in the magnetic field called magnetic north, situated in northern Canada. The dial sits on a fine-jeweled pivot point in a pool of light oil (which dampens its rotation as the boat turns) under

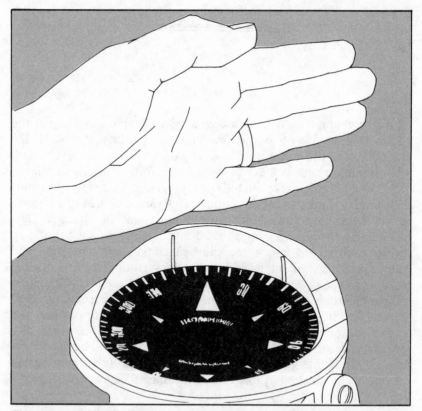

The course is the compass direction in which the boat is heading, as indicated by the forward lubber's line. A bearing is the compass direction to another object. Cut a bearing across the compass with the hand or use a handbearing compass.

a Plexiglas dome that magnifies its print and allows it to be read from the side. Vertical sighting sticks called lubber's lines provide reference points for steering or taking bearings, and they and the dial card are gimballed so they stay level when the boat heels or pitches.

Local magnetic fields surrounding nearby metal objects—like a flashlight, a tool, another compass, or a wrist watch—may deviate the compass so that the north arrow points off to one side of magnetic north. Deviation can be eliminated by removing the metal object or adjusting compensating magnets in the compass base. If the deviation remains, a correction sheet called a deviation table may be constructed to allow the pilot to compensate for errors. All this work is both difficult and important, and is best left to a professional compass adjuster.

The reading of a corrected or undeviated compass is the single constant on board a boat. Regardless of the wind direction and visibility, north is north and 170 degrees is 170 degrees. Like death and taxes, a correctly installed and compensated compass can always be depended on to provide an accurate course and bearing.

Compass courses are courses steered by the compass, in which the steerer uses the compass rather than the sails, a buoy, or some other object as his or her reference. To steer a course, say, of 170 degrees, the helmsperson adjusts the helm until the forward lubber's line is directly over 170, or one of the side lubber's lines is over a number 45 or 90 degrees either side of 170 (125 or 80 degrees for the port lubber's lines, 215 or 260 degrees for the starboard ones). Depending on her size and the wind and sea conditions, even a well-steered boat will wander several degrees either side of that heading. Since it's easier to steer by the thick lines at 5- or 10-degree intervals on the compass card than by the thin ones every 1 or 2 degrees, the pilot will help the helmsman by giving the course in 5- or 10-degree increments (for example, 095 degrees instead of 093 or 097).

Compass bearings are the compass directions from the boat to another object. To take a bearing, close one eye and sight the object down the forefinger of your outstretched hand. Then drop the hand straight down to the compass dome. The bearing is the number under your straight little finger on the far side of the card. Because your hand acts somewhat like a knife, this is often called "cutting a bearing." In rough weather and at night, cut at least three bearings and average them. For greater accuracy, either aim the boat right at the object and read the heading on the forward lubber's line, or use a portable compass called a hand bearing compass.

Compass bearings can be either absolute or relative. A cut

bearing is an absolute one—the number on the dial under your hand or in the viewfinder of the hand bearing compass. A relative bearing is the included angle between the boat's compass course and the absolute bearing. For example, when you're sailing a course of 100 degrees and take a bearing of 150 degrees on a lighthouse, the absolute compass bearing is 150 degrees but the relative compass bearing is 050 degrees (150 − 100 = 050). The side lubber's lines on the compass automatically indicate relative bearings of 45 or 90 degrees. Although a navigator uses absolute bearings more frequently, relative bearings can help when determining if you're on a collision course with another moving vessel (you'll collide if the relative bearing stays the same over a period of time).

The Chart

Knowing the compass course and taking bearings to navigation aids opens the door to the chart, that scale model of your surroundings on which your pencil mimics your every move in miniature. The modern marine chart is a wondrous thing, beautiful in its coloration and its logical, clear expression of mounds of information. The charts that most American sailors use are distributed by the National Ocean Survey, a division of the National Oceanographic and Atmospheric Administration, and sold by the N.O.S. and its authorized agents, including many chandleries and seaside town hardware stores. Chart order forms and catalogs are available from: Distribution Division, C44, National Ocean Survey, Riverdale, MD 20840.

The most obvious difference among individual charts is the scale, or the size of the area of land and sea that they cover. The N.O.S. breaks down its charts into five types. Going from the smallest scale (the largest area) to the largest scale (the smallest area) they are as follows:

✓ **Sailing charts** include very large areas of coastline, show no details of bays and harbors, and are used on long offshore passages.

✓ **General charts** cover about 15 percent the area of the sailing chart, show some coastal details and the entrances to major harbors, and are used on shorter passages along outer shorelines.

✓ **Coast charts** show bays, sounds, and large harbors in considerable detail, and are the charts most used on cruising boats.

✓ **Harbor charts** cover small harbors in great detail and are helpful when returning to port.

✓ **Small-craft charts** are fold-out collections of harbor charts for popular cruising grounds along bays, sounds, and large harbors. (The N.O.S. is gradually eliminating this type of chart.)

Most cruising navigators quickly find that almost all their plotting is done on coast charts. Harbor and small-craft charts cover areas so small that, except in fog, you can get around quite safely just by eyeballing the aids to navigation and landmarks as you stand in the cockpit, chart in hand. And sailing and general charts show nowhere near enough detail for normal alongshore sailing. The extremely helpful information shown on a coast chart includes navigation aids (buoys and lighthouses), water depths, radio beacons, landmarks (such as water tanks, tall buildings, and bridges), and time difference lines used to navigate with a loran electronic device.

The compass rose is a chart's most important feature for normal piloting. It is a replica of the card in the cockpit compass and it serves as a sailor's Rosetta Stone to translate courses and bearings onto paper. The several roses scattered across the chart actually include two concentric compass dials. The outer dial is oriented to polar or true north—the spot that geographers have decided is the top of the world and toward which, at least in the Mercator projection used on saltwater charts, the vertical meridians of longitude ascend in parallel (on the polyconic projection of Great Lakes charts, the meridians gradually converge, more or less as they do on a globe). The rose's inner dial, like the compass on deck, is oriented to the earth's magnetic field and so usually is skewed to the meridians. The angular difference between north on the true, outer dial and north on the magnetic, inner dial is called variation, and is labeled inside the rose. As the magnetic field is mobile, the small annual changes in variation are also labeled.

The Plotter and Dividers

All right, you have your course and some bearings on deck, and you've got your chart spread out on the chart table below, well out of the spray and crew traffic. Now you need some tools to help convert deck compass degrees to chart compass rose degrees, and to display distances to scale. Start out with a soft #2 pencil sharpened to a fine point. Then get out a plotter and a pair of dividers.

The plotter provides both a straight edge to draw courses and bearings and a way to duplicate them on the chart. There are different types of plotters. Some, called parallel rulers (or rules), are laid across the magnetic dial to find the course or bearing that has been reported from the cockpit, and are then slid (or "walked") across the chart to the boat's approximate position. When plotting a course, a plotter's edge is laid over the last known position and a

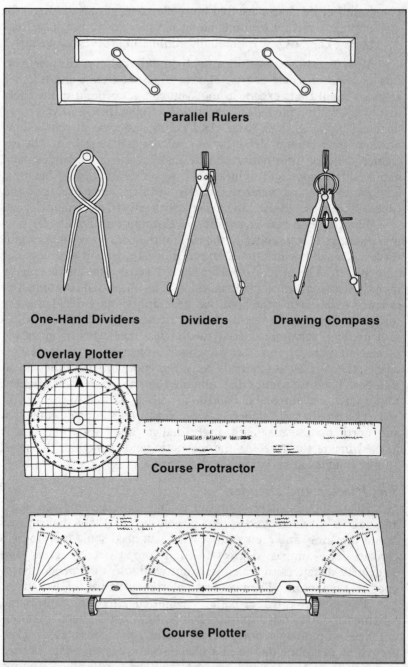

Parallel Rulers

One-Hand Dividers   **Dividers**   **Drawing Compass**

Overlay Plotter

Course Protractor

Course Plotter

These are the pilot's basic plotting tools. Add a soft pencil, calcula-
tor, watch, cruising guide, tide table (if needed), and the necessary
charts and you're ready to go.

course line is drawn from it. On the other hand, when plotting a bearing, an edge is placed over the symbol of the sighted object and a bearing line is laid off on the chart.

Since parallel rulers can slide around when the boat is rolling or pitching, many navigators prefer to use another type of plotter— a 360-degree protractor with an adjustable arm. The protractor is laid over an intersection of a north-south running meridian of longitude and an east-west running parallel of latitude, and then turned until it mimics the local variation as shown on the closest rose. The protractor is adjusted until the arm passes at the reported compass course through the last position, or at the reported bearing through the sighted object. Then the line is drawn.

Dividers —a drawing compass with a point at each end—are used to measure distances on the chart, referring either to the mileage scale near the large chart label or to the latitude scale on the side (since the scale varies due to the distortion of the Mercator projection, be sure to use the latitude scale exactly alongside your position).

Plotting: The D.R., E.P., and Fix

Three types of position plotting are used on sailboats: dead reckoning with no bearings (the D.R.), estimating a position with one bearing (the E.P.), and fixing a position with two or more bearings (the fix). The last is the most reliable, but until you can make a fix on sighted objects or radio beacons, you must keep up the D.R. plot.

The Dead Reckoning Plot (D.R.)

Dead stands for "ded" or "deduced." The D.R. plot is the best possible way for the crew to stay in tune with the boat's progress without relying on aids to navigation. *It depends solely on information found on board*: the boat's course, read off the compass and reported (accurately, we trust) by the helmsperson; and her speed, read off a distance-run indicator or averaged from the boat's speedometer. If the boat does not have speed or distance-run indicators, you can estimate her speed with remarkable accuracy using the speed/time/distance formula:

$$\text{speed} = \frac{(60 \times \text{distance run})}{\text{time}}$$

Speed is in knots (or, on the Great Lakes, miles per hour), *distance* is in nautical miles (or, on the Lakes, statute miles), and *time* is in minutes. Add or subtract favorable or unfavorable current to or from speed.

You can use this formula in many helpful ways: run up and down a measured mile or half-mile set on shore by the government and shown clearly on charts; time your run between two charted buoys; or simply time how long it takes the boat to pass a floating object and enter her overall length for distance.

No matter how you calculate speed, once confident of your figures you may determine distance run (or how far you've sailed at a known speed for a known length of time) by changing the formula around:

$$\text{distance run} = \frac{(\text{speed} \times \text{time})}{60}$$

If you have sailed at 6 knots for 28 minutes, you've covered 2.8 nautical miles; for 70 minutes, 7 miles; and so on.

With course and distance run known, you can plot the D.R. Let's use this example: it's 7:34 P.M. and since you last plotted your position at 7:00 P.M. you have averaged 5.5 knots on a course of 165 degrees. What is your new D.R. position?

Here are the steps you take:

1. **Plot the course.** From your last position, use the plotter to draw a short, light line on the chart at 165 degrees, being careful to use the inner, magnetic dial on the compass rose. Above the line, print *C 165 M* to show that the line represents a course of 165 magnetic degrees. Below the line print *S 5.5* to remind you of your average speed.

2. **Calculate the distance run.** Using the formula

$$\text{distance run} = \frac{(\text{speed} \times \text{time})}{60}$$

calculate how far you've sailed since 7 o'clock. Here the distance is 3.12 miles, which, to be safe, we'll round up to 3.2 miles.

3. **Plot the distance run.** Using the latitude scale alongside the position, spread the dividers over 3.2 miles, pick them up, and place one point at the 7 o'clock position and the other point on the new course or its extension, just pricking the paper. Remove the dividers and, if necessary, complete the line to the prick.

4. **Label the D.R.** Make a pencil dot over the prick and draw a

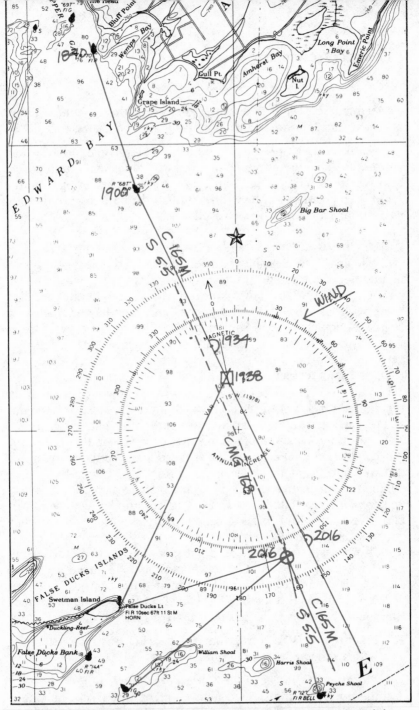

This portion of a Great Lakes chart shows a compass rose and three types of plots. The semicircle (at 1934 and 2016 hours) is a dead reckoning (D.R.) position. It's plotted by drawing a course line and measuring off the distance run since the last position. The box (1938) is an estimated position (E.P.) plotted by crossing the D.R. with one bearing. And the circle (2016) is a fix made by crossing two bearings.

semicircle over it. Label it *1934*; using the 24-hour military clock is insurance against confusing A.M. with P.M. times.

With the D.R. position, you now have a reliable plot of where you are. If there are any tidal or wind-driven currents, unreported helmsperson's wanderings from course, or mistakes in figuring the speed, this position will be wrong, but it's the best you can do until you can take a bearing on a charted object.

The Estimated Position (E.P.)

Each compass bearing you take on a charted object—a buoy, a lighthouse, a water tank, whatever—provides what's called a line of position or L.O.P. Another kind of L.O.P. is a depth sounding made with an echo or hand sounder, since depths are labeled on charts. Major changes in soundings can provide good evidence of your position. In fact, an excellent tactic when sailing in fog is to get over a contour line that links points of the same depth and, using the sounder as your eyes, follow it to your destination.

A single L.O.P. does not tell you exactly how far you are from the sighted object; but it does allow you to picture a clear, straight, and repeatable path to it—an invisible path, but a path all the same. Your position is somewhere along that path. In landbound terms, this connection is like an avenue that stretches between you and a distant house. Not the least of the virtues of a single bearing or depth sounding is that it will give you a fairly clear picture of where you are *not*; since piloting is meant partially to help you avoid certain places, that information can be extremely comforting when you're sailing near reefs and land.

While a single L.O.P. does not give the whole picture, combined with the D.R. it may tell you enough to make a reliable estimate of your whereabouts—an estimated position, or E.P. This position is plotted by crossing the single L.O.P. with the D.R. track (the course between D.R. positions). Here's how to plot an E.P.:

1. **Update the D.R. to the time the bearing was taken.** Label it with a semicircle and the time.

2. **Plot the L.O.P.** Using the plotter, draw the L.O.P.—the bearing line from the sighted object—across the track, making it only as long as necessary to indicate the object on which the bearing was taken. If there is the possibility of any confusion, label the line with the bearing angle.

3. **Label the E.P.** If the L.O.P. exactly crosses the D.R. semicircle, draw a small square around the intersection and label it with the time, using the 24-hour clock. However, if the line

crosses the course ahead of or behind the D.R. semicircle, extend the L.O.P. until a right angle from it crosses the D.R. position, and there draw the square and write the label. (In other words, drop a perpendicular from the D.R. to the bearing line.) The right angle brings the D.R. and E.P. as close to each other as possible. If the E.P. is based on a depth sounding, draw a square around the sounding and label it with *sounding* and the time.

The Fix

If there were some way to measure exactly how far along the single L.O.P. you are, you could improve on that estimate with a fixed position (called a fix). Of course, you can estimate the distance, but poor visibility or eyesight usually make that an unreliable gauge. Better yet, find another L.O.P. (to another charted object) that crosses the first one—preferably at as near to a right angle as possible so that any errors made while taking the bearings are minimized. When using three L.O.P.'s, try to cross them at 60-degree angles.

To make a fix, follow these steps:

1. **Update the D.R.** This will be a check against the accuracy of the bearings.
2. **Take and plot two or more bearings.** They should be taken as near to simultaneously as possible. Plot the L.O.P.'s, clearly indicating the objects that the bearings were taken on.
3. **Label the fix.** Where the L.O.P.'s intersect or form a small triangle, draw a circle and label it with the time in the 24-hour clock. If you're using two L.O.P.'s and one of them puts the boat surprisingly far from the D.R., retake them both. If one of three L.O.P.'s skews the fix by making a large triangle, either consider this an area of position rather than a fix, or discard that bearing as an aberration, or start over again by retaking the bearings.

The new D.R. plot then begins at the circle marking the fix. If the difference between a reliable fix and the last D.R. is large—say one mile after ten miles of sailing—try to figure out why. The cause could be as simple as a speedometer that reads too high or a helmsperson overly optimistic about his or her ability to sail the course. Maybe the boat is making a lot of leeway and you should compensate when you set the new course. (Sailing close-hauled or on a reach in rough weather, most boats make 10 to 15 degrees of leeway.) Or perhaps the tidal current shoved the boat to one side, forward, or backward.

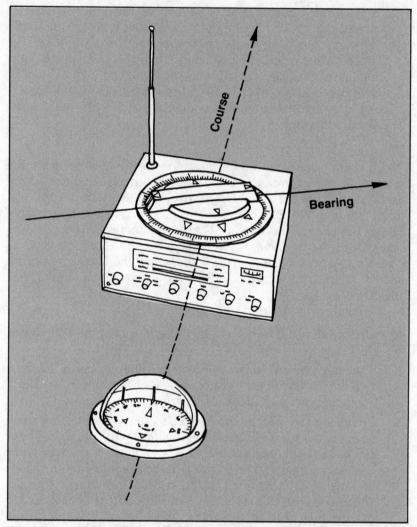

The radio direction finder (R.D.F.) takes bearings on radio beacons. First tune to a nearby station and align its outer ring with the compass heading (dotted line)—but keep it well away from the cockpit compass. Then rotate the pointer until the dot-dash signal is inaudible (solid line). That's the null. Read the bearing off the ring.

Electronic Navigation: R.D.F. and Loran

The two electronic navigation instruments most commonly found on pleasure boats are the radio direction finder (R.D.F.) and loran. The former is the less expensive and accurate; the latter costs somewhat more and is very precise. They have one problem in common, and that's a tendency to go haywire when there is atmospheric disturbance around dawn, in the evening, and during thunderstorms (when their antennas may also attract lightning).

The Radio Direction Finder

The R.D.F. works like a long-range, hand bearing compass, picking up and taking bearings on radio signals sent from towers and lighthouses as far as 200 miles away. The navigator places the radio on the cabin sole or a sturdy table and, guided by somebody watching the cockpit compass, turns a ring that is like a compass dial until an arrow on the forward side of the box is directly over the compass course. He or she tunes to the frequency of a radio beacon—indicated on charts and in the Coast Guard publication *Light List*—and rotates the antenna until the signal is inaudible. This point is called the *null*. He or she reads the bearing to the beacon under the antenna pointer. All this time, the helmsperson must remain on the original course.

Bearings are plotted as lines of position and labeled with a box (for E.P.) or circle (for a fix), the time, and the label *R.D.F. E.P.* or *R.D.F. Fix*. This special identification is necessary because an R.D.F. bearing is considered less reliable than a sighted one.

One of the best uses for an R.D.F. is homing in on a beacon at a harbor entrance in poor visibility. Simply tune it to the beacon and turn up the sound so the helmsperson can hear the signal when the boat's off course. The silent null tells him or her that the boat's on course.

Loran

Loran—*long range navigation*—is an extremely accurate, nearly automatic electronic system that does not depend on plotting straight L.O.P.'s to a source. Instead, the machine displays the time difference in reception of two signals sent simultaneously by two distant beacons. The navigator locates curved L.O.P.'s (called time difference or T.D. lines) that represent the time differences on a coast or general chart, and then plots a fixed position where two or three lines meet. The accuracy can be as good as plus or minus 50 feet. Many loran sets simplify plotting by automatically translating the T.D.'s into latitude and longitude, by calculating the bearing and distance to the destination, and by figuring the boat's exact speed over the sea bottom. Even more remarkable than their performance is the fact that as loran receivers get more sophisticated, they get less expensive.

Old-time navigators become very squeamish when they hear

praise for devices like loran and its more expensive and versatile cousin satellite navigation, which are quickly obsoleting many traditional skills, including celestial navigation. Like everything else (celestial navigation included), these remarkable devices have their limitations and their place, yet they should not be blithely ignored by *anybody* who cares about knowing where he or she is on the water. Expense is no longer an excuse not to own loran; receivers that in 1980 cost more than $2,000 are available in 1985 for less than $500—roughly the price of two suits of good foul-weather gear. A selling point for loran that I've only recently discovered is that, unlike celestial navigation and advanced piloting, loran fascinates many bright people—some of them computer "hackers," others unathletic adolescents—who find nothing else of interest on a boat. This gadget allows many intellectual people to feel that they are making a contribution in a place where they would otherwise be passively and unenjoyably hanging on.

Nonetheless, too much can be made of a good thing. Once, the owner of the boat I was sailing on went wild when the loran packed up ten minutes before the start of a long race. Everything else—sail stowage, starting sequences, crew assignments—was ignored while the machine and its wires and antenna were attacked with screwdrivers, pliers, and voltmeters. He finally relaxed a bit after I pointed out that Long Island Sound at night is, after all, about as well lit as an interstate highway. He obviously had become addicted to electronics. Having bought this wonderful gadget, he wanted not only to use it but to *depend* on it. To avoid or minimize the dangerous and distracting effects of this addiction, the navigator must back up the secure belt of electronic navigation with the sturdy suspenders of standard piloting techniques. Just as the early navigators learned to place less than full trust in the magnetic compass (the oldest kind of electronic navigation device), so should the nautical beneficiaries of the silicon chip revolution be cautious about relying entirely on their magic blinking boxes.

A problem with these systems is that radio waves are not infallible. Not only do they jump all over the place at dawn and dusk and in electrical storms, but they can be redirected by land formations in "lane skips." A receiver's computer may misinterpret them because filters have not been adjusted or a nearby fluorescent light is turned on. For example, in 1980 a loran T.D. lane skip near Bermuda produced some rather surprising landfalls for many navigators on the Newport-Bermuda race. On *Elixir*, our hardworking and extremely thorough navigator, Ted Bilkey, spotted the error because the readout did not fit in the pattern of previous fixes, which he had carefully logged. Ted (whose caution earned us second place in the race) also compared loran fixes with celestial sights and with his meticulous dead reckoning plot, based on half-hourly log entries.

While each of the traditional navigation techniques is valuable, the importance of the D.R. cannot be overestimated. Because it is based solely on the evidence right there in front of your eyes, it is the only consistent backup and check on all of the other techniques.

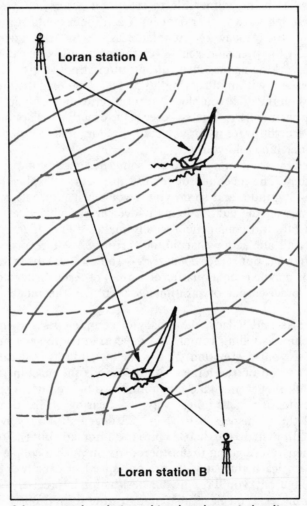

Loran station A

Loran station B

A loran receiver is tuned to signals sent simultaneously by a pair of stations, and displays the time difference (T.D.) in their reception. By matching the T.D.'s to lines printed on the chart, the pilot can plot an extremely accurate fix.

To make a D.R., you simply determine the boat's distance run over a known period of time, sailing on a known heading. All you need is a compass, a clock, and some way to determine speed. Of course, the compass can always be in error by a couple of degrees or the helmsperson might read the speedometer a tenth of a knot high or low, but given time and opportunity, those errors can be deduced and compensated for. At least with the D.R. your safety isn't wholly in the invisible hands of radio waves.

Besides being vulnerable to reception errors, electronics addicts are open to two other dangers. I call them the fallacy of precision and the fallacy of completeness. First, the instrument's reputation for precision can lower the navigator's guard. When a loran is working as designed, in optimum atmospheric conditions, its accuracy is within plus or minus 50 feet. You read the little green numbers on the dial; you plot your position; you mark your position with an encircled X. There—precisely, exactly, indisputably *there* —is where you were when you read the numbers. No doubt about it. The machine told you so.

Well, yes and no. There are some necessary compromises in the system. The machine rounds off numbers to display T.D. and latitude-longitude, and so do you if you must interpolate between T.D. lines on the chart. Your dividers or straight edge may be a fraction off, and your pencil usually makes a line thick enough to account, all alone, for that 50-foot error. So you're probably not *there*, after all, but rather *about there*—somewhere within about 100 yards (or maybe even a quarter of a mile) of *there*. Instead of marking the precise spot of position, X identifies the reliable area of position.

The second fallacy, the fallacy of completeness, assumes that the machine is telling you all you have to know to get from where you are to your destination. You go below and push the range-and-bearing button on the loran; within seconds the machine tells you something that would take five minutes to figure out on the chart: your destination is 10 miles away at a bearing of 323 degrees. So you tell the helmsperson to steer 323 degrees (or, if you're thoroughly automated, you dial 323 into the automatic pilot). Somebody asks when you're going to get there, so you push a couple of other buttons to learn that at your present speed of exactly 5.38 knots over the bottom, you'll reach your destination in precisely one hour, 51.52 minutes. You have just enough time to find out who killed Roger Ackroyd; you lean back and open up your Agatha Christie mystery. That's how simple it is. You don't have to look at the chart or plot your position or take a depth sounding or even go to the considerable effort of asking a shipmate sunbathing up on the foredeck to roll over and take a glance ahead. And then, Wham! The rock that the chart or a depth sounding or a lookout would have warned you about—an obstruction that a loran receiver has no capability of discovering—suddenly appears in precisely the wrong place, through the cabin sole.

So while electronic instruments can tell you a lot that is important and helpful and accurate, they do not and cannot tell you everything that is relevant to your situation and your intentions. It is a truism of our age that to depend too much on a machine, to expect a gadget—no matter how consequential it may be—to do more or better than it is capable of is to risk idolatry and invite disaster. Every time a navigator turns on one of these extraordinary machines, he or she must consciously declare the limits of his or her reliance on it, and be prepared to assume personal and human responsibility for safe navigation.

Keeping Up the Log

The log is the "ship's journal or day by day record of events, observations, courses steered, weather experienced, etc.," according to the *Encyclopedia of Nautical Knowledge*. This combination legal journal and diary can be a simple, ruled notebook or a fancy, leatherbound volume with the boat's name embossed in gold leaf. Plain or fancy, either way it should have enough room for the crew to record what's important to the boat's and their own welfare, to meet a legal requirement, and to provide some entertainment.

What information should be recorded? Anticipating the worst, you should write down anything that an investigator would need to know in order to recreate the important events of a cruise if nobody were there to tell about it: the names of crew and guests; ports of call and departure times; destinations and arrival times. The Coast Guard requires that all radio transmissions concerning safety be logged, so list times of calls, names of boats, call signals, and messages, even if they are merely overheard and not acted on. By law you must also sign each summary of a safety transmission. To keep a record of developments that might lead to trouble, note any rapid rises or drops in the barometer, buildup of heavy clouds, or increase in wave size that may herald bad weather. Report the sighting and progress of another vessel that threatens collision, and write down the changing bearings. Maintenance observations should be recorded in the log much the way you write grocery lists on the backs of envelopes: a change of engine oil; a shortage of toilet paper or ice; a request for honey for the tea; a lost batten in the mainsail. Announce a strange clank in the engine, a frayed halyard, a drop in voltage, a loss of stove fuel pressure.

But the log needn't be all business. It's a place to wax poetic about a glowing sunset, to repeat a good joke that deserves immortality, to tell about the dolphins that slipped under the bow wave all afternoon, to list the ingredients of a good rum punch, to tease the overseriousness out of the skipper at the beginning of a cruise.

The log's format should be structured in some places and loose in the other places. Here's a possible organization for a looseleaf notebook's page:

Log of yacht LYNX (Summer 1984)

8/5, Camden—Katherine, Peter, Anthony, & Sandy R.; Will, Dana, & John R.; Jim R., Sr. aboard for sail to Cape Cod Canal

Date/Time	Wind	Sea	Barom.	Course	Comments
8/5 1400	SW 12k	mod	30.0	190	Under way after fueling
1600	SW 15k	mod	"	"	Beautiful beat under Camden Hills toward sea
1640	Chan. 16 SOS from *R. H. Dana* on fire nr Camden. Relay SOS to USCG				
1650	USCG notifies standing by *Dana*, no serious damage or injury. SIGNED: *John Rousmaniere*				
1715	Back to normal after all the excitement. Last-minute top-off of engine oil (451 hrs), change to full stove gas tank. Forecast for SW going fresh NW tonight for fast reach across Gulf of Maine and Cape Cod Bay, so change down from #2 to #3 jib. Children issued life jackets and given seasick pills. "I'm on your watch, Dad" says Sandy—dead to the world 10 minutes later. Ah, the endurance of youth!				
1900	WSW 15	choppy	30.1	200	Clearing to NW and cooler. Hash & eggs for dinner
1930	Nav lights switched on. Replace dead bulb in port running light.				
2000	WSW 18	rough	30.1	210	Start watches: 1-P,K, A; 2-John, W; 3-Dad,D. 2 hour watches but nobody seems to want to go below.

The Pilot's Mind and Routine

Like any sort of detailed calculating, piloting is only as accurate as the data that are used. "Garbage in, garbage out" applies here just as it does in computer programming. There is one big difference, though: the pilot can often get into trouble by having too much faith in the accuracy of his information, which for a variety of good and solid reasons usually has a sizable fudge factor. Though many sailors aim for pin-point navigation, they rarely achieve it. Expecting too much accuracy will lead to frustration, time-consuming repetitions of bearings and calculations, and overly optimistic projections that may cut corners and leave the boat high and dry on a reef. Experienced navigators know that although the tiny circle they draw on the chart looks like a precise position, it's more like a fairly broad area of position. Rather than drawing an *X* and saying, "We're right there!", the pilot is better off saying that there's a 75 percent chance of being within two miles of the fixed position. Once made, promises are hard to go back on.

A good pilot also knows that even in calm weather no seaman can steer a course or take a compass bearing on (or toward) an object that is a mile or more away with an accuracy better than plus or minus 3 degrees; when the boat is rolling in steep waves, the error expands to 5 or even 10 degrees. Therefore, depending on the conditions, a "right on" course or bearing of 270 degrees might actually be anywhere between 265 and 275 degrees. At a range of one mile, that's an error of 300 yards; at five miles, three-quarters of a mile. Obviously, then, the pilot should take every opportunity available to check on a position.

Stick to a Routine

The lowest common denominator of good piloting is to keep in safe water. There are other reasons for taking bearings and plotting positions, but none is better than that one. Good pilots may not always know precisely where they are, but they usually know where they are *not*—and that is where rocks, shoals, fish nets, and other hazards *are*. Only a fool would navigate in fog or heavy weather without such a conservative approach, but defensive piloting should be standard operating procedure all the time. The many groundings and collisions that occur in perfectly clear weather suggest that even expert mariners let down their guard when the sailing becomes easy. Somehow, the routines that we follow so rigorously in poor visibility are forgotten when the sun comes out, and we cut corners and take other risks that may well pile us up on the nearest rocks.

These steps need not be pursued with the fervor of a Bligh;

just establish a reasonable ship's routine to be followed all the time she is under sail. Here's the one I like to use:

✓   At all times one person is assigned as navigator and has the primary responsibility for taking bearings, plotting positions on the chart, and advising the skipper about the boat's position and progress. The pilot may be the skipper or somebody with less experience (over whose shoulder the skipper takes an occasional peek). The actual mechanics of piloting are simple enough for anybody to do; it's the interpretation of apparently contradictory evidence that requires some experience. The essential skills can be mastered by anybody who can focus the mind, concentrate for extended periods of time, read a map, draw a straight line, and perform elementary mathematics. Twelve-year-olds make excellent pilots, as do computer whizzes and crossword puzzle buffs.

✓   All potential problems must be anticipated and talked through before they appear. For example, the times of tide changes should be calculated ahead of time, and charts should be arranged in the probable order of use.

✓   The plot and logbook must be kept up to date. The boat's position is noted regularly in clear weather. Near shore, this means plotting the position at every turning point and inspecting the upcoming route on the chart (to save chart wear and tear, the position need not be written down). In bad weather, the position is always written down on the chart at every turning point near shore and at every hour (or more frequently) offshore. In addition, the most important courses, distances run, and turning marks are listed in order in the logbook. That way, the pilot can backtrack to find mistakes.

A little system, care, and routine—that's all we're encouraging. In the long run, the five minutes you spend over the chart and tide tables every hour will save you many hours of worry. Much of the time, what worries a navigator most is the threat of running into something—either land or another vessel. In Chapter 10, we'll see how the risk of collisions can be minimized.

CHAPTER 10

How to Avoid Running into Things

The United States government has created or played a part in creating two legal systems that, when observed by mariners, keep vessels from colliding with land and each other. Called the lateral buoyage system and the rules of the road, these sets of regulations feature sound and sight signals, many of them redundant, that warn which kinds of hazards to anticipate and indicate how to avoid them. Once you have taken the time to learn the vocabulary and grammar of these two systems, you will find them ingeniously unambiguous.

Avoiding Running Aground: The Lateral Buoyage System

Buoys that serve as aids to navigation are large floating metal objects with distinctive characteristics—shapes, colors, and lights—that tell approaching sailors on which side to pass. Their purpose is to guide boats away from shoals and land and into channels, and to keep them there. In the United States and Canada, an arrangement of buoys called the lateral system governs. In it, the buoys mark the side of the channel much the way the curb marks the side of the road. Most of the rest of the world relies on the cardinal system, in which buoy characteristics indicate the compass direction

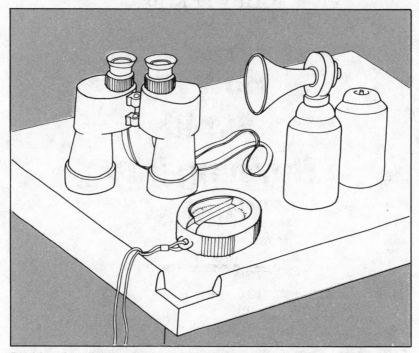

Besides the chart and a knowledge of the rules of the road, these three items may be your best protection against running into land or another boat: binoculars for identifying distant objects, a handbearing compass for taking extremely accurate bearings, and a horn for making required signals.

to a hazard. The cardinal system is also the basis of the U.S. Uniform State Waterway Marking System, used on inland lakes and rivers within the boundaries of one state and therefore outside the jurisdiction of the Coast Guard.

The Two Key Terms: Leave *and* Enter

Before we move on to describe the buoys, we should discuss the meaning of two important words that must be understood if the lateral system is to make any sense. Those terms are *leave* and *enter*.

To leave a buoy to port or starboard (also called *on the port or starboard hand*) means to pass it so that the buoy is on the designated side of the boat. When a buoy is left to port, it's passed on the boat's port (left) side. When left to starboard, a buoy is passed on the boat's starboard (right) side.

To enter means to sail into a harbor, or into a smaller body of water—from, say, an ocean into a bay or from a bay into a river mouth. On the other hand, *to depart* means to sail out of a port or into a larger body of water. Sometimes *return* and *leave* are used instead of *enter* and *depart*.

The lateral system doesn't make any sense unless you are aware whether you're entering or departing, because almost all buoys must be left on one side when entering and on the other when departing. Knowing when you are entering or departing may not always be easy, since the size of the two bodies of water may be similar. A helpful rule of thumb is that you're entering if you're sailing toward the most likely place to anchor, but leaving if you're moving toward the sea.

Buoy Characteristics and What They Mean

Within the lateral system there are seven families of navigation buoys: cans, nuns, junction buoys, daybeacons, midchannel buoys, lighted buoys, and special buoys. Each has two or more characteristics of shape, color, number, and light; if you can distinguish only one characteristic, you'll still know which side of the buoy to pass on.

Most of the time, the most visible buoy characteristic is its color or the color of its light, and so long as you know if you are entering or departing, this simple rule will be your guide:

> Red right returning,
> Green or black right departing.

This means that when *entering* (returning), leave red buoys and lights to starboard and green or black buoys and green lights to port. The opposite applies when *departing*: red buoys and lights are left to port and green or black buoys and green lights are left to starboard. Another important rule is that buoy numbers increase on the way into the harbor.

Here are the seven types of buoys:

✓ **Cans** are green or black and flat-topped, carry reflective odd numbers, and have no lights. (Since 1983, high-visibility green has gradually been replacing black as the color of can buoys.) Cans always mark the left-hand side of a channel when you're entering: you leave them to port (left) on entering and to starboard (right) on departing. The chart symbol for a can is a green or black diamond, the letter *C*, and the buoy's number.

✓ **Nuns** are red, have pointed tops, carry reflective even numbers, and have no lights. Nuns line the starboard (right) side of the channel on entering and the port (left) side on departing.

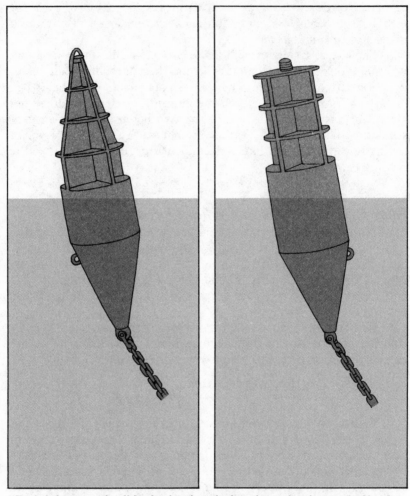

"Red right returning" is the basic rule for observing buoys in North America. Leave red nun buoys (pictured left) to starboard when entering a harbor, green and black can buoys (pictured right) to port.

On a chart, a nun is indicated by a red diamond, the letter *N*, and the buoy's number.

✓ **Junction buoys** have red and green (or black) horizontal stripes, are shaped like nuns or cans, may carry letters (but not numbers), and may carry lights. They mark rocks or shoals in a channel and may be left to either side, but the shape and color scheme indicate the preferred side for the safest navigation. A can-shaped junction buoy whose top stripe is green or

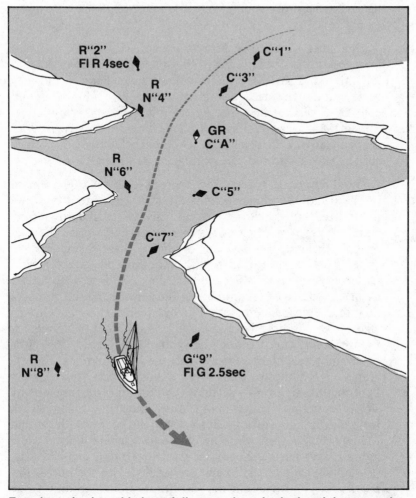

Entering a harbor, this boat follows a clear, logical path between the curbs defined by the various buoys, whose chart symbols are shown here.

black should be treated like a can. Its chart symbol is a green and red diamond labeled *GR*. A nun-shaped one with a red top stripe should be treated like a nun. A red and green diamond and *RG* are its chart symbol and label.

✓ **Daybeacons** are stakes pounded into the bottoms of rivers and waterways with visible plaques called *daymarks*, which have the same arrangement of color schemes, numbers, symbols, labels, and meanings as cans, nuns, and junction buoys. Green, port-hand daymarks are square; red, starboard-hand ones are triangular.

✓ **Midchannel or fairway buoys** are spherical, have red and white vertical stripes (if lighted they have tall frameworks), and are lettered. They mark the middle of wide channels and may be left to either side. Their chart symbol is a white diamond split by a vertical line, the letters *RW*, and the buoy letter. (Since 1983, these midchannel buoys have been replacing can-shaped buoys with black and white vertical stripes and nun-shaped buoys with red and white vertical stripes.)

✓ **Lighted buoys** are painted red or green (or black). Their main job is to indicate channels at night with green, red, or white lights. Red buoys with red lights mark the starboard side on entering; green or black buoys with green lights mark the port side. Their lights can have one of several phase characteristics, either fixed (always lit at night) or flashing in one of several patterns. A green or black lighted buoy is odd-numbered (like a can), a red one even-numbered (like a nun), and the numbers fit into the sequence of other buoys in the channel. On the chart, green and red lighted buoys are indicated by a green or red diamond, a purple dot (the symbol for a light), the light's color and phase characteristic, and the buoy number. For example, *F R* indicates a fixed red light and *Fl G 4sec* a green light that flashes every 4 seconds (you can time the intervals by slowly counting "one-thousand, two-thousand," and so on from one flash to the next. Since 1983, the policy has been that the only buoys with white lights are midchannel buoys; these lights always have a short-long-short-long phase characteristic (the Morse code letter *A*) and are labeled with the purple dot and *MoA*. To provide further identification, lighted buoys may carry bells, gongs (bells with several notes), whistles, or horns.

✓ **Special buoys** are lighted or unlighted, and yellow, white, or white-and-orange striped. They indicate anchorages and quarantine areas and warn of fish nets, dredges, and other dangers.

Hints on Using Buoys

The beauty of the lateral system is that it *is* a *system*; all its pieces intermesh to define "roads" around hazards. Once you're on the road, keep track of your position by following the increasing buoy numbers if you're entering or the decreasing numbers if you're departing. Where the water is shallow and the channel twisting, it's easy to get confused unless you plan and trace your progress on a large-scale harbor chart. Be attentive to low-tide water depths, or soundings, marked in small black numbers on the chart; provide yourself a safety factor of at least three feet below your keel. Broken black contour lines link points of equal depth at approximately ten-foot intervals, and areas of shoal water may be identified by blue shading. An elaborate symbolic language has been developed to show hazards on charts; it is described in a booklet called *Nautical Chart Symbols and Abbreviations*, available from authorized N.O.S. chart agents. Among the symbols most frequently found on harbor and coast charts are + (submerged rock) and * (rock visible at low tide).

Many buoys in large, deep bodies of water are laid out for large commercial ships and may be safely passed on either side by a shoal-draft pleasure boat. But most buoys in harbors and shallow bays must be properly passed. Even if the chart suggests that there's safe water outside the imaginary curb marked by buoys, it's safer to stick to the middle of the channel because buoys may have drifted or the bottom around them may have silted up. However, swing toward the outside of bends in rivers or tidal waters, where the inside tends to shoal more quickly than the outside.

In poor visibility you may have trouble locating or identifying buoys and lights. When looking for one, keep your eyes moving across the horizon—staring invites double vision—and don't panic if it doesn't immediately appear where you think it should. Land, another boat, or waves may be obscuring it, or your eyes may be tired. Slow the boat down and rest for a moment, or get a fresh pair of eyes working on the problem.

The Coast Guard frequently relocates buoys and changes their characteristics during the winter. Your best protection against chaos is an up-to-date chart and the official publication *Local Notice to Mariners*, available at many chandleries and by subscription from your local Coast Guard District headquarters (their addresses are listed in Appendix II of *The Annapolis Book of Seamanship*).

Avoiding Collisions:
The Inland Rules of the Road

Over the centuries, each maritime community has developed its own driving rules to keep vessels within sight of each other from colliding. These rules have gradually been internationalized and standardized. Today, there are two sets of very similar rules of the road (as they're informally known): the International Regulations for Preventing Collisions at Sea, known as COLREGS; and the Inland

Navigational Rules of the United States, known as the *inland rules of the road*.

COLREGS applies in waters beyond an offshore purple demarcation line shown on U.S. charts; if you sail far out into salt water or into foreign waters, you'll be subject to COLREGS. The inland rules apply inside those lines, in U.S. coastal, lake, and river waters. The rules differ in minor ways (mainly in the sound signals that are made when vessels are near each other), and even those differences may soon end. Since the inland rules cover the waters plied by the vast majority of American sailors, we'll devote the remainder of this chapter to a summary of their most important provisions. Both sets of rules are given verbatim in the Coast Guard booklet *Navigation Rules, International-Inland*, available at many N.O.S. chart outlets.

Definitions, Signals, and Navigation Lights

A few rules apply all the time in the form of definitions and required signals and lights for nighttime sailing.

Give-way vessels are responsible for staying out of the way of *stand-on* vessels. When a collision threatens, the rules specify which boat is the give-way vessel and must alter course. While she changes course, the stand-on vessel must do what that name implies—continue on her course so as not to confuse the give-way vessel.

A *powerboat* is a boat whose engine is running and in gear. Even when your sails are set, if your engine is in gear, your boat is a powerboat under the rules.

Signals between vessels are made by a horn or loud whistle in short blasts of 1 second or long blasts of 4 to 6 seconds, or in combinations of the two. Whenever there is any risk of imminent collision, the *danger signal* of five or more short blasts is sounded.

Navigation lights must be turned on at sunset. Different combinations and types of lights identify different types of boats. Sailboats shorter than 23 feet can legally get by with a bright flashlight, but most larger sailboats must carry the following navigation lights:

✓ **Sidelights** showing red for port and green for starboard, aimed ahead and slightly to the side. Sidelights are usually placed on the bow but they may be at the top of the mast.

✓ **A white masthead (also called a bow or powering) light** about two-thirds of the way up the mast. This light aims ahead and slightly to the sides and is turned on only when the boat is under power.

✓ **A white sternlight** that aims astern and slightly to the sides.

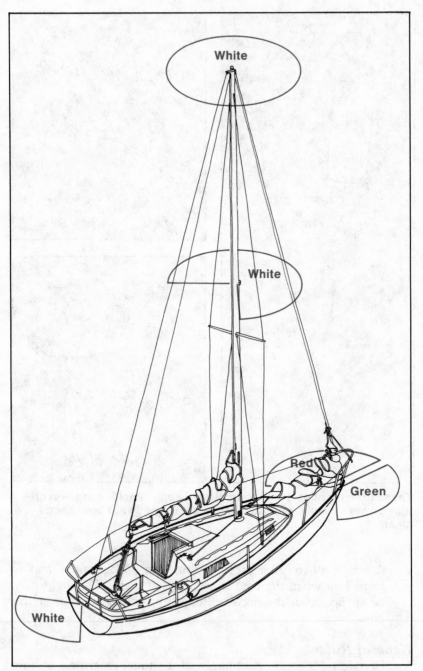

These legally required navigation lights must be lit at night on most sailboats larger than 23 feet. The masthead light partway up the mast is used only when under power.

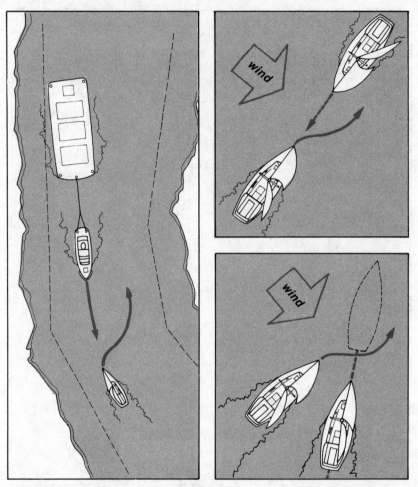

These general rules of the road always apply: avoid unmaneuverable power vessels; port tack keeps clear; windward boat keeps clear.

✔ **A white all-round light** that shines in all directions and is turned on when the boat is anchored at night. This light may be at the top of the mast or hung from the headstay over the bow.

General Rules

Certain rules of the road apply all the time, regardless of how boats are approaching each other.

✔ When sailboats—boats under sail with their engines off or out

of gear—are near each other:
- On different tacks, the give-way vessel is the one on port tack (the one with the wind coming over her port side). If a collision threatens, she must alter course to avoid the stand-on, starboard-tack boat, which must continue on her course. *"Port tack keep clear."*
- On the same tack, the give-way vessel is the one to windward, or upwind of the stand-on vessel. *"Windward boat keep clear."*

✓ In all other situations, the boat with the better maneuverability —the one most able to change course quickly—is the give-way vessel, and the less maneuverable boat is the stand-on vessel. For example:
- When a powerboat is near a sailboat, the powerboat is the give-way vessel. *Exceptions:* sailboats must give way to large powerboats in channels and traffic separation zones, to powerboats engaged in fishing or trawling, to vessels that are out of control, and to cumbersome vessels such as tows, dredges, and ferries.
- In a narrow channel or traffic separation zone, boats smaller than 66 feet, fishing boats, and sailboats are the give-way vessels when near a large vessel that must use the center of the channel.
- A moving vessel must stay out of the way of an anchored, moored, or otherwise stationary vessel.

When Powerboats Meet

Certain rules apply when powerboats (including sailboats under power) meet. Echoing *intent-agreement* horn or whistle signals must be exchanged by the boats involved *before* the give-way vessel alters course. The give-way boat first signals her intentions and the other boat responds either by repeating the signal to indicate "go ahead" or by sounding the danger signal (five short blasts) to indicate "no." If the former, they take the action that has been signaled. If the latter, they take "appropriate cautionary action," usually by stopping or slowing down. If the signals *cross* (contradict each other), both boats must make the danger signal and take appropriate cautionary action until they have reached agreement.

Situations and required signals are as follows:

✓ **When powerboats are meeting bow to bow** and are likely to pass within one-half mile of each other, each boat is a give-way vessel with a responsibility for altering course, preferably sharply to starboard so that they pass port side to port side at a

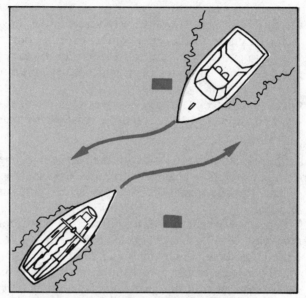

**Sound one blast if you intend to alter course to
starboard and two if you plan to alter course to
port. Wait for the other vessel's agreement.
Three short blasts mean you're backing down,
five short blasts is the danger signal. These rules
apply whether you are overtaking, meeting
(shown here), or crossing another boat.**

safe distance. At night, you know you're in this situation if you
see the other boat's red and green sidelights, and her masthead,
or powering, light.

- If they intend to pass port side to port side or turn to
  starboard away from each other, they signal one short
  blast.
- If they intend to pass starboard side to starboard side and
  turn to port, they make two short blasts.
- If they intend to back down away from each other, they
  signal three short blasts.

✓ **When powerboats are on converging, crossing courses,** the
one to port (the left side) of the other is the give-way vessel. At
night, you know you're in this situation if you see a green light
to port or a red light to starboard and the compass bearing to it
doesn't seem to change. The give-way vessel's turn should be
abrupt and she should pass well away from the stand-on vessel.

- If she intends to avoid the stand-on vessel by altering

course to starboard and passing astern of her, the give-way vessel gives one short blast but does not alter course until the other vessel gives one short blast.

- If she plans to turn to port, the give-way vessel gives two short blasts and waits before turning for the stand-on vessel to echo her signal.
- If she plans to back down, the give-way vessel makes three short blasts.

✓ **When one powerboat is overtaking another** —passing from astern but not yet even—she is the give-way vessel and the boat ahead is the stand-on vessel. At night, you know you're the stand-on vessel if you see red and green lights approaching from astern. You're the give-way vessel if a low white stern light ahead seems to be getting nearer.

- If the trailing boat intends to pass on the leading boat's starboard side, she makes one short blast and waits for an agreement.
- If she intends to pass on the leading boat's port side, she makes two short blasts and waits for an agreement.
- If for some reason she must back down, the trailing boat makes three short blasts. Once again, the give-way vessel must not make her move until the stand-on vessel signals agreement with her intentions.

Anticipating Possible Collisions

Keep your eyes open; a big problem is seeing the other boat in

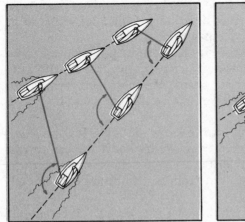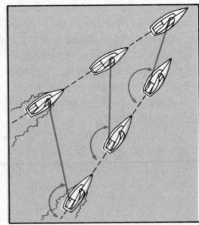

(left) If bearings taken on another boat move aft, you'll pass ahead. (right) If they move forward, she'll pass ahead.

the first place. You must be able to answer these questions within a minute of spotting another vessel: How big is she? Which direction is she headed in? How fast is she moving?

At night, analyze her lights and their arrangement. If all you see is a red or green sidelight, she's probably a boat under sail; a white powering light higher than the sidelight indicates that she's under power. Commercial ships such as tows, freighters, and tankers show special light combinations (described in Chapter 11 of *The Annapolis Book of Seamanship* and in other seamanship and navigation manuals). After a few minutes of this hard work, your eyes may get tired and your mind may turn to jelly; if this happens, ask somebody else to study the other boat. Anybody taking over as lookout or helmsperson must be carefully briefed about nearby boats and possible collision situations.

Be extremely cautious when near big ships, whose maneuverability is limited (if there's nobody at the helm, it's nonexistent) and whose speed is greater than you may at first think.

When you see another boat coming toward you, try to figure out her heading. Study the arrangement of her rigging and, at night, her navigation lights. Unless both boats take evasive action, a collision is certain to occur under one or more of the following circumstances: if her headstay and mast line up; if her stern can't be seen; if the windward and leeward sides of her sails alternately appear; if her red and green sidelights are both visible; or, on ships, if two elevated white masthead range lights—one forward and the other aft—line up.

When another vessel is alongside and closing on you, take a series of compass bearings on her. If the bearings don't change, you definitely will converge and collide. When near a boat that is between you and the land, try to determine if the land seems to be moving behind her; if not, you may collide.

If you're the give-way vessel, take abrupt and obvious evasive action. When meeting, "show her your port or your red" with a 20-degree (or greater) turn to starboard. When passing behind the other boat, pass far astern. However, if you're the stand-on vessel, hold your course.

Don't trust the other skipper to know the rules. If there is any question of his or her competence (or yours), or if you can't make any sense of lights or behavior, either stop and wait for the other vessel to pass or alter course away from her. Clearheaded caution is your best guide.

CHAPTER 11

Painless Docking and Anchoring

Once a boat and her crew have left her marina or mooring, they often proceed, slowly or otherwise, toward a place to stop for the night, a meal, a swim, or just a nap. Here we'll talk about the mechanics of anchoring, docking, and using the dinghy. In Part III we'll have a lot to say about what to do once you've stopped.

Before heading off, the crew should agree on a secure destination (multiply the number of hours you want to be under way by your anticipated average speed to figure how far you'll sail) and at least one closer, more protected alternative, just in case the wind dies or the weather worsens. Depending on the area, the destination will be either an anchorage, where you may drop an anchor or pick up a mooring, or a marina or pier, where you'll dock. Many sailing areas offer both alternatives, each of which has advantages and disadvantages spelled out in the *U.S. Coast Pilot* (a government guide to coastlines and waterways available at chart stores) and in commercially published books that go under the generic term "cruising guide." Anchoring is free and can be done in many places near shore, but it requires some skill, and an anchored boat should not be left unattended longer than a few hours. Moorings and slips at yacht clubs, boat yards, and town docks usually are secure and provide access to showers, shops, and entertainment, but they're noisy and crowded and can be expensive. In 1984, overnight fees in

New England and Long Island Sound ran $1 to $2 per foot of overall length for a marina slip (water and electricity included) and $10 to $20 for a mooring (often with shoreboat service included). Many experienced cruising sailors anchor out away from civilization most of the time, breaking their cruise every several days with a night spent on a mooring or in a dock near a town. One money-saving tactic is to anchor at night and, every couple of days, tie up for a short while at a fuel dock (generally at no cost beyond the fuel or ice you purchase) for short shore trips. Remember, too, that you can drop somebody off on a pier for a shopping expedition and slowly circle under power until he or she returns.

How to Dock and Undock

A dock is the spot of water that a boat sits in when she's tied to a pier, float, or wharf, so docking is the act of tying up and undocking is the act of leaving.

Docking Equipment

To dock properly you'll need two or more fenders (rubber bumpers) to hang between the boat and pier and four docking lines, each preferably about 20 feet long and made of ⅜-inch or larger nylon rope. Nylon is less expensive, stronger, and more resistant to chafe (abrasion) than Dacron, so don't use the Dacron jib or spinnaker sheets as docking lines; they'll quickly be worn so badly that they may break when used for their primary purpose. In a pinch, the long nylon anchor rode (line) may be rigged as a continuous docking line, but since each of the four lines has a unique function and often must be rigged and unrigged quickly, it's better to have separate short ones. Some docking lines have large loops spliced in one end to hang over cleats or posts on the pier, but you can do just as well if you know how to tie a bowline or cleat a line properly.

The four docking lines and their uses are as follows:

✓ **The bow line** runs from a cleat on the bow through a chock (a metal groove that minimizes chafe) and slightly forward to a cleat or post on the pier. The bow line keeps the bow from swinging out from the pier.

✓ **The stern line** runs from the stern slightly aft to the pier to prevent the stern from swinging out.

✓ **The after spring line** runs from the foredeck, about one-fourth the boat's length aft of the bow, to a cleat on the pier, about one-fourth of her length forward of the stern. The after spring restrains the boat from surging forward.

✓ **The forward spring line** crosses the after spring in a shallow X. It runs forward from the after deck, about one-fourth of the boat's length forward of the stern, to a cleat on the pier, about one-fourth of her length aft of the bow. The forward spring stops the boat from surging aft.

The bow and stern lines serve mainly to keep the boat parallel to the pier. The main load is taken by the two crisscrossed spring lines, which should be led around winches or large cleats. All the docking lines should be dead-ended at (secured with one end at) the cleats or posts on the pier, float, or wharf, leaving plenty of line at the other end so that they can be adjusted by the crew on board. Lines tied to piers or wharfs, which aren't buoyant, usually must be lengthened and shortened as the boat falls and rises with the tide, although spreading them out at very shallow angles may minimize or even eliminate the need for adjustment. (Floats, however, rise and fall with the water.) Reinforce docking lines with backups in threatening or stormy weather.

How to Dock

Small, light daysailers may be docked under sail by jogging toward the pier with sails luffing, then heading the bow into the

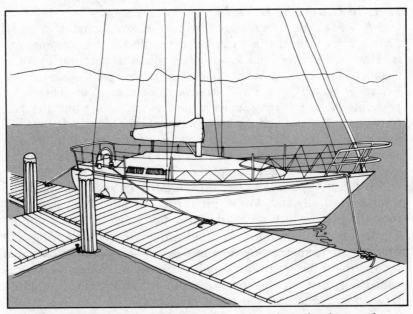

This properly docked C & C racer-cruiser has three fenders and bow, stern, and spring lines between her and the float.

wind and toward the dock. Don't try to dock on a reach or run; you'll just ram the pier and scratch up your boat's sides. Hang the boat downwind off the float or pier with a bow line.

Most cruising-boat docking is done under power. Approach fast enough to have steerageway but not so fast that you can't stop within about five feet by going into reverse. Hang the fenders over the side at the height of the side of the pier, tying them to a plastic-coated lifeline or a fitting on the rail using a double half-hitch or bowline, and lay out the four docking lines on deck. The boat should be parallel to the pier as you make the final approach. Put the engine into neutral or slow reverse gear—shifting suddenly into hard reverse may damage the transmission—and toss or hand the bow and stern lines to people on the pier (or have two of your crew step onto it). Adjust the lines at the bow and stern as she slows and stops, and then rig the two spring lines and adjust them until the boat lies parallel. Heavy boats or boats docking in a high stern wind or rough seas may need the help of the after spring line—that's the one running from the bow aft to the pier—to brake to a stop. Hand that line across and have it cleated first. The stern will swing out as she slows, so rig the stern line next.

Larger boats have boarding gates (openings in the lifelines); they should be positioned as close to the float or pier as possible.

How to Leave the Dock

A boat has no steerageway when she makes a standing start, so getting away from the pier can be more difficult than coming into it. Here the spring lines are used to aim the boat out into the channel. The basic principle is that *as a boat pulls against a line secured at one end of her hull, the other end swings out.* Therefore, powering aft in reverse gear with the forward spring line attached forces the stern into and the bow away from the pier, and powering forward with the after spring attached forces the bow into the pier and the stern away from it. Be careful to keep lines from dangling overboard and fouling the propeller when the engine is in gear.

It's best to power out of a dock in forward gear since sailboats reverse erratically and slowly. First, the bow must be swung away from the pier—which means that the stern must be swung into it. Throw off the bow line and after spring (that's the spring line running aft from the bow to the pier). Then gently back down against the forward spring to pull the stern in. When the bow is aimed out, cast off the stern line and forward spring, shift into forward gear, and head out.

Sometimes, though, you'll have to back out of a dock, first swinging the bow into and the stern away from the pier. Throw off

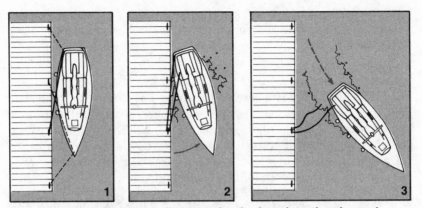

Undocking, use the spring lines to aim the bow into the channel. First, power aft against the forward spring line, then throw off the spring and power out.

the stern and forward spring lines and power slow ahead. When the stern is aimed out into the channel, throw off the bow and after spring lines and back out.

Because single-propeller boats like the average cruising sailboat are inherently asymmetrical and therefore handle poorly under power at low speeds, you'll never be bored while docking and undocking. Yet while it can spoil maneuverability, the propeller's built-in asymmetry can be a help. When a right-handed, clockwise-turning propeller is put into reverse gear and the throttle is given a quick burst, the stern will initially walk (slide) to port more than it will go aft. Left-handed, counterclockwise-spinning propellers will walk the stern to starboard in reverse. Used properly, this trick will give you an eggshell landing every time; all you need to know is which direction the propeller turns. Don't try it in forward gear, though, unless you want to ram the boat ahead.

How to Anchor

The anchor and its connecting rode (nylon line, chain, or a combination of both) are called *ground tackle* because they secure the boat to the ground beneath the water. There are several types of anchor—plow, lightweight, Bruce, yachtsman's, and others. Of the more manageable, smaller anchors, the CQR-type plow seems to work well in just about all bottoms and the Danforth-type lightweight and Bruce are especially good in the soft sand and mud found in many cruising areas. The anchor's weight and the rode's strength must be carefully matched to the boat's size. Typically, the rode is made of nylon line except for the last 6 to 10 feet, where chain is used to add weight, improving the horizontal pull down near the bottom.

Selecting an Anchorage

The anchorage is where you anchor. The Coast Guard has laid out areas called Special Anchorages where boats need not show white anchor lights at night and where the holding ground presumably is good and will grab an anchor well; these areas are delineated clearly on charts. But you can anchor just about anywhere, so long as you comply with certain important guidelines.

✓ For the greatest possible security when anchoring overnight, the depth of water at high tide should be about one-quarter to one-eighth the length of your rode. If the rode is 160 feet long, you're entirely safe if you anchor in 20 feet of water, all right in 30 feet, but tempting fate in 40. The reason for this is that to make the hook dig in, you must maximize the horizontal pull by narrowing the angle between the rode and the bottom. To do that, you let out much more rode than the water is deep. The ratio of rode to depth is called *scope*. The ideal scope ranges from 4:1 (4 feet of rode for every 1 foot of water) in light conditions to 7:1 or more in storms. To determine the high-tide depth, find the low-tide depth on the chart and add the local tidal range to it.

✓ Choose a soft mud or sand bottom rather than one that has hard rocks, hard mud, or (worst of all) weed. Chart labels show the type of holding ground.

✓ Anchor with some protective land between you and the wind —a shoreline, a peninsula, even a sandbar—so that the waves are broken before they get to you.

✓ Anchor at least 50 feet from other boats (100 feet in rough weather).

✓ Anticipate changes in wind direction and their effect on your position, keeping in mind a quick escape route if you must up-anchor and leave the harbor in the middle of the night in a rising gale.

Dropping the Hook

Pull the anchor and about 50 feet of rode on deck and tighten all the shackles with a wrench, spike, or pliers. The shackle pins should then be *moused*, or secured with wraps of light wire or line.

Lead the anchor so the rode will run smoothly from the bow cleat through the bow chock and down to the water. Tie the bitter end of the rode to the mast or some other strong, permanently fixed object just in case it runs out all the way.

Meanwhile, the skipper steers the boat toward the anchorage, powers dead into the wind to the chosen spot, and goes into slow reverse to stop her there. (Though power provides better maneuverability, you can anchor under sail in light and moderate wind under mainsail alone, beating up to the spot, then heading into the wind.) As the boat makes her approach, the crew should quickly reevaluate

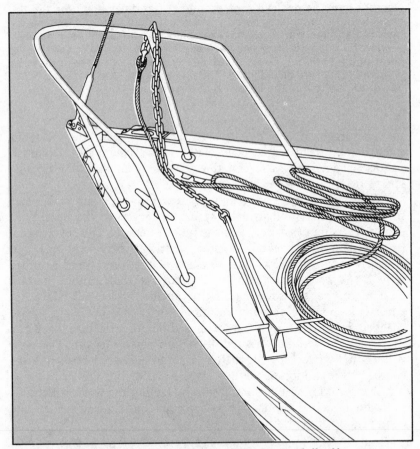

Before anchoring, prepare the ground tackle carefully. Here a Danforth-type lightweight anchor, perhaps the most widely used anchor in the United States, is ready to be dropped. Its chain and rope rode are faked out in long loops. All shackles should be moused (securely lashed) and the rode's bitter end should be tied to the boat with a bowline.

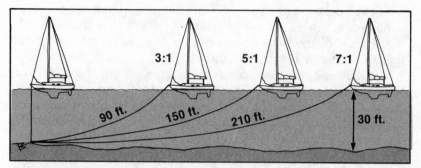

(left to right) To anchor, first bring the boat slowly into the wind and stop her over the desired spot, then back her down and drop the hook. Let out considerable rode to make a shallow angle between the rode and the water, so that the pull is as horizontal as possible —up to 7:1 scope in fresh winds. Keep checking to make sure you're not dragging anchor. To weigh anchor, power forward while the rode is pulled up. When directly over the anchor, cleat the rode and power ahead to pull the hook out of the bottom.

the anchorage. When she falls back about 50 feet, will she swing safely distant from nearby boats? Will she be lying out of a channel? Is this harbor *really* safe? Or does it just seem that way because you're tired?

The skipper keeps the bow pointed into the wind and, when the boat begins to drift backwards, orders that the anchor be dropped. As it goes over, he or she puts the engine into reverse gear (or the mainsail is backed) to gather sternway (reverse speed). The crew on the bow throws out, to start, about three times as much rode as the water is deep and takes a turn of rode around the bow cleat. The boat's sternway pulls the anchor back until it digs in. The hook should grab within a minute or two; if not, it may have snagged an obstruction like a cardboard box or a big clam shell and must be retrieved and cleaned off before you try again. The crew will know by checking for drift relative to anchored boats and the shore; by the motion of the bow, which will bob if the anchor's set but swing to one side if it isn't; and by feeling the rode, which will jerk and twitch if the anchor is dragging but quietly stretch and compress if it has grabbed the bottom.

By far the most common mistake made when anchoring is not having enough scope. If the anchor drags or doesn't immediately catch, throw out more rode—not just a foot or two but many yards of it. The greater the scope, the more horizontal is the rode's pull on the anchor and the more likely it is that the flukes will dig in. If great scope doesn't stop dragging, haul up and clean off the anchor, move somewhere else, and try again. Once the anchor is set, the scope should be increased to approximately 6:1, or about 120 feet of rode in water that will be 20 feet deep at high tide. If you become nervous during the night, and find yourself waking frequently to take bearings on nearby stationary objects to see if you're dragging, the best sleeping pill is even greater scope.

How to Weigh Anchor

Weigh anchor under power only. While you can drop a mooring under sail (backing the jib to swing the bow off), few boats under sail can accelerate sufficiently from a standing stop to pull the anchor out of the bottom. With a crewmember pulling in the rode, power slowly toward the anchor. Somebody should point down the line of the rode to keep the skipper aimed properly. When the rode is straight up and down, the crew notifies the helm by raising an arm. The engine is shifted into neutral as the rode is cleated on the bow cleat. With a wave, the crew tells the skipper to power forward, and the boat's momentum trips the anchor from the bottom. The crew then hauls the rest of the rode and the anchor on deck, carefully avoiding scratching the topsides with the anchor's sharp flukes. If the hook is muddy, it may be washed off by bouncing it up and down in the bow wave and scrubbing it overboard or on deck with a long-handled brush. Keep mud off sails and lines. Once on deck, the cleaned anchor and coiled rode should be immediately tied down and left to dry.

Rafting-Up and Other Anchoring Tricks

A sociable way to spend an evening is to tie one or more boats alongside each other in a raft. The largest boat first drops and securely digs in her heaviest anchor at greater scope than she would use if anchoring alone. Then the other boats tie up alongside using fenders and bow, stern, and spring lines just as they would when docking. The main danger from rafting-up is that the masts and spreaders may tangle when the boats roll; alert adjustments to the spring lines should keep the rigging well separated. Another problem is dragging, in which case the raft should be broken up immediately. Caution suggests that raft-ups should not be left unattended and that they be broken up before everybody goes to bed.

Setting two anchors has the triple advantage of increasing the holding power, using less scope, and limiting swinging around in currents and gusty winds. Two anchors may be dropped over the bow either on the same rode or on separate rodes. With the two-rode system, drop the first anchor the way we described earlier, then using the dinghy set the second anchor so that the included

When rafting-up, the biggest boat first digs in her largest anchor, then the other boats come alongside using fenders and bow, stern, and spring lines. Be sure to keep the masts well separated so they don't roll into each other when a powerboat passes by. Break up the raft and go your separate ways if the wind blows hard or the sea gets very rough.

angle between the rodes is 60 to 90 degrees. Dual anchoring over the bow and stern is used in narrow, crowded anchorages where boats may swing into each other. Drop the first anchor over the stern and, making sure the rode doesn't tangle in the propeller, keep going forward until the scope is 8:1. Then drop the second anchor over the bow and back down to dig it in until the scope on both is 4:1. She'll now lie quietly between the two, like a shirt on a clothesline.

The Dinghy

A great help in an anchorage—for transportation and pleasure —is the boat's dinghy, a small rubber or fiberglass rowing or sailing boat usually towed astern but sometimes carried aboard. Whole books have been written about dinghies and their use, but what's important here is to know how to tow them and get in and out of them.

Hard fiberglass dinghies, of which the best-known is the Dyer Dhow, come in both rowing and sailing versions. The latter has a centerboard, rudder, and small rig, and can be great fun. Once in

Edgartown Harbor on Martha's Vineyard, my ingenious brother Arthur figured out how to sail a Dyer Dhow close-hauled *backwards* (don't ask me how). These boats should normally be towed so they're riding comfortably in the second wave astern, except in close quarters (for example, a crowded anchorage), when the bow line should be shortened until the bow nudges the big boat's stern. Remove the oars before towing. In fact, for security, keep the oars out of the dinghy except when she's actually being rowed; thieves don't normally walk around with oars looking for a dinghy to steal.

Getting in and out of a fiberglass rowing or sailing dinghy can be the most challenging part of the sailor's day. Keep your weight in the middle of the boat, stepping onto and off the middle of the center seat and lowering or raising yourself gradually with a hand on each rail. If another person is already aboard, balance his or her weight. For example, if someone is sitting on the stern seat, lower yourself onto the forward seat. Never make a sudden move in a crowded dinghy.

An inflatable rubber dinghy under tow can easily capsize in crosswinds and rough seas unless the bow is pulled right up on the big boat's transom with only the after half dragging. Better yet, partially or wholly deflate it and tie it on deck or, after a thorough

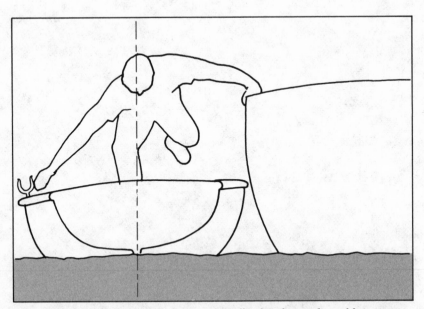

When climbing in and out of an empty dinghy, face aft and keep your weight in the middle of the boat. If somebody's already aboard in the bow or stern, step into the opposite end to balance the weight. Remove the inside oarlock so it doesn't scratch the yacht's hull.

drying, stow it below. Inflatables used in salt water should be hosed off with fresh water and then dried before being put below, since dry salt crystals will attract moisture and cause mildew. The advantages of an inflatable are that you don't have to tow it and that, with its buoyant sides, it's much more stable than a hard dinghy when loaded. The disadvantage is that there's not a whole lot you can do with it in the water except run it with a small outboard engine. Inflatables can't be sailed, and when rowed in rough seas they make very little way unless the wind is from astern.

Dinghy painters (bow lines) are usually made of buoyant polypropylene rope that won't sink and foul the propeller.

Unfortunately, this rope is also extremely hard and slippery and, under load, liable to slip off a cleat or cause rope burns.

The last eight chapters have provided a survey of the fundamental skills of sailing, piloting, and seamanship. In Part IV, we'll have more to say about the technical side—particularly about getting along in challenging conditions and situations. But the next four chapters are given over to the sybaritic pleasure of living aboard a boat, which (for me, at least) is what sailing is about.

PART III

Cooking and Gracious Living Afloat

CHAPTER 12

The View from the Galley

F or many people, cruising has very little to do with sailing and a lot to do with relaxed eating. Even more than life in Ernest Hemingway's Paris in the 1920s, life aboard a boat on a vacation is a movable feast. Just how movable and elaborate the feast will be is up to the crew and, to a great extent, to the cooking tools at hand. Some people prefer simplicity, others relative luxury. Whichever, all seasoned sailing cooks and sailing eaters have evolved a system that meets their needs and that provides nutrition, comfort, a degree of ease, and a modicum of graciousness—the little things that make living and eating aboard a boat a special pleasure, adding a touch of quiet elegance to what is, after all, not much more than camping out. The next three chapters are about the cruising lifestyle below decks: galley equipment, food and recipes, and that intangible called gracious living. Since children are frequently aboard, I have appended a short chapter on the challenges and delights of sailing with kids.

To help with these chapters I called upon fifteen widely experienced cruising cooks (and their mates). Two of them have sailed around the world, several have crossed the Atlantic more than once, and one has cruised to the Arctic Circle. I estimate that among them they have spent a total of three centuries and 200,000 miles under sail. Responding to a five-page, thirty-nine-item questionnaire,

these experts (whose names are on the acknowledgments page) provided an immense amount of information about life below. While
they agree on many key items, each has her or his equipment preferences, favorite recipes, and own way of doing things. The sheer
range of opinions and the undisputed success of their sailing careers
suggest that, unlike on-deck routines, cook's chores rarely have a
right and a wrong way.

The Right Galley Equipment

As when cooking ashore, you must make sure to begin with
that you have the right equipment and know how to use it safely
and efficiently. The main difference between a house's and a boat's
kitchen is that limitations on electrical power mean that most sailing
cooks have few equipment options; while large powerboats with
generators may have goodies like electric ranges, freezers, micro-
wave and toaster ovens, and dishwashers, the average 30-foot to 40-
foot cruising sailboat is considered luxurious if she has a refrigerator
(in place of an icebox) and hot and cold running water. For every
appliance a boat carries, the engine must be run another hour or so
a day just to keep the batteries charged to operate it; and while the
cook gains in one way by having the appliance, he or she only
suffers in another since the noisy, vibrating, hot diesel is usually
thundering away right next to the galley. Another difference is that
storage space is greatly limited in a boat's galley. There's not much
room for even a few multipurpose tools, much less many specialized
ones. Knives, especially, are at a premium because there may not
be sufficient, secure drawer spaces to stow them so that they won't
fly out dangerously every time the boat heels or slams into a wave.

The Essential Gear

At the beginning of the questionnaire I asked the experts what
galley equipment they found essential. The answers to this question
reveal perhaps more than any others just how simple a sailing
kitchen can be.

Besides a good stove with at least two burners and an oven, the
"essential" item most frequently mentioned was a foot-operated
pump for the water system, which gives the cook access to water
when hands are full. This is no small consideration in rough
weather, when one hand is seriously engaged in holding on while
the other may be clutching a pot. Some correspondents said they
found hot-and-cold pressurized tap water essential. Many sailors
have strong opinions concerning the design and number of a galley's
sinks. As several cooks emphasized, a good galley has two deep

Every cruising cook's dream, this galley has deep double sinks with fresh- and seawater faucets worked by the two foot pedals, many deep drawers (heavy items go in the lower ones), and high fiddles around the stove and counters. In rough weather, the cook will be able to wedge in securely and, with the aid of a restraining belt, stay there.

sinks side by side. *Deep* means sufficiently recessed to hold large dinner plates on-edge while they soak in soapy water or wait to be rinsed or dried. The second sink is then available for rinsing or, on rough days and nights, to hold food, bottles, cups, or other items in the intermediate stage between stowage lockers and a sailor's hands.

Another "essential" item mentioned was a holder for a roll of paper towels. On a boat, sponges, tea towels, and handkerchiefs (for wiping eyeglasses) aren't much help since once used they never dry out entirely in the humid marine environment. Always take one roll of paper towels for every day or two of cruising.

Important—and Not So—Tools and Gadgets

We asked our informants to list five tools that they find indispensable in the galley, as well as any standard home kitchen gadgets that are helpful on board. Many of the tools deal with the never-ending cruising problems of food preservation and energy conservation. Reflecting how difficult and important it is to save leftovers, two chefs put Ziploc food storage bags at the top of their lists, and several people advise stocking plenty of plastic containers with lids. Others recommend using pressure cookers, which, because they boil water and cook stews, soups, and vegetables more quickly than regular pots, save on cooking fuel. Cooks who use block ice, which is less expensive and melts slower than cubes, recommend ice picks. Other tools and gadgets mentioned include a sharp knife (with a sharpening stone), several small and medium-sized pots (so you don't have to heat more water than necessary, again in the interest of fuel conservation), *The Joy of Cooking*, a cavernous six-quart pot for cooking lobsters purchased from fishermen while cruising in Maine, a big all-purpose iron frying pan, a fold-up metal gadget for making toast over an open burner, and a kitchen timer.

To help decide which kitchen gadgets to take along, transatlantic veteran voyager Sheila McCurdy proposes a simple rule of thumb that is well worth making a commandment:

> Not helpful: anything that takes up space and is not
> used often; for example, a waffle iron.

Items that are worth the space they take up include a simple vegetable peeler, a folding dish rack, a wire wisk, a jar opener, a cheese grater, and a coffee pot for brewed coffee (but not a drip pot—"too tippy," says one expert). As for waffle irons and their discarded kin, almost everybody agrees that electric gadgets like Cuisinarts have no place on board. "Forget about a toaster or Waring blender on a boat," says one cook. On the other hand, Steve and Linda Dashew, who made a circumnavigation in two boats with good electrical systems (and who wrote an excellent book about world voyaging, *The Circumnavigator's Handbook*), carry an electric blender and a popcorn popper, which on their sloop *Intermezzo II* is used often enough to satisfy the McCurdy rule.

We asked how cooks keep metal cookware from rusting in a salt atmosphere. One answers, simply, "We don't," and circumnavigator Mimi Dyer cheerfully responds, "A rusty can opener works swell." Suggested remedies include rubbing cooking oil onto iron pans, careful drying before stowage in a dry locker, and frequent use and washing.

Stainless steel eating implements are vastly preferred over plastic knives and forks. While some cooks use paper plates for sandwiches or other simple meals, paper becomes soggy and takes up too much valuable garbage space to be worth the saving in cleanup time. (These days, is it necessary to say that garbage is dumped ashore, not in the water? I hope not.) Plastic or ceramic plates, bowls, and cups—preferably with nonskid rubber rings inset in their bases—are the choice on most boats. Any boat going out into rough weather ought to have a big, wide-mouth, flat-bottom plastic bowl for each crew member. You'll be eating more than your breakfast cereal out of it in sloppy going, when nothing stays on a plate.

Other helpful gear includes a good cutting board, preferably one that nests in the sink top (to save space); Teflon scrubbers (steel wool corrodes); and an ice cooler with a secure lid, for drinks.

The Stove, a Mixed Blessing

Since it's the largest, most complicated, and most frequently used galley item, we asked several questions about the stove and its use. The two main variables are the type of fuel and the number of burners.

Liquid and Gas Fuels

As all the cooks in our survey acknowledge, there is no one perfect fuel. The main advantages of the liquid fuels—alcohol and kerosene—are that they are very unlikely to explode and their tanks can be located below deck. But to quote one experienced sea cook, they are "not for the unwary" because lighting them requires an elaborate routine of priming and preheating to convert the liquid

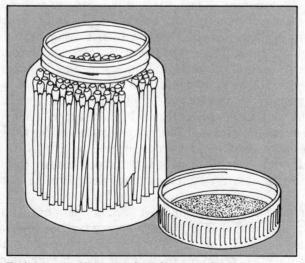

To keep wooden matches from getting soggy, store them in a plastic container or an empty peanut butter jar. Glue a strip of sandpaper into the lid for striking.

into a gas. If the stove jets clog or the preparations are done carelessly, the equipment may flare up or even cause a bad fire. (Later, we'll tell how to light an alcohol stove and look at general cooking safety.) Alcohol also heats poorly and slowly, has an unpleasant smell, is expensive and, frequently, is difficult to find in out-of-the-way places (in some Caribbean islands, local high-proof rums may be cheaper and more accessible). Since kerosene burns hotter than alcohol and is easier to find and less expensive to buy, it's often the fuel of choice on board boats heading off on very long voyages or circumnavigations.

The stoves on most of today's cruising boats use a gas fuel, either propane, butane, or compressed or liquid natural gas (known as CNG and LNG). All light with the flick of a match and burn clean and, except for CNG, very hot. However, propane and butane are heavier than air and, therefore, extremely dangerous if their lines, valves, or on-deck containers leak and drop gas into the bilge; any nearby exposed flame or spark will blow the boat to pieces. Compressed natural gas (CNG) is lighter than air and may be stored below, but it is used up quickly and is sometimes difficult to find.

Burners and an Oven

As to how many burners are needed, and whether an oven is necessary, our panel of sea cooks split into two camps. One favors simplicity: "Two burners are essential, all else is luxury." The other side likes a stove with as many as four burners and an oven (at least to heat up casseroles and rolls, warm the cabin, and dry socks). Just how many of these elements are used at once depends on the cook's ambition and taste. Those who like to prepare elaborate meals use all elements most of the time, and those who aim for simplicity use few of them. It's nice, though, to have a choice. Sailing around the world in their 37-footer *Rabbit*, Mimi and Dan Dyer used only one burner 60 percent of the time and the oven every couple of weeks and on special occasions—"We always had turkey for Christmas."

No matter how many burners it has, an alcohol or kerosene stove will rarely have them all lit at once both because fuel is expensive and because safely lighting a new burner can be complicated and time-consuming. One fuel-conserving alternative is to move pots around from active to inactive burners; another is to double-deck pots in an actual or improvised double boiler—say, one of rice or potatoes below another of vegetables. Unfortunately, since liquid fuel doesn't burn very hot, ovens in alcohol and kerosene stoves may not be very efficient. Yet even the 300 to 350 degrees that they can produce is enough for most purposes.

Most stoves are gimballed, which means that a hinge and counterweights allow them to self-level when the boat heels. Still, the stove's swing may be slow or fast and containers may fall off unless they are secured on the burners with metal fiddle rails and in the oven by a securely locked door.

A one-burner stove is usually the primary cooker on boats smaller than about 25 feet and can also be a helpful backup for heating water on a larger boat. Sea Swing, the brand name of one type, has become the generic name for all one-burner stoves. Some are heated by Sterno cans, which work very inefficiently and smell even worse; others burn butane from a small canister. A few members of our panel say they use these stoves at night, others prefer to make hot water on the big stove and store it in Thermos bottles (obviously ones without glass liners) for night use.

How to Use a Liquid-Fuel Stove Safely

An alcohol stove can be dangerous. The cooks agree with Betty Noyes that "only people who are *thoroughly* familiar with the stove may light it." On some boats, only the cook and captain are allowed to apply match to burner. If liquid-fuel stoves aren't lit correctly, there may be a dangerous flare-up; if the fuel is gas, the boat may be blown up.

Alcohol and kerosene stoves are lit by preheating (often called priming) the burner jet so the liquid fuel passing through it is vaporized and can burn evenly. If the preheating is incomplete, liquid fuel instead of vapor will spurt out and cause a flare-up or fire.

Here's how to light a liquid-fuel stove:

1. Fill a medium-sized pot or a kettle with water and put it on a spare burner. In case of fire, this may be the first and only extinguisher you'll need (although a regular fire extinguisher and an asbestos fireproof blanket, for smothering flames, should also be within reach).

2. Open the valve from the tank to the stove (ideally, the cook should be able to turn this valve without reaching through a stove flare-up or fire).

3. Pump the handle in the fuel tank to build up sufficient pressure to force fuel to the stove. If the pump has a pressure gauge, it probably is marked at the proper pressure. If not, keep pumping until you meet some resistance.

4. Slightly open the burner valve handle for a couple of seconds to let some drops of alcohol drip onto the cup under the burner

until there is a very shallow pool of alcohol. With a kerosene stove, use a funnel to drip a bit of alcohol into the cup. Close this valve.

5. Double check that the burner valve is closed completely. Then ignite the alcohol with a long wooden match or a commercial gun-shaped spark-making instrument.

6. Watch the alcohol burn. When it is just extinguished—*and no sooner*—open the burner valve about a quarter-turn.

7. If the preheating has been successful, you will hear a low hiss of pressurized alcohol (or kerosene) vapor escaping. You may light it with a match or the spark-maker. When you are sure that there's a flame and that no liquid fuel is gurgling or spurting out of the jet, you may safely start cooking. *However, if drops of liquid appear, the jet has not been sufficiently preheated and you must immediately shut off the valve and return to step 5.*

Lighting an oven is generally more difficult since the burner, jet, and preheating cup are usually all but inaccessible. You may have to lie on the cabin sole (floor) and remove a part of the stove in order to get a clear view. Follow the same step-by-step procedure described above (or the instructions that, frequently, are printed on the stove), keeping all distractions at bay until the oven is going properly.

When you're finished cooking and want to turn off the burners, first shut off the fuel-line valve closest to the tank. This allows the fuel between it and the stove to be burned off so none remains to leak onto the preheating cup through an accidentally opened burner valve. Once the fires are out, turn off the burner valves.

Why Alcohol Fires Occur

Fires and flare-ups happen when large amounts of standing liquid alcohol, or small amounts of pressurized fuel, are suddenly ignited. Five sources of trouble are:

✓ Too much alcohol is allowed into the cup, and it spills over, ignites, and spreads flames across the stove.

✓ The valve is not completely shut before the cup of alcohol is ignited for preheating, and liquid fuel spurts out into the flame to spread the fire. This may happen because the handle is loose or the valve is stuck; don't use the burner until you've tightened the handle's set screw or lubricated the valve.

✓ During the preheating (priming) steps, if the cook is not able to see the almost transparent flame, he or she may think it has gone out and will open the valve, only to have liquid fuel surge out into the flame.

✓ The valve is opened prematurely and a lighted match is applied before the jet has been sufficiently heated for proper vaporization, so liquid fuel is ignited.

✓ The jet or burner is clogged and liquid fuel dribbles out. If this is the case, clear the obstruction with a pin or fine brush. If that doesn't work, don't use the burner; cover it and the valve handle with tape to alert your shipmates.

How to Use a Gas Stove

A gas burner is lit much like one on a home stove without a pilot light. First open the valve nearest the tank and any valves in the line, then open the burner valve and apply a match. There may be flare-ups; if the flame seems to be surging, turn the burner off, shut the fuel-line valve, and inspect the jets for obstructions (which may be cleaned out with a fine brush or pin) and the valves for air leaks. Don't use a doubtful burner.

The main danger with a propane or butane stove is that unburned gas may leak out of the fuel line, a jet, or a partially opened valve, fall into the bilge, and lurk there waiting for a match to set it off. A safety device called a *sniffer* should set off an alarm when there's a leak.

The best way to make sure that gas doesn't find its way into the bilge is to clear the line of unburned fuel. When you're finished cooking, before turning off the burner valve, shut off the fuel line at the tank (or as close to the tank as possible). Allow the fire to burn itself out, and then close the burner valve. This way, an accidental opening of a burner valve—say, when the cook bumps against it in rough weather—will release air, not a gaseous time-bomb.

"Don't Fry Bacon in Your Birthday Suit" and Other Galley Safety Hints

Working on an unstable platform in a very tight area with plenty of distractions, a sea cook is exposed to more hazards than a chef working at home. Certain procedures and equipment, carefully and alertly followed and used, will cut most of the risks down to tolerable levels.

The combination of rocky boat, cramped quarters, hot food, and skimpy summer clothing has led to all too many accidents in the galley. Most stoves are gimballed to keep the top surface level when the boat is heeling up to about 40 degrees. However, her motion may be so quick that the gimballing is always a second or two behind, or off-center heavy pots or casseroles may throw the balancing system off, so the chef should be alert to surprising lurches and spills even when cooking in a calm harbor, where a powerboat's wake may roll the boat. In rough conditions, then, be careful. Don't fill pots so far that they'll spill over, and avoid using grease or oil (which may be out of the question anyway, since greasy food tends to stimulate seasickness). Fiddles (support rails) will keep pots from sliding about and capsizing, and a strong protective bar across the front of the stove will prevent the cook from falling directly on the burners. Experienced offshore cooks keep the floor beneath their feet absolutely clear of grease and oil, and also rig restraining straps or harnesses around their hips. Still, there will be spills, and the cook must dress appropriately. Mimi and Dan Dyer proclaim this valuable rule of thumb: "Don't fry bacon in your birthday suit." One female chef never cooks in a bikini, and she keeps an aloe plant in the galley to treat small burns.

If anybody on board is likely to get seasick, it's the cook in the cramped, airless, hot galley. Seasickness pills should be taken long before coming on board, and the diet a day or two before the start of the cruise should be grease- and liquor-free. If the misery does attack, the best thing to do is go on deck, get some fresh air, look at the horizon, and shed the malaise through activity. If you're not totally incapacitated, a stint at the helm will meet all three requirements.

Stove Fires

As our long discussion of stove-lighting procedures has probably made clear, the main safety worry on a boat is a galley fire. Half of our guest experts have experienced fires and flare-ups, and one suffered arm and hand burns due to a propane flare-up. Anybody using the stove *must* be competent (read *sober*) and observe these rules:

✓ Light the stove with great care and never leave it unattended (except perhaps when heating water in a kettle in a calm sea).

✓ Keep the stove and pans free of grease.

✓ Have a pot or kettle of water at hand.

✓ Know the location of fire-fighting devices such as an asbestos blanket (for smothering flames) and fire extinguishers.

✓ Know where the fuel-line shut-off valve is and how to operate it.

The Coast Guard requires that at least one charged fire extinguisher be carried on every boat equipped with an inboard engine or having a compartment in which fumes may be trapped. The Coast Guard doesn't say where to install it, but common sense requires that at least one extinguisher be located within arm's length of the cook, but not in a place where the cook must reach through flames to get at it.

Fighting a Fire

With a minor flare-up or fire, your first step is to cut off the fuel supply by closing the valve on the feeder line from the tank. This will allow a minor fire to burn itself out in the burner, or at least prevent it from becoming a major one while you fight it in other ways. If shutting off the fuel supply is not sufficient and the fire threatens to burn flammable objects, douse it with the water in the pot, smother it with a wet or asbestos blanket, or put it out with the fire extinguisher, which will choke off its supply of air. A fire in a large puddle of alcohol may well spread if doused with water. This kind of fire should be smothered with a blanket or put out with the extinguisher.

Energy and Water Conservation

Few boats run out of water and cooking fuel, but since both may be hard to find and bring aboard and fuel is expensive, conservation is a good practice. Most Americans are much more aware of natural resource and energy conservation than they were just ten years ago, and the same OPEC-stimulated common-sense procedures that we follow at home work on the boat.

Boiling water requires more energy than heating almost anything else. Many years of nervous pot-watching have taught me that one full kettle of water boils more slowly than two half-filled kettles. One of our informants advises, "Avoid heating too much water, use any leftover hot water for cleanup or face-washing, keep hot water in a Thermos, and avoid using food that has to be cooked in a large amount of water." Marcia Wiley, executive editor of *Yachting* magazine, suggests always steaming, rather than boiling, vegetables. Another cook has two recommendations for saving fuel, one of which might strike some people as slightly radical: before sailing, partially precook some food, like bacon, roasts, and chicken; and carry a lot of nutritious ready-made food, specifically "a case of peanut butter and a lot of crackers.''

Our experts had several suggestions for water conservation while washing dishes. Dishes should first be scraped very thoroughly and given a hard rub with a brush or paper towel, then washed in cold water using a liquid soap. Uncontaminated left-over cooking water can be saved for washing up. One cook we surveyed even uses leftover egg-boiling water for making tea and instant coffee (but another reported an English superstition that reused egg water causes warts!). Clean outdoors water is an excellent resource on boats, especially on offshore passages. To conserve fresh water in the boat's tanks, dishes are often scraped and rinsed in the salt or fresh water the boat's sitting in, drawn either by a foot-operated galley pump or with a bucket. Since salt deposits absorb moisture, do the last rinse in fresh water, or at least wipe the dishes with a sponge or towel damp with fresh water. Salt water may be used in small quantities for cooking eggs or potatoes. While research and the experience of abandoned sailors in life rafts strongly suggest that salt water not be drunk straight, perhaps it may be used in small doses to save fresh water. During the 1972 Trans-Atlantic Race, as we sat becalmed and worrying about our water supply in a huge stagnant high-pressure system west of the Azores, our cook (an M.D.) made powdered lemonade with a mix of fresh and salt water. Of course, fresh-water sailors have it all over ocean-going seamen here; during the Great Lakes races that I've sailed on, once a safe distance from big cities we got our drinking water by pulling it from Lake Michigan or Lake Huron with a bucket.

With that foundation laid, let's now look at how some experienced seafaring cooks prepare for and cook their meals, while leaving themselves enough time to enjoy the sailing, too.

CHAPTER 13

Eating
Simply and
Well

W hile few people go to sea in order to eat gourmet meals—
most are escaping from hot kitchens and complicated cooking—everybody on a boat still must eat, preferably in a way that
complements the pleasures of living under sail. Just how you provide sustenance depends to a great extent on your original goals. If
you've set out to get away from a frantic shore life, you'll probably
choose to live and eat with relative simplicity and flexibility, relying
on frozen precooked casseroles and sauceless two-course meals, frequently cooking while under way, changing your menus to fit the
day's weather and your itinerary, and inserting small, special frills
here and there. On the other hand, if you like to carry your luxury
with you like a turtle's shell, you may well fit your sailing activities
around your culinary tastes and demands, staying under way for
relatively short distances and anchoring frequently to allow the chef
to spin out elaborate meals on a level platform.

The first of these lifestyles is the one that most people who
enjoy sailing and the footloose freedom of the sailing life usually
end up choosing, even if they originally wanted the second. Unless
they are willing to go ashore in search of three-star restaurants,
sybarites who sail discover quickly that culinary compromises must
be made, starting with the sea cook's tools, which, as we saw in the
last chapter, simply aren't up to a shore kitchen's standards. Most

boat stoves are small, stowage lockers tiny, refrigerators and ice chests none too efficient. On the human side, even the most ambitious sailing gastronomes usually realize with a day or two that they are, after all, on a vacation. Given a choice between the joys of relaxing on deck on a warm sunny afternoon in a beautiful and isolated bay, on the one hand, and stopping daily for fresh provisions so they can slave away in a tiny, steaming galley over a four-course meal, on the other, most sailing chefs soon find themselves moving radically in the direction of simplicity.

This does not mean, however, that sailors have to live like Boy Scouts camping in the woods, scooping half-warm beef stew out of cans. Tasty, nutrutious meals made from fresh meat and vegetables are within the realm of possibility of any cook whose boat has an ice chest and a two-burner stove. Add an oven and a well-filled spice rack and you can cook almost as successfully as you do at home—more so, in fact, since cooking afloat always improves the smell and taste of good, simple food. Neither does simplicity require dispensing entirely with formality. As we'll see in the next chapter, seasoned cruising sailors strive to create an atmosphere of gracious living by observing two or three fairly impractical but highly pleasurable customs, much the way English explorers used to dress for dinner no matter what swamp they were slogging through.

Where and How to Stow the Food

The most important limits on the type and amount of food to be carried are storage space and refrigeration. Nonperishables can be crammed in just about anywhere. The primary stowage area is the set of cabinets and bins in the galley, but most crews soon find themselves sticking food in lockers ostensibly set aside for other purposes. One of the experienced cooks that I surveyed reports that her biggest problem with stowage was competing with the crew's clothes.

Most boats have deep, relatively inaccessible bins under bunks and in the head that are perfect for stowing nonperishables. Use caution, however; an excess of heavy items, such as canned goods, in bins way forward will weigh down the bow and throw the boat out of balance. Given a choice, stow light stuff—cereal, noodles, paper goods—forward, and put the cans aft, where there is more buoyancy. One boat I know well has a huge storage bin under the cockpit that is reached by crawling way aft in a quarter berth. Because it is deep and square, this pantry soon came to be called the "lobster pound." Besides its size, it has the advantages of being low in the boat and far from traffic; unlike goods stored on high shelves, the cans there don't fly about and risk injuring people in rough seas. Stowing cans in the bilge under the cabin sole (or floor) offers the same benefit but with two disadvantages: when water gets into the bilge (which is inevitable) the paper wrappers will peel off and the cans may rust. A solution is to tear off the wrapper, label the contents on the can top with an indelible pen, and put the cans in plastic bags.

Food stowage should follow a logic. Many people organize by meals, putting all the ingredients for an individual dinner together. Others group by type—for example, stowing all the canned fruits in one place and all the canned vegetables in another. As a disaster back-up, it's a good idea to set aside two days' worth of emergency canned or dried rations and fresh water in jugs in an especially secure, dry place. With so many items scattered in so many places, the cook should make a written record of their whereabouts. A simple list might do, but it may be better to draw a map using the boat's overhead accommodation plan, available from the builder or designer.

Perishables

Several members of our cooks' survey stress that the best way to keep perishable food from rotting is to buy only as much as you need, stow it so you won't forget about it, and eat it quickly. Even then, certain foods require special attention. Vegetables and fruits should be purchased as fresh as possible and stowed in a dark, cool, well-ventilated place. Many cooks hang them in string bags that must be secured so they won't swing against the hull or a bulkhead and bruise the produce. Bread will mildew extremely rapidly in the marine atmosphere; stowing it in two tightly secured plastic bags usually keeps it dry.

Eggs present a challenging stowage problem. They should be as fresh as possible when purchased, and their life will be longer if they have never been refrigerated or washed. Before a long cruise, one cook I questioned likes to buy the eggs right at the farm, and when under way turn them every few days to keep the yolks from settling. To delay spoilage, many cooks coat eggs with petroleum jelly or melted wax. Eggs may be put away in special plastic egg crates in the icebox or refrigerator, or stowed with and cushioned by towels and paper goods in a dry locker in the head.

Ice and Iceboxes

The standard way to preserve perishables is to keep them cold. On most boats I know, there are two cold places: a portable ice chest reserved solely for soft drinks, beer, and jugs of cold water;

and the main icebox or refrigerator, where milk, eggs, meat, butter, and other perishable foods are stored. This way, the cool items most in demand on hot summer days are accessible without having to open the main cold storage, letting cold air escape. (In cool climates and water, canned drinks may be stored in the bilge.) Many cruising boats today have refrigerators that run, one way or another, off the engine and the ship's batteries, and if the boat you are sailing on is so blessed you may skip the next three paragraphs and simply worry about whether the damn thing will break down and how you're going to fix it.

Loading ice is an art. Assuming that there's no old ice, start by emptying the icebox and thoroughly cleaning it out with scrub brush, sponge, and liquid cleanser. Then dry it with paper towels before leaving the top off so the box can air for at least an hour. The spoiled milk and rotting bologna left over from the last cruise may be appalling in both quantity and malodorousness. Be especially attentive to the drains, the sump where the run-off settles, and the various corners and dividers. Wash the cans and containers that you

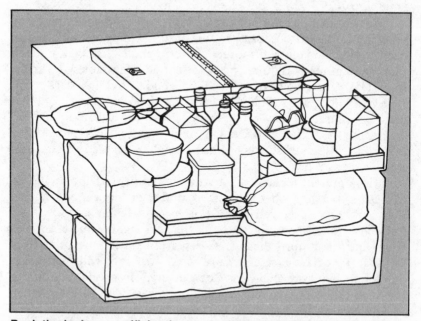

Pack the icebox as efficiently as possible, using block ice shaped with an ice pick, so that the blocks brick the bottom and sides. Wrap perishables carefully with one or two layers of plastic, and store milk, snacks, and drinks so that they may be reached quickly, with little loss of cold air. Sealable plastic containers are worth their weight in gold.

plan to put back, and don't forget to clean and air the lid, where many spills and crumbs accumulate.

Once the icebox is washed and aired out, load the ice. It must be block ice—not fast-melting cubes—brought aboard with old-fashioned ice tongs or, more frequently these days, in plastic bags. Don't skimp, especially if the weather is warm and your cruise is long; you'll probably need to load at least sixty pounds at the beginning. Shape the blocks with an ice pick until they brick the box's floor with no wasted space either underneath or between, then build walls of ice up the sides. Water will run off through a drain into a sump or the bilge, which should be periodically pumped dry and scrubbed clean to keep it free of spilled milk and moldy food. If there is no drain use a small hand pump, or water will eventually seep into food storage bags. It's a good idea to leave some blocks in their plastic delivery bags so you'll have several quarts of clean ice water when the ice melts.

Just how long the ice will last depends on the thickness of insulation in the box's walls, the quantity of food that must be cooled, the air and water temperature, and the amount of use the box receives. In hot weather, or in warm weather when it is opened frequently, a fully loaded icebox may remain cold enough with its original load of ice to preserve milk and meat for four days. But don't count on it; as the ice melts, replace it with another twenty or thirty pounds every two or three days. One way to increase efficiency is to bring all your food, and even frozen drinking water in milk jugs, aboard directly from your home refrigerator or freezer. Camping stores and some chandleries sell freeze packs to freeze at home and take aboard to lengthen the life of the ice.

Plastics, Plastics, Plastics

Because the icebox's temperature is relatively high as well as variable, all perishables should be protected in plastic wrap, bags, boxes, or bottles. *Avoid using glass containers whenever possible.* No matter how secure it seems, glass eventually will break, causing a mess and probably cutting somebody's foot or hand. If you must use a glass jar or bottle, stow it in a secure locker low in the boat or wrap it with tape or a towel.

Dairy products are the biggest worries. If milk spills, the icebox and, possibly, the bilge will begin to smell like a sewer. Some people have had such bad experiences with liquid milk that they won't allow it on board and use the powdered or canned variety instead. But if you can't live without whole milk, stow it with great care—not in cardboard containers, which will almost certainly leak, but in plastic jugs with secure lids. The very best way to stow milk is the system recommended by Betty Noyes: pour it into plastic bottles with wide, screw-on tops that allow the entire bottle to be washed in hot water later. Sticks of butter and margarine can easily get lost between the cracks of ice blocks, will inevitably melt, and are difficult to slice one-handed; instead, take plastic tubs of margarine or other spreads, which preserve well and are easy to use. Empty tubs are handy storage containers for leftovers as well as for change and loose nuts and bolts.

Plastic jugs should also be used for other liquids, like orange juice, but because the consequences of a juice spill are less disastrous than with milk, a cardboard container may do for short passages as long as the top is kept closed with tape or a paper clip.

Judging from their responses to questions about preservation, the cooks I surveyed have obviously learned the hard way about keeping solid perishables. Several stressed that plastic is a much more secure and permanent wrap than aluminum foil. "Put *everything* in Ziploc bags," one insisted, and another uses two layers—first a plastic wrap and then a left-over bread bag or some other plastic bag. If you do use open plastic bags, secure them with rubber bands instead of metal twist ties, which will rust when they get wet.

Finding the container you want in a dark, crowded icebox will be difficult unless the food is stowed systematically. You may, for instance, put vegetables on one side, meat on the other, cans on the bottom, and dairy products on top. Whichever way you pack the food, do it as simply and logically as possible. No system is good if it can't be explained in common English or if basic items aren't easy to find. You'll know there's something wrong if every time a crewmember wants a drink or a peanut butter and jelly sandwich, the cook has to be asked to go below to hunt down the ingredients.

Meal-Planning Hints

While one of the joys of cooking on a vacation is that you can shrug off the burden of culinary conventions accumulated over a lifetime and eat what you want when you want it, good cooks feel that they haven't done their jobs if they haven't anticipated and provisioned for their shipmates' tastes, needs, and appetites. Some sailors stick to a breakfast-lunch-dinner schedule but take on more and larger helpings than they would ashore. Others eat about the same amount at meals but gorge on snacks. A well-provisioned boat with a crew that includes both types of eater will carry plenty of both types of food—meals and snacks—plus a varied supply of drinks.

Since space is limited and there's no store around the corner, everything depends on good planning. Before provisioning for a cruise, sit down and write out the menus, keeping everybody's preferences in mind. Before heading out to cook for people whose tastes are unfamiliar to you, it may be a good idea to send out a questionnaire like the one that Susie Page mails to the crew of *Pageant*, a 37-foot ocean racer that normally carries eight men and women in her crew.

Pageant Crew Food Preferences

I. BREAKFAST

Check one:
( ) cereal and bread stuff
( ) eggs and bread stuff
( ) cereal, eggs, and bread stuff

Check one or two:
( ) tea
( ) caffeinated coffee
( ) decaffeinated coffee
( ) milk
( ) other _____

II. LUNCH

Check one:
( ) white bread ( ) whole wheat bread

Number five sandwich preferences in order:
( ) ham & cheese
( ) turkey slices
( ) roast beef slices
( ) chicken salad
( ) egg salad
( ) tuna salad
( ) bologna
( ) liverwurst
( ) salami
( ) deviled ham
( ) peanut butter & jelly
( ) other _____

III. DINNER
Number three casserole preferences in order:
( ) beef stroganoff
( ) turkey
( ) lasagna
( ) chicken
( ) meat loaf
( ) other _____
Number two canned meat preferences in order:
( ) corned beef hash
( ) spaghetti & meat balls
( ) beef stew
( ) ravioli
( ) other _____

IV. DRINKS AND SNACKS
List three favorite:
Drinks _____
Fruits _____
Snacks _____
Treats _____

As at home, the food trade-off is usually between convenience and taste, but it doesn't always have to be that way. There's no reason why you can't buy take-out from your favorite ribs or Chinese restaurant and carry the goodies aboard in the ice chest to be reheated for dinner on the first or second night. On a week's cruise, in fact, you may find yourself eating as many precooked meals as you do freshly made ones, alternating them with an occasional cook's-night-off at a cheerful local seafood restaurant. (Dinner ashore is a good time for the guests to thank their hosts by picking up the check; that's why it's traditionally called a "crew dinner.")

Although some cooks shy away from them because of their grease and smoke, many boats carry charcoal-fired barbecue grills. For obvious reasons, grills should always be used either ashore or hanging over the water, suspended from a sturdy clamp on the after pulpit. The same common-sense rules that apply for shoreside grilling should be followed on board, with the added provisos that you be alert to sparks or smoke blowing onto your neighbor's boat downwind, and that, after cooking, you carefully stow the leftover charcoal and dirty, greasy grill. Two heavy-duty plastic garbage bags and a cardboard box should suffice to isolate them from your sails, fenders, and sheets.

Depending on your tolerance for preservatives, you may even eat meals out of cans. I do, very occasionally. Cans are the best long-term packages for sauces, fruits, and vegetables, while canned butter and bacon keep longer without refrigeration than the fresh kind. There's no reason why canned meat stews have to remain as tasteless as the manufacturer made them. Even the blandest soup or stew can be enlivened by some spices and a cup of wine. Over several years of cruising my sons have gradually been initiated into the opinion that the best breakfast afloat is corned beef hash mixed with a dash of Worcestershire sauce and capped by a fried egg. Now that I think of it, their enthusiasm for—or at least acceptance of—this delicacy may be due to the fact that we never eat it ashore. They associate it with cruising's other and more profound pleasures, much the way Pavlov's dogs drooled with joy at the sound of a bell. If you, too, can convince your crew that heaven is a can of hash or stew, well, your cooking problems may be over. *Digestive* problems, no.

Some Recipes

We have devoted many pages to equipment, provisioning, and preparation; it is time to speak of cooking.

"Tasty simplicity" is the best description of a good meal afloat, and recipes should be chosen (or invented) with that objective in mind. This approach is neatly summarized by Sheila McCurdy, who has cooked across oceans and into tiny Caribbean harbors on many cruises, races, and yacht delivery trips:

> My philosophy of the galley is to keep matters as simple as possible. Good cooking enhances a cruise, but it is still secondary to the sailing. Those who wish to indulge epicurean desires do not seek out sailboats. The best sea cooks I know are not valued for their exotic dishes but for their flexibility, creativity, and persistence under dreadful conditions. It helps to have a sense of humor. One reassuring fact that a cook should keep in mind is that, on a boat, people will eat just about anything and be happy. With imagination and a little effort, a meal becomes a special occasion.
>
> I learned to cook at sea and so, unlike most people, had to adapt to land cooking. For me the same rules apply wherever I cook. I tend toward simple, nutritious, well-seasoned meals. I try to minimize mess and avoid recipes with critical re-

quirements such as timing, oven temperature, or rare ingredients, like fresh coconut milk in Maine or maple syrup in Portugal. Quantities can be difficult to guess when one does not know the crew. No one should go away hungry, yet a nightly feast is uncalled for. Common sense prevails. I have never known anybody to starve on a cruise.

Plan meals around other activities. One should never cut short snorkeling over a coral reef to peel potatoes.

Like most good cooks, Sheila is an improviser. "I have rarely, if ever, followed a recipe from beginning to end," she adds. "I freely change ingredients and proportions based on whim and availability." Once, during a transatlantic passage on a boat lacking yeast and baking soda, she found a way to bake bread using Alka-Seltzer as the riser. While Sheila didn't send us those proportions, we are printing her recipe for beer beef stew, followed by five other relatively simple recipes for dinners, salads, snacks, and desserts that were suggested by other sea cooks.*

Beer Beef Stew, from Sheila McCurdy

2 lb. beef chuck in 1-inch cubes
3 tablespoons shortening, butter, or margarine
2 large sliced onions
4 carrots, cut up
4 medium potatoes, cubed
2 large, hard, sweet apples, cut up
2 tablespoons flour
½ cup beef bouillon
1 cup (approximately) beer
1 tablespoon fresh basil (or ½ teaspoon dried basil)
pepper and salt to taste

1. Melt shortening in a dutch oven or other deep, heavy pot. Pat the meat dry and brown a few pieces at a time. Set aside. Sauté

---

* Many more good, simple recipes can be found in three books specifically about on-board cooking: Barbara Davis (editor), *The Best of People and Food* (Newport, R.I.: Seven Seas Press, 1983); Alex W. Moffat and Porter C. Burnham, *The Galley Guide Updated*, 2nd ed. (New York: Dodd, Mead, 1977); and Lin Pardey, *The Care and Feeding of the Offshore Crew* (New York: W. W. Norton, 1981).

onions until tender. Sprinkle in flour. Add salt, pepper, and basil. Stir in liquids.

2. Return meat to pot. Bring to a boil, then simmer, covered, for one hour or so.

3. Add carrots, potatoes, apples, and (if needed) more beer. Continue cooking 20–30 minutes until vegetables are tender. Serve whenever the crew is assembled with a tasty bread, perhaps a rye or anadama, and a salad.

Serves about 6. (The better the beer, the better the flavor.)

Cioppino (Fish Stew), from Linda Dashew

> *1½ lb. halibut, mahi-mahi, or other catch of the day*
> *½ lb. raw shrimp, shelled and cleaned*
> *3 cans (6½ oz.) crab meat with cartilage removed, drained*
> *   (or 1 lb. fresh crab meat or a 2 lb. lobster tail)*
> *1 jar (1½ oz.) whole clams*
> *½ cup olive or salad oil*
> *3 cloves garlic, finely chopped*
> *1¼ cups chopped onions*
> *¾ cup chopped green pepper*
> *1 can (1 lb. 12 oz.) tomatoes*
> *1 can (6 oz.) tomato paste*
> *1¾ cups Burgundy wine*
> *⅓ cup chopped parsley*
> *2 teaspoons oregano*
> *½ teaspoon basil*
> *¼ teaspoon pepper*

1. In hot oil in a 6-quart pot, sauté garlic, onions, and green pepper until tender (about 10 minutes), stirring occasionally.

2. To sautéed vegetables add undrained tomatoes, tomato paste, Burgundy, parsley, oregano, basil, salt, pepper, and ¾ cup water, mixing well. Bring to boil. Reduce heat and simmer uncovered and stirring for 10 minutes.

3. Drain clams, reserving ¼ cup liquid. Cut halibut (or other fish) into 1-inch pieces, discarding skin and bones. Add with clams, shrimp, and crab (or lobster) to tomato mixture. Simmer uncovered 15 minutes. Serve with hot crunchy bread.

Serves 8.

Turkey Divan Casserole, from Susie Page

1. Cook 2 packages frozen broccoli spears. Drain and put in bottom of casserole dish.
2. Put 8 (or more) slices of turkey on top of broccoli.
3. Mix 2 cans cream of chicken soup, ⅔ cup mayonnaise, 1 teaspoon curry, and 1 teaspoon lemon juice, and pour over turkey and broccoli.
4. Sprinkle with topping of 4 tablespoons melted butter, ½ cup soft bread crumbs, 1 cup shredded cheese. Bake at 350 degrees for 25 minutes.

Serves 6–8. May be made ashore and frozen before taking aboard.

Note: When cooking or heating casseroles in the boat's oven, make sure the door is latched shut whether or not the stove gimbals are engaged; the pan will slide around, sometimes violently, and may end up on the floor or, worse, somebody's lap.

Corn Pancakes, from Carol Nicklaus

Substitute 1 can creamed corn for the portion of liquid called for in pancake mix, and cook as usual. Result: pancakes with little nuggets of corn.

Five-Bean Salad, from Adra Kober

1 can wax beans, drained
1 can green beans, drained
1 can kidney beans, drained
1 can garbanzo beans, drained
1 can lima beans, drained
¾ cup sliced celery
1 medium red onion, sliced
½ cup sugar
¼ cup salad oil
¼ cup olive oil
1 teaspoon dried basil
¼ cup vinegar
¼ cup lemon juice

1. Toss beans, celery, and onion together in large bowl.
2. Thoroughly mix sugar, oils, vinegar, lemon juice, and basil. Pour over vegetables and toss gently.
3. Cover, set in refrigerator overnight, tossing now and then.

Quick-Mix Plain Cake, from Linda Dashew

1. Measure into a bowl 2 cups self-rising flour and ¼ teaspoon salt.
2. Add 1 cup sugar, ½ cup soft margarine, 2 eggs, ½ cup milk.
3. Beat for 2 minutes and pour into a well-greased tin.

Bake at 325 degrees (gas stove) or 375 degrees (electric stove) for these times:

> 7″ shallow layer pan, 30–35 minutes
> 8″ ring pan, 40–45 minutes
> 10″ × 4½″ bar pan, 40–45 minutes
> 11″ × 7″ laminated pan, 25–30 minutes

Cool for 5 minutes before turning out. May be frosted or served with fruit, ice cream, or whipped cream.

For banana cake, add ¾ cup mashed banana to batter before baking.

Wine and Beer

As we'll see in the next chapter, a bottle of wine or two can be a valuable asset to gracious living on a boat (but only if—like all alcohol on board—it is sampled judiciously when under way). There are certain built-in limitations to provisioning wine. One, of course, is its fragile glass container. Some wineries have begun to distribute their products in cardboard cartons, and you may always decant your own favorites into a plastic bottle or jug. If you must use glass wine or liquor bottles, wrap them with towels or, better yet, stuff them in thick wool socks or shoe bags. Another problem is that while the quality of packaged foods doesn't suffer in a boat's bouncy, warm interior, that of many wines does. Older wines, which have sediment, suffer more than unsedimented younger ones, so if you can't live without vintage wine, carry along a strainer. Wine may be chilled overboard, several feet deep into cool water, at the end of a line—use a clove hitch cinched by a half-hitch—or in a string bag. When you use a bottle, try to finish it off in one sitting so that you won't have to worry about leakage around the loosened cork.

Champagne anyone? It will take the abuse. One evening in September 1979, in Newport, Rhode Island, a gang of cheerful English sailors were distributing some good bubbly that they had carried with them a month earlier on the very rough Fastnet Race in Britain, then in the same boat across to America. It tasted just fine.

As to beer—well, beer drinkers know what they like, and now

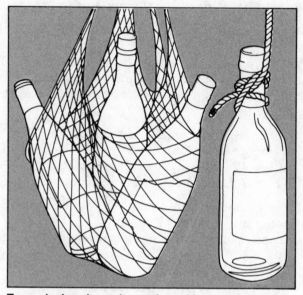

To cool wine, hang it overboard in a string bag or at the end of a line.

that some premium beers are available in cans, you may be able to give it to them. The only caveat is that anybody who normally downs a couple of brews on a quiet Saturday afternoon at home will easily put away twice that many on a busy Saturday afternoon on an active boat, not so much for the taste of it but to quench a raging thirst. Therefore, low-calorie "light" beers and the new low-alcohol brands may be healthier than their weightier and more potent cousins. Many years ago Sir Francis Chichester survived a one-stop circumnavigation with the help of several kegs of beer wedged into the cabin of *Gipsy Moth IV*.

Other Drinks

Cold liquids used on board vary with the crew's tastes. Canned —*never* bottled—soft drinks are of course very popular, and everybody has a favorite. Colas may be in special demand because they help settle queasy stomachs. Powdered drinks mixed with cold water in plastic bottles or pitchers are convenient but can be messy. As ashore, the best way to quench thirst is to take a drink of cool water; add a lemon slice or a teaspoon of powdered lemonade to override the faint fiberglass taste of the water tank. Better yet, at home fill some clean milk jugs or plastic bottles most of the way

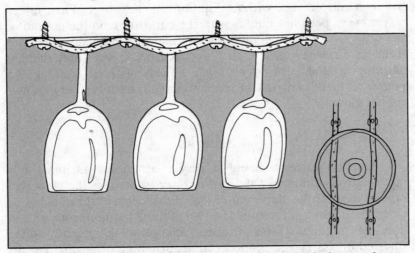

Some attractive plastic wineglasses are now available for gracious nautical sipping, if you can figure out how to stow them. On board *Revelation*, Carol Nicklaus and Eric Camiel hang their glasses upside down, the bases slipped under two lengths of shockcord screwed to the underside of a galley cabinet.

with tap water and freeze them. On board, the jugs of frozen water will help lower temperatures in iceboxes and ice chests and, when they melt, will provide chilled drinking water without depleting the boat's tanks.

Popular hot drinks include the usual coffee and tea flavored with powdered "creamers" and sugar or honey (store sweets in secure plastic containers to keep flies out of the galley). Worrying about spills and coffee grounds, some skippers will not allow fresh coffee on board. Obviously, they either are tea drinkers or couldn't care less how bland their morning caffeine fix tastes, yet their concern about safety is legitimate. Coffee pots, whose high center of gravity invites capsize, must be used with great care when the boat is under sail. Hot cocoa is a wonderful treat on a cold day. Many people like chicken or beef bouillon made from cubes, perhaps with a drop or two of wine or sherry stirred in. Canned soup can make a meal in itself, but is more awkward to make than instant powdered soup, which, to me, tastes like salted dishwater.

The worst part of hot drinks is heating the water and juggling to pour them. Instead of boiling a pot of water for each cup, wasting both time and fuel, at the start of the day fill a large Thermos bottle with boiling water and leave it in a secure, visible place, say in the sink. Anybody who needs a hot drink may then make it at his or her own convenience without lighting up the stove. When under way, always pour hot liquids with the cup sitting on the bottom of the sink. One boat I sail on has a cup rack, undoubtedly borrowed from an airplane's galley, that fits securely in the sink, thereby allowing several cups to be filled quickly without scalding the pourer. If there's any risk of spills, wear your foul-weather gear and rubber gloves.

Snacks

Snacks and treats should be easy to assemble, nutritious, filling, relatively unmessy, and not too dry (otherwise the crew will rapidly deplete the ship's water and drink supply). Peanut butter on crackers meets all but the last two of these requirements, and so does that children's favorite called "ants on a log": peanut butter smeared on celery and topped with a sprinkling of raisins. Peanut butter is my favorite snack, but when it smears, drips, or (God forbid) is sat upon, its protein oozes messily all over the boat. (Noting this, owners of boats with fine wooden decks will not allow peanut butter, potato chips, nuts, or any other oily snack out of the cabin.) Another problem with peanut butter is that it is sold mostly in glass jars. To protect yourself against broken glass, either scoop the stuff into a plastic container or wrap the glass jars with a couple of layers of heavy tape.

Among the other filling, sweet, and energy-producing snacks and treats that our survey of cooks recommended are: plain crackers (greasy ones will leave their imprint on sails, decks, clothes, and cushions), cheese, raisins, cookies, chocolate bars, sour balls, M & M's (which, unlike plain candy bars, melt in your mouth, not in the galley locker), chopped vegetables, nuts, and fresh fruit (especially grapes, apples, and oranges; bananas rot quickly). I'd add chewing gum, which is both a temporary hunger-appeaser and a wonderful breath-freshener for a crowded locale where bad breath is both easily come by and quickly noticed.

Fruits and nuts are especially valuable snacks because they function as natural laxatives to help cure one of the sailor's biggest problems—constipation brought on by hours and hours of sitting. A bran breakfast cereal is another cure for this malaise. So is taking a long row or daily walk or jog ashore, which has the added benefit of providing a release from the tensions that inevitably accumulate when several people live almost on top of each other.

CHAPTER 14

Fun and Gracious Living

Y ou've probably noticed that the words *cautious, should,* and *must* have appeared more frequently up to now than *fun, may,* and *if you please.* Sailing, after all, is always challenging, can be difficult, and is sometimes even dangerous. Still, many of the most relaxed and enjoyable moments of my own life have been spent on the decks and in the cabins of racing and cruising sailboats, bathing in the warm and joking camaraderie of my shipmates, including children.

The foundation of these pleasures is the joy of living in an active community of other people with nature. From that base spring the handful of simple habits and rituals that make up gracious living: the little and not-so-little things that add to enjoyment, comfort, and civilized life aboard a conveyance that quite frequently is uncomfortable and wet. Some of these customs are touches of formality that would seem inconsequential in our homes ashore but that add a gratifying sense of ritual and gentility to our moments afloat. Others are seafaring versions of those rules of decent behavior that we all learn as we grow up and that we intuitively fall back on in order to get through life's crises. From a distance, sailing may not seem to need such backstops, but like any activity that crams people together in tight quarters in a difficult environment, it demands civility, a sense of humor, and tolerance.

Here, then, are some suggestions for improving and enjoying the quality of life on board a boat.

The Evening Rituals

We have made and quoted many praises of simplicity afloat—simple food, simple galleys, simple sail-handling rules, simple clothing. So often have we repeated this advice that we run the risk of being considered simple-minded. This emphasis is important because sailing is an extremely complicated, variable-ridden pastime that most full-time sailors (much less weekenders) aren't able to master completely even in a long lifetime. If we're to have any chance of making sense of the pastime's complexities, they must be sorted out, organized, and reduced to easily remembered rules of thumb; some of these complexities, in fact, must be eliminated.

Although simplicity is clearly a benefit on board a boat, we should not become so obsessed with it that all the quirky fun is taken from a sport that, like life itself, overflows with unpredictability, humor, contradictions, and irony. In life ashore, we need rituals and ceremonies to keep chaos at bay. So, too, on a boat.

Most of the sea cooks surveyed report that when afloat, usually

"Gracious dining is only limited if one is under sail and not at anchor." This Trintella racer-cruiser is obviously at anchor.

before and during dinner, they follow one or two formal routines. Whether or not they also adhere to these rituals in their houses, they choose to make these embellishments an important part of their lives on board. A few hard-nosed types might think some of these little luxuries irrelevant, superficial, and, in some cases, unsafe. There was a time when I felt that way, too, but incipient middle age has finally convinced me that a hair shirt is not only uncomfortable and unbecoming, but unnecessary.

If cruising sailors, a contentious lot, can agree about anything, they agree about in-harbor evening routines. In the afternoon, once the anchor is set or the docking lines are secure and the boat is cleaned up, most people feel freed for a nap, a row, a swim, a walk or a shower ashore—whatever allows them a moment of privacy and reflection. They need that psychological "one hand for yourself" to get them through the day.

Rum and Gab

Later, when the sun is "over the yardarm"—about 6 P.M.—many crews gather in the cockpit under the shade of an awning (or, in miserable weather, around the cabin table) for a cocktail hour consisting of simple hors d'oeuvres, good conversation, and a rum drink or two, using ice chipped from a block in the icebox. (Beware: a tiring day in the hot sun may leave you weak and helpless before the onslaught of 86-proof alcohol.) With the skipper's permission, an invitation to join in may be shouted, waved, radioed, or rowed across to a nearby boat containing friends or attractive-looking strangers. While acquaintances are made easily on the water, privacy is important, too; don't feel slighted if your invitation is turned down. Using the largest boat's biggest anchor, several boats may be rafted-up side by side, their masts and shrouds carefully kept apart through the judicious use of spring lines. The raft should be broken up immediately if the weather worsens. For their own relief—and that of adults who would enjoy some purely grown-up company—this is a good time for children to play card games way up on the foredeck or to get away from the old folks for a swim or a short row.

Wine, Wildflowers, and Candlelight

Although most cooks don't allow obsessive food preparation to get in the way of this informal party, the smart ones time dinner so that it's served before everybody is too drunk to eat. The time of sunset has nothing to do with it, as I learned the hard way while cruising one July down the Caledonian Canal in the Scottish highlands, where the summer sun finally goes down at around 11 P.M. Used to 8-ish New England sunsets, we kept sip-sip-sipping away

A kerosene lamp (shown here next to a barometer and ship's clock) makes a cheerful warm light that suffuses the entire cabin. However, because it has a glass dome and flammable fuel, it should be watched with care.

on splendid single-malt whisky, waiting for darkness to settle over Loch Ness and herald dinnertime. By the time the sun finally sank, the only crewmember competent to handle the stove was the single abstainer, my then thirteen-year-old sister, Kate.

How fancy can dinner be? Susie Page, who has cruised for many years, tells us, "Gracious dining is only limited if one is under sail and not at anchor." Amenities have a lot to do with it. On *Pageant,* the Pages set a vase of freshly picked wildflowers on the table, and they and most of the other cooks I surveyed report that dinner at anchor is usually eaten under candlelight and served with wine. Many boats have neat brackets for wineglasses and wine and liquor bottles, but you can make do by wrapping glassware in towels or by using the new cardboard wine jugs. Sometimes a change in the usual amenities is an important ritual. When they sailed around the world in *Rabbit,* Mimi and Dan Dyer celebrated every arrival in a new port by using crystal glasses and special "harbor" coffee mugs, which they carefully put back in storage when they weighed anchor. Of course, what you eat makes a difference, too. Once again, the little things are important. Adra and Chuck Kober drink only regular coffee ("we never use instant") when they cruise in *Shibui* off Southern California; other cooks take along special items like herbs, spices, loose tea, a pepper grinder, and after-dinner mints.

Lighted candles, wineglasses, a coffee pot, and mints all demand a certain amount of special preparation and concentrated attention if they're to be used in a jumpy, damp sailboat. The sacrifice is well worth making if any one of them contributes to the crew's happiness. The clear lesson here is that while some of these items may be utterly impractical some of the time—for example, it's not a good idea to light candles when the boat is wildly rolling in rough seas—every sailor will have a short list of "nice-to-haves" that may be treated as essentials.

Order and Neatness Count

A cruising boat's interior is roughly the size of a large closet, her galley about the size of a large bureau. It doesn't take much thought to realize that the ingenious choreography of floor space, lockers, shelves, bins, and bunks will not work at all—in fact may be counterproductive—if things are not kept organized and neat. Good housekeeping is important. So is a common-sense approach to using what little room is available.

First off, the galley should not be cluttered with willing, eager, but unnecessary bodies. Let the cook do the job the way he or she wants to do it, which often means doing it alone because the space is so tiny and the tools so few. "Offer the cook help," one experienced chef recommends to potential cutters, choppers, and stirrers, "but if not helping, stay out of the way." Eager shipmates should avoid making the cook worry about hurt feelings if, of necessity, he or she spurns their requests to assist. The dishes, stove, sink, and cutting boards should be washed as soon as possible after each meal not only to free up space and materials for the next one but also to avoid attracting insects. Every boat has her own dish-washing system. For reasons we outlined in Chapter 5, a clean-up routine that depends on volunteers may be the worst, since it often leads to unconscious misunderstandings and hurt feelings. Sometimes the cook assumes responsibility in a defensive maneuver to keep other people from taking over "my" galley. That's the cook's prerogative, and the others can work off their sense of responsibility by enjoying their after-dinner mints and liqueurs while he or she washes up. Usually, however, the job rotates among the crewmembers from meal to meal, day to day, according to an announced schedule.

Nuisances at home, cockroaches and other bugs are horrible creatures to be forced to live with on a boat since the galley, where they generally congregate, overlaps the sleeping and eating areas. Keeping the galley clean is one way to deal with them, and you can always fumigate, but the best protection is not to let them on board in the first place. Roaches are most likely to arrive uninvited in the corners and recesses of cardboard boxes and paper bags; many experienced cooks always transfer their food to tote bags before carrying it aboard, leaving the paper containers ashore.

Don't let the garbage take over the galley or cabin. Rotten or unwanted leftover food may be heaved overboard to feed the fish and birds (throw it to *leeward,* thank you), but dump everything else into a garbage can lined with a sturdy plastic bag—or perhaps two bags, one inside the other, if you're worried about sharp edges poking through. Most people prefer to put the garbage can under a step in the companionway ladder, where it's automatically ventilated as well as visible and accessible to just about everybody who has a piece of trash in hand. When the bag's about two-thirds full, pull it out and tie up its neck so that the contents are loose (otherwise it might explode). If you can't take the bag ashore right away, store it in a big locker, the forepeak, or—best yet—the dinghy towed astern. In some ports, the harbor master (a paid official who supervises moorings, aids to navigation, and other essential services) sends a boat around to pick up garbage, for a fee.

The cabin as a whole must be kept tidy. Because the cook spends more time below than most other crewmembers, she or he frequently is the best judge of cabin neatness and serves as a combination housemother and inspector general. Locker doors and

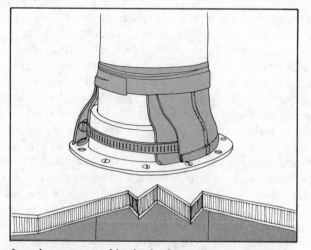

A major source of leaks is the partners, the deck hole for the mast. It should be sealed by a mast boot, a rubber gasket held in place by a large hose clamp and covered by a well-taped canvas hood.

drawers must be shut. Everybody should keep clothes in lockers, bunks, or seabags and foul-weather gear in the assigned locker or bin. The head should receive a daily cleaning; the toilet must be scrubbed out and its lid left shut. In the interest of keeping the toilet's immediate surroundings from smelling bad, men when the weather is rough should not try to urinate below while standing up. "Gentlemen always sit," as old-timers say.

Finally, do everything you can to keep the cabin dry. Pump the bilge to prevent messy, oily water from slopping over onto the cabin sole. The moment spray begins to fly or rain begins to fall, shut the ports and hatches. If you notice water drops on the mast below the partners (the mast hole in the ceiling), tighten the rubber mast boot on deck. Sponge up puddles of water as soon as they form, and wipe any interior surface exposed to salt water with a paper towel damp with fresh water. Once clothes get wet (and they will), be sure to isolate them. If the weather permits, clothespin wet clothes on the lifelines to dry in the sun after a fierce shaking to "spin-dry" much of the superficial moisture off. Later, shake the salt crystals off dry clothes, too. In rainy or overcast weather, store wet clothes in plastic bags until you can get to a laundry.

Be Sensitive to Smells

The cook has to be alert to the indirect ways in which cooking affects living aboard the boat. The most obvious concern is that food preparation and cooking should not overflow from the galley. But of almost equal importance is keeping the cabin smelling nice. One of the most gratifying aspects of cruising is that while almost all food tastes good on a boat, it smells even better in the neutral air away from land. Several days at sea will rest and reprogram a sailor's olfactory nerves to pick up even the meekest odors that, ashore, would be lost in the swirl of civilization. For example, one of the many pleasures of sailing to Bermuda is that the landfall is usually made not by sighting the archipelago's low coral outgrowths but by sniffing the moist perfume of its oleander shrubs. Scents are enhanced even on western Long Island Sound, that busy near-lake in the middle of New York City's urban and suburban hurly-burly. During an overnight race there several years ago, my cold night watch was made special by the unmistakable, soulful smell of baking bread. It obviously did not originate in our galley. I finally solved the mystery by mentally backtracking up the path of the north wind, which was wafting the sweet exhaust of the Arnold bakery down to us from Greenwich, Connecticut. If odors in the atmosphere around the boat are more distinguishable, so too are smells on board. Spices are sharper, fruits are juicier, rum drinks are more tropical. Consciously or unconsciously, good sea chefs combine foods for their pungency as well as for their tastes, much the way Oriental cooks design a stir-fried meal around its appearance. This doesn't take much work in the morning, for while its light grease may make frying risky, the meld of bacon's sharp tang with the rich steam of good brewed coffee is the most pleasant alarm clock that I know.

It's easy to go too far in this direction and create or permit overpowering, lingering odors. Keep the cabin well ventilated; open the hatches and ports, and if you have one, rig an air scoop through the forward hatch. Yet even on warm, windy days, when you would think there is plenty of ventilation, the smell of thick grease, over-fried onions, or rotten bananas will find its way into every locker and bunk—even every sleeping bag—and nauseate shipmates to the point of seasickness.

Keep Your Sense of Humor

Like any other part of life, sailing can fall into a deadly routine unless the crew works hard to do something about it. Long hours of sitting and gazing at the same shoreline, the same ocean, and the same faces can produce a malaise much worse than cabin fever. Call it cockpit fever or boat fever, it usually responds to a mix of laughter, song, variety, and privacy.

The evening cocktail hour is a great time for a group pick-me-up, and with the forbearance of neighboring crews it can go on late into the night. An extroverted shipmate with a good voice and repertory of cheerful songs is a wonderful addition. Some of my fondest sailing memories include late-night concerts by Bob and Harvey Loomis, who are members of an amateur Gilbert and Sullivan troupe. W. S. Gilbert's patter-song lyrics never sound more silly nor Arthur Sullivan's ballads so sweet as when sung in a boat's cockpit. Of course, there is the possibility of too much of a good thing, but the Loomises—like most other good singers I know—are careful not to spread their talents too thin with overuse.

A good way to add some spice to a cruise is to break it with a celebration of some kind—a birthday party, say, or a national holiday—when most rules are off and everybody's hair is let down. Crews sailing long distances often plan for a special event and prepare for it by provisioning party favors, special food and drinks, and other pleasant impracticalities.

On the other hand, spontaneity is an important part of good fun. In early July 1972, before we went off on the Trans-Atlantic Race from Bermuda to Spain in Clayton Ewing's 55-foot yawl *Dyna,*

I asked my watch captain, Steve Colgate (proprietor of the well-known Offshore Sailing School), if and when we might be served a cocktail. Steve said that if the skipper followed his normal, cautious policy we might be favored with a single glass of sherry on Bastille Day. However, after ten days of painfully slow sailing, during which we fell way behind schedule and everybody's enthusiasm for sailing quietly faded into bare tolerance, Clayt emphatically changed his policy. One evening, as the off-going watch sat down to eat, he reached into the ship's liquor locker under his bunk and pulled out the first bottle he touched, a fifth of scotch. He then asked the cook to grab the first can his fingers brushed in the refrigerator. It was a Coke, but that was good enough for Clayt, and we all had a small, harmless scotch and Coke. It tasted like slag, but the inspired foolishness did wonders for our morale. The next night, the same stab-in-the-dark selection process came up with bourbon and lemonade. This nonsense went on every night until, in late July, after an agonizing three weeks of sailing, we finally crawled to the finish. A couple of times we chanced upon a conventional combination of liquor and mixer, but in light of our absurd circumstances—eleven men drifting around in the middle of an ocean for no other reason than to try to beat some other people doing the same thing—it was much more fun to break the rules.

When Sailing Gets Gloomy

There are times when no amount of joyful song and good cheer will make up for sustained bad weather or a poor mix of personalities, and somebody (or everybody) becomes unhappy. The first to notice and try to do something about it may be the cook. Sheila McCurdy offers some wise words:

> An additional duty the cook often takes on is that
> of morale officer, probably because the galley is the
> primary source of diversion when weather or some
> other conditions have turned sour. Some special
> treat at teatime, or a few gentle, joking words, can
> keep close living spaces more tolerable.

A sympathetic cook—usually, but not necessarily, a female one—can do wonders with someone's burgeoning depression. So, too, can a cook who plays the kidding Fool to an overserious skipper's Lear. But often the greatest help is for unhappy crewmembers to find some diversion and privacy ashore or, if shore is inaccessible, to enjoy a few hours to themselves on board, often in the bunk with a book. Couples especially may find it hard to adjust to the exuberant chaos of a crowded boat. While they may have a cabin to themselves, they sometimes find that the kind of privacy they need for their normal intimate life (for which read *sex*) is totally lacking. One solution is for the various couples to go their separate ways every now and then in order to allow each pair a private evening either on board or ashore.

Keep Your Priorities Straight

Cheering-up aside, the cook's primary concern is to see that everybody gets enough tasty food to survive a cruise without both malnutrition and boredom. The cook should aim to provide properly for him- or herself, and then multiply that serving by the number of people on board. After all, cooks like cruising, too, as I found when I asked sea cooks what they enjoy most about sailing. Most say nothing about cooking, little about actual sailing, and a lot about activities once the boat reaches her destination and drops anchor. Several cooks say their greatest pleasure is "a quiet anchorage." Others mention exploring harbors or rivers in dinghies or going ashore to paint and draw. One skipper who also cooks describes his rewards as "the challenge of the navigation, the finding of new places, the remote and quiet anchorage, and self-reliance, with no umbilical cords to the rest of society." Yet others say that they enjoy meeting new people, just as long as the anchorage isn't crowded. The closest anybody comes to the galley is "picnic lunches or early dinners on a deserted beach or rock"—perhaps with some lobster bought from a passing fisherman and boiled over a wood fire.

Gracious living on board a boat, then, requires that cooking be kept in perspective. Flexibility and a sense of humor are important if the cook is going to have a good time, and if the cook's having fun, so probably is the rest of the crew.

CHAPTER 15

Sailing
with
Children

The world consists of two kinds of people: those who can get along with and understand children and those who can't. Parents are not necessarily in one group or the other, and neither are nonparents; that makes taking kids along on a boat somewhat problematical. Having sailed with my sons, Will and Dana, for many years, I'm not about to romanticize the experience any more than I would single parenthood (or parenthood itself, for that matter). At worst, it's like the normal, harried, noisy, somewhat thankless experience of living with kids, but one compressed geographically into a tiny arena from which there is almost no escape. At best, it overflows with joyous surprises and offers a complete change from the usual daily routine. It can be one of the most satisfying experiences that a parent and child can share.

If you want to find out how your children take to sailing, why, take them sailing. You'll soon get a sense of their interest in and aptitude for the pastime as you expose them to the sailing life, with all its pleasures and challenges, and some of its fears. Like adults, children learn how to sail faster on small boats than on large ones. A capsizable dinghy works best partly because her small gear can be managed by small bodies, but primarily because it rewards good technique and punishes bad with decisive quickness. If you do it wrong you get very wet; if you do it right you stay dry. After many years of teaching beginning sailing in relatively large three-person boats, instructors have begun to use singlehanders such as Lasers (with cut-down rigs) in order to leave kids on their own and maximize the amount of time they spend at the helm—an excellent idea that is turning out new generations of better and more independent sailors. Sailboards work well for the same reason (and also because they're a great platform for showing off, which every child needs to do from time to time).

Perhaps an outline of one youngster's sailing life will suggest some possibilities. Until I was ten my family lived in Ohio, and I first sailed with my father on vacations at his boyhood home on Long Island, New York. He gave me the run of the boat on short daysails, wisely allowing me to discover if I liked it before imposing detailed instruction and complicated terminology. I liked it. That settled, my first sailing lessons came at a summer camp on Maine's Kennebec River. A year or so later, we moved to Long Island and I and my brothers were given two 13½-foot Blue Jay sloops, boxy and roomy and made of plywood. My boat was bright red and was called *Lucivee*, which I was told means "baby lynx" and which was inspired by a family tradition of boats named *Lynx*.

That's where I began to sail in earnest, at first knocking around Cold Spring Harbor under the watchful eye of a couple of college-student sailing instructors, later venturing out onto Long Island Sound for races, in which I did creditably enough to inspire a child's dreams of glory. Like all adolescents I was hungry for success in whichever arena worked best for me. Some find it in Little League, others in gymnastics, still others in academics. Sailing and learning about its history and traditions—that was my turf. (Many years later, when I worked with America's Cup winner Dennis Conner on his autobiography, *No Excuse to Lose*, I was fascinated to discover that he had made the same discovery in much the same way in San Diego, although his interest was more competitive than mine.)

As often happens, the rewards of early success stimulated harder work and greater ambitions, all fertilized by a library of sailing instructional and history books given to me by my father (and to him by his). An annual, week-long family cruise aboard a chartered boat in Maine or Massachusetts opened another door of the pastime. Like many teenagers before and since, I became captivated by the never-ending complexity of piloting and rigging, the relaxed camaraderie of a crew, and the almost spiritual satisfaction that comes when a sailor helps a boat sail well. The energy and knowledge accumulated during those years eventually led to wider-ranging boating experiences. In 1964, when I was nineteen, I was fortunate to be invited to join a four-month voyage in a 77-foot ketch from San Diego to Sicily, and eight years later—after college, graduate school, and army duty—I sailed in a race from Bermuda to Spain. My writing about that transatlantic race led to a position on the staff of *Yachting* magazine, where sailing was a part of the job, and five years later I set out on my own to write books about the pastime that had been such an important part of my life for so many years.

I was lucky: my father, who knew and loved sailing, encouraged me in many ways, and my family moved in circles that involved yacht clubs, which, until the early 1970s, were almost the only places where a child could receive thorough sailing instruction and go out on the water every day of the summer. Fortunately, alternatives to that expensive exclusivity have long since made sailing available to many more people. After several summers of off-and-on sailing with me to find out if they liked it, my boys were enrolled in a local public sailing school—one of many that have sprung up in waterfront city parks all over the country—to learn sailing theory, terminology, and boat handling. At first, when they were nine and ten, the boys mastered the basic skills in a boat called a Puffer, which is a lighter, faster version of a Blue Jay. The next summer, they moved on to the much racier and tippier Laser, and Dana (when he was ten) earned his beginner's certificate on a Windsurfer—a type of boat that did not even exist until 1969, three years before he was born. Although I don't own a cruising boat, both boys have enjoyed the side benefits of having a father who is a sailor. By the time they were in junior high, they had been on a few short cruises, and we often sail together on annual boat delivery trips from Maine, usually with my father in a delightful three-generational crew whose cumulative experience stretches from the 1920s to the 1980s.

Along the way, I—like all sailing parents of sailing children—have been forced to cope with a variety of problems, including allowing the children to learn at their own speed and even leaving them ashore if that's their pleasure. Among the other concerns were (and continue to be) clothing, safety, enjoyment, and living together on a boat in relative harmony. Other parents may benefit from my experiences.

What to Wear

The same questions concerning adult clothing apply to children's gear. Theoretically, the amount and quality of gear that *you* purchase will depend on the amount and type of sailing that *they* do —and, especially, on how cold and wet they'll get. In fine weather,

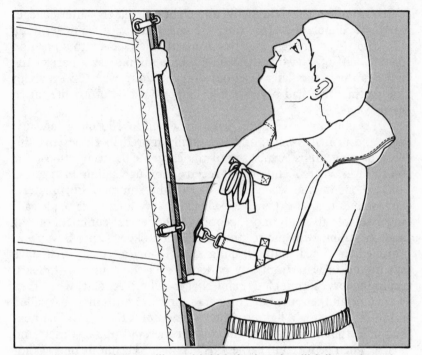

The main worry about sailing with kids is that they'll fall overboard. Less than expert swimmers are usually required to wear life jackets like this horseshoe type, which is less confining than a vest. Most cruising families have very definite rules about when and where children may go on deck in rough weather.

a T-shirt and bathing suit will work well, along with sneakers for any sailing on boats with deck fittings. Be alert to sunburn; have the child wear a long-sleeved cotton shirt most of the time until he or she is well tanned. Like time and distance, the wind-chill factor is an abstraction ungraspable by the average twelve-year-old mind. Dressing a child properly for cool weather, therefore, is a herculean chore that often meets with protests along the lines of "But I'll look like a polar bear!" A diplomatic solution is to pack—*you* pack—a seabag with another, skimpier outfit that the child may exchange for the bulky clothes that he or she finds so distasteful, or (more likely) put on over or under them upon discovering that you were correct from the beginning. If your children are like mine, you'll also take along plenty of extra socks; Dana, who once "accidentally" fell into the reflecting pool in front of the Lincoln Memorial in Washington, D.C., takes pleasure in dangling from anchor rodes and docking lines with his toes in the water.

Since Dana is not the only child who enjoys getting wet, any special protective gear you provide may never be used. Normal, zip-up, $15 knee-length raincoats worked fine on board whenever I was able to cram my sons into them. Now they have, and sometimes even wear, $40 PVC foul-weather jackets bought at a local chandlery. Normal rubber boots serve in place of seaboots. Every child who goes out on the water regularly must have his own vest-style Type III life jacket.

Safety Worries

Most mothers and (secretly) most fathers, too, worry deeply about their children's safety on board a boat. The same rough guidelines that careful, loving parents follow at home apply on board, but there are some special rules that apply uniquely to a sailing environment. The ones that I find most important are:

✓ Always know where your children are on the boat, especially when they're on deck. It may help to have them wear a shirt or sweater with a distinctive color.

✓ Make sure that children know who on deck is in charge, and that that person's commands must be obeyed implicitly. Since kids like and need limits in their lives, observing this guideline will be as reassuring to them as it is to their parents.

✓ Develop a tone of voice that means and is understood as *"Listen to me! This is important!"*

✓ As soon as a child old enough to follow instructions comes aboard for the first time, demonstrate the safety equipment and any potential hazards. If you don't feel qualified to do it, ask somebody who knows the boat well to give the child a careful tour. You should go along to translate warnings into the child's language.

✓ With all that understood, let your child roam anywhere within the confines of the lifelines.

Drown-Proofing

Your weightiest fear, obviously, is drowning. Teaching the child to swim early and well is the first step toward dealing with this problem, and winter swimming lessons at the local YMCA or YWCA are a good investment. But any young child and all children (or, for that matter, adults) whose swimming ability is unproven should follow these rules, from the most elementary for normal weather to the most restrictive for rough weather:

✓ Wear a life jacket whenever on deck or in the cockpit.

✓ Stay below or in the cockpit.

✓ Wear a safety harness and hook it to an object near the middle of the boat whenever on deck or in the cockpit.

In easy conditions, older children who can prove they are good swimmers by, say, swimming twice around the boat need not observe these rules, but the skipper's word is law when the weather gets rough. Toddlers present the most serious safety problems. Infants are rarely mobile enough to get out of the cockpit, and older children, if they have been lovingly disciplined, respect and are proud to observe the rules. But children from about one to four are too mobile, unbalanced, and vague about instructions to be trusted to stay where their parents leave them. For that reason, the decks of many toddler-crewed cruising boats are fenced in by mesh strung along the lifelines.

Falling, Cold and Strains

Two health hazards endemic to adults rarely affect children because of their small size and relatively large fat content. One of these is an injury caused by a fall; a fall that's serious for a tall adult is usually shaken off quickly by a four-footer. The other hazard is hypothermia, or drastic loss of body heat. A scrawny kid may get cold quickly and a distracted parent may not notice the usual symptoms—shivering, vagueness, passivity—but most children probably resist hypothermia better than most adults. On the other hand, children may be injured because they become unrealistically confident of their ability to perform chores best left to larger, stronger people—chores like trimming heavily strained sheets, handling docking lines, and lugging anchors. It's a good idea, once the boat is under way, to give the children an idea of the forces involved by having them trim a sheet or pull on a halyard. It looks easy until they try to do it. Once children realize how large the strains are, they usually stay well (and safely) away from big loads.

But don't be *too* protective, especially of near- and actual adolescents. That's the age when kids are constantly taking new risks, and when a good parent, at the price of many gray hairs, is encouraging the taking of those risks. Until about the age of eleven or twelve, the children's world is often so benign that they can't imagine getting hurt, but beginning at this age they want to (and, for the sake of maturation, must) discover that possibility. If there's any way that a sailor this age or older can catch a small but healthy dose of reasonable fear without being scared so badly that he or she swears off boats for life, parents should take advantage of it. Sailing a dinghy or sailboard in windy weather is one of those experiences; so is rowing a dinghy into rough seas.

Kids' Jobs

What jobs can children perform? Quite a few are available, but, remembering that they are only children, an adult should not demand either total dedication or absolute perfection in the performance of the vast majority of them. Certainly children should be requested and expected to pick up after themselves and, observing a written schedule, to help with communal chores such as washing dishes and swabbing the deck with a mop or scrub brush. But when it comes to sailing and piloting the boat, there will be much less contention and disappointment if adults put themselves in a frame of mind where they are gratified and surprised if the kids volunteer to help.

One place where most children will be more than happy to serve is at the helm, and that's also where they may make their greatest contribution to the vessel's welfare while larger people are exercising their bigger muscles on sheets, halyards, sails, and anchors. Some awful day, in an emergency, a grown-up swimming after a rapidly disappearing boat may wish that he'd taught his child how to steer. For those reasons—and also because steering is a lot of fun—any child who shows an interest in handling the tiller or wheel should be given it once the boat is clear of land and traffic. Let the child steer just as long as desired so that he or she may learn by making mistakes. While the child is working at it, gradually show the novice helmsperson something about the points of sail, which way to shove the helm to alter course, and how to trim sails, steer by the compass, and tack and jibe. Other jobs that children may enjoy performing are taking bearings, spotting aids to navigation, watching the read-out on the depth sounder, listening to radio weather forecasts, making log entries, and clearing tangled halyards. Many children are fascinated by piloting skills, perhaps because so much of their own energy is dedicated to pinpointing their own positions on the great chart of life. Kids who are computer buffs frequently master the intricacies of a loran receiver or other electronic device more quickly than computer-illiterate adults. Whatever the job, tell them how important a contribution they're making and reward them by taking them seriously.

Besides the immediate, utilitarian benefits, plenty of rewards fall out from a child's sailing accomplishments, whether or not he or she is sailing with his or her parents. Kids who are good at something and see their skill properly recognized often develop a confidence that they carry fruitfully into other parts of their lives. As the child develops, so too does the parent. I was recently reminded of this during a cruise on a complicated and powerful 51-foot ocean racer. We had to douse a big genoa jib, and I handed the helm over to a shipmate and went forward. So that the jib would drop directly on deck and not fall overboard into the bow wave, I shouted aft, "Bring her up a little." The helmsman headed up to a forereach exactly as I would have done, we let go the halyard, and the sail collapsed on itself in neat folds on the foredeck as he professionally swung the bow off, bringing the boat back on course. As I walked aft after tying the sail, it finally sank in that this skillful helmsman was my ten-year-old son—the one who falls into reflecting pools, loses his baseball mitts, forgets his homework, and is surprised whenever he does something well. Right then, he looked like another Dennis Conner as his hands caressed the wheel with gentle strength. He was still a child, of course, and too much should not have been expected of him; but that, I reflected, would soon change.

Having Fun on the Big Gym

For a child, a sailboat has all the advantages of both a big gymnasium and a small castle, and a normally eager, athletic, and individualistic boy or girl will find plenty to do all day. If the exercise is balanced by some private time spent alone and by plenty of rest, everybody on board regardless of age will enjoy the child's presence.

Most obvious when a child first comes aboard are all the things to swing on—the boom, halyards, sheets, bowlines, and mast. By the time they reach adolescence, kids become as obsessed about climbing the mast as mountaineers are about scaling Mt. Everest. This urge may be satisfied at first by strapping the child securely into a bosun's chair—usually a big Dacron diaper—and hauling him or her up to the top of the spar with a halyard. Be sure to tie a line to the chair so you can pull a light child back down. By the time he or she is hauled up about 20 feet, the child will know whether this is fun or not. Parents should be sure to praise the anxious child who sensibly calls a halt to the adventure as well as the daredevil who wants to keep going. As children get stronger and their hands tougher, they may try shinning up the mast on the halyards. It will be easier when the boat is heeled, when they can

The boat herself is a huge, safe gymnasium. Just keep your eyes on the young athletes.

almost walk up the windward side. While I've never known a kid (including myself at that age) to fall off a mast, if this activity makes a parent nervous to the point of acute distraction, perhaps it should be left to school gyms (or postponed until that parent is below taking a nap).

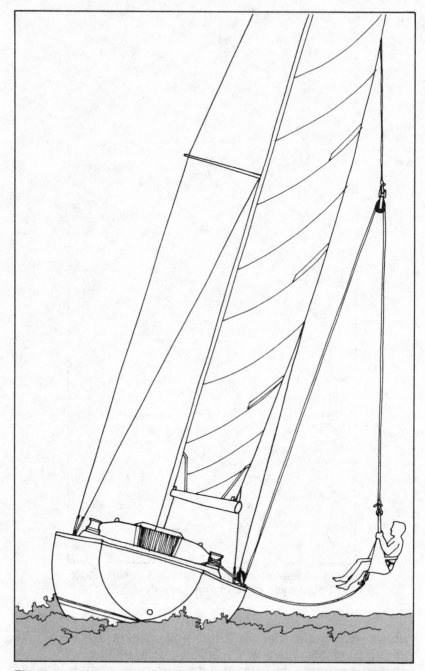

The trapeze is a wonderful diversion on a breezy, warm afternoon for adults as well as children. The fore and aft position of the deck block for the guy line determines how far forward the rider swings.

The Rousmaniere Trapeze

A lot of fun can be had by swinging out from a sailing boat on a trapeze rigged from a halyard. I modestly take credit for refining this adventure to a science through many hours of experimenting with delighted children. It works only on a boat with powerful sheet winches and only when there is enough wind to heel her over at least 20 degrees, until her leeward rail is just kissing the water. Here's how the trapeze is set up:

1. Working on the leeward side, snap a block into the shackle of the highest free halyard—usually a spare jib or spinnaker halyard—and lead a very long, relatively heavy line such as a spinnaker or jib sheet through the block.

2. Tying one end of the line to the lifelines, haul up the halyard as you feed out the line, until the block is about two-thirds of the way up the mast. Wrap the halyard several times around its winch and cleat it. You now have a rope guy line running through a block suspended from the mast.

3. Lead the guy line through a block snapped to the rail about halfway between the leeward shrouds and the boat's widest point, and then back to the largest winch in the cockpit. You probably will have to lead the line through another block to make it lead up to the winch drum at an angle about 15 degrees below the horizontal; if the line comes in at or above the horizontal, there will be a riding turn, jamming it on the drum.

4. Now shackle or tie (with a bowline) the other end of the guy line to the bosun's chair. To be doubly safe, wrap the pin of this and all other shackles in the system with a layer of tape.

5. Tie or shackle a retrieval line to the bottom of the bosun's chair and lead it through a block on the rail at the boat's widest point. If there is a boarding gate in the lifelines (a section of lifeline that can be disconnected to facilitate boarding and unboarding), open it.

The trapeze is now ready. Wearing a bathing suit, the rider steps into the bosun's chair, a strong adult trims the guy line (perhaps with the help of a winch handle grinder), and the rider rises from the deck and flies out to leeward through the boarding gate, directly abeam of the widest point. If he or she is forward of that point and threatening to swing into the leeward shrouds, move the lead block on the rail aft; if aft of the widest point, move the lead block forward.

The guy-line tender controls the swinger's altitude, raising or

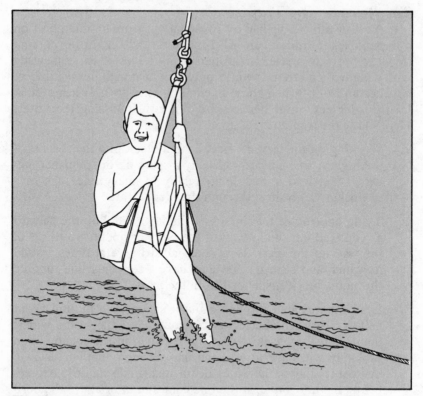

The diaper-type bosun's chair provides great security for the swinger. Tape the pin of the guy line's shackle so that it doesn't open accidentally.

dropping him or her into the water as whim allows. To pull the swinger back, haul on the retrieval line and have an adult sitting or standing on the leeward deck to make the grab.

The excitement is enhanced if as the swinger's toes dangle in the water twenty feet to leeward of the boat, somebody loudly cries "shark!" In fact, my friend Eric Camiel tells me that a version of the trapeze—in which the bosun's chair dangles off the end of the boom while the boat is running—is called "shark bait."

Spinnaker Flying

A riskier type of trapeze artistry, spinnaker flying is done at anchor on boats larger than about 40 feet. Because this exercise is controlled by the wind and can be wild, if not dangerous, I do not recommend it for use in gusting winds and by anybody younger than about sixteen.

1. Anchor the boat by her stern, with her bow pointed downwind. Set the smallest spinnaker with sheets but without a pole, and with a line about 1½ times the length of the foot tied between the two clews. Hoist the spinnaker about two-thirds of the way so that when filled it flies *well* ahead of the bow.

2. Shackle the bosun's chair to the line—either to a knot in its middle or with a snatch block that can slide back and forth between the clews. The snatch block gives the wilder ride. Let one spinnaker sheet go, letting the sail flag out before the boat and the chair drop to the water.

3. The swinger jumps into the water and climbs into the chair, and the sheet is trimmed to fill the sail, which will lift high above the water and, as it oscillates, throw the rider around unpredictably. To drop the rider into the water, collapse the spinnaker by letting go a sheet *only* when he or she is well forward of the pulpit. Serious accidents have been caused by falls onto the pulpit and bow.

Quiet Fun

Crazy swinging is not the only fun a child can have on a sailboat. A row in the boat's dinghy, a spin on her sailboard, a swim to a nearby island—all can provide both pleasure and the short daily vacation from adults that every child (and every parent) requires. On board, too, there are many ways kids can enjoy themselves quietly. Some of these go with the nautical surroundings. Practicing the basic knots—the bowline, double half-hitch, and rolling hitch —can be fun, especially if it is a group effort involving an adult expert. Tutored by an experienced grown-up or by a book like the classic *Ashley Book of Knots*, a boy or girl who enjoys detailed work may learn the basics of traditional marlinspike seamanship, including splicing and decorative rope work. On the other hand, the child who shows an interest in the history and technical aspects of sailing may, as I did, hole up with a specialized book for hours. One endlessly fascinating activity is to tow a model boat or wooden stick astern at the end of a long string (for some reason lost in time, we called those sticks "weewogs" when I was a boy). After some practice, you can make the thing submarine and dance in the air. Bird-watching seems to interest more adults than children, but a well-illustrated natural history guide to the area you're cruising in may well attract a young reader or two.

When you pack for a cruise with children, include a tote bag or seabag full of the kinds of entertainment that they and you enjoy at home: their favorite books, a couple of decks of cards (and a guide to card games), a magnetized chess or Scrabble set (but keep it away from the compass!), some puzzle or word game books, crayons and drawing paper, and on and on. You and they know what pleases them. Cassette music and story tapes are wonderful to have aboard for adults as well as children. An excellent source of story tapes is The Mind's Eye (Box 6727, San Francisco, CA 94101), whose dramatizations of J. R. R. Tolkien's *The Hobbit* and *The Lord of the Rings* have given great pleasure to my family for several years now. Earphones, whether on a plain recorder or a fancy Walkman type, are well worth their price, since they allow a crewmember to listen to what he or she likes without worrying whether the music will offend shipmates' tastes. Another benefit of earphones is that they provide the solitude that every child needs for an hour or so each day. Even on a crowded boat, a little privacy is essential to gracious living.

PART IV

When Sailing Gets Difficult

CHAPTER 16

Night Sailing, Getting Lost, Heavy Weather, and Five Other Problems

W e can talk all we want to about how well everything should go in normal conditions, but (like life ashore) sailing often consists of extended periods of relative ease punctuated by brief moments of legitimate fear. Someday you'll have to sail in the dark or in fog, or the weather will get rough, or a sail will rip. These things and more may, in fact, all happen at once. We're concerned with problems here, not life-threatening emergencies (which we'll discuss in the next chapter). This chapter describes eight hassles that cause discomfort and, if not dealt with quickly, can lead to an emergency. Alertness, calm, good leadership and followership, and good attention to detail are important when dealing with them, but you must also know some specific steps to take. If any of these eight problems turns into an emergency, it probably will be because the crew panics and allows common sense and their knowledge of basic mechanical and sailing skills to fly overboard.

When faced with potential danger, head, if possible, to a sheltered harbor and anchor. Sometimes, however, you can't get to port. In that case, sail or power away from crowded channels and threatening shorelines and stop or drastically slow the boat. In smooth water, you can stop her simply by turning off the engine or lowering the sails and letting her drift, but if there's any seaway (waves) you'll have to steady her motion by leaving some sails up.

Too many people panic in a situation like this because, being auto-
mobile-addicted modernists, they are used to relying on engines to
get them out of trouble. But sails can do the job just about as well.
To stop the boat, heave-to: back the jib, trim the mainsail flat, and
sail just above a close-hauled course, with the mainsail partially
luffing. She'll jog along comfortably at a speed of about one knot.
Alternatively, get on a beam reach, let the main boom all the way
out to the leeward shrouds, and hold it there with a line. With the
jib lowered, she'll slide very slowly to leeward while making about
one knot ahead. In neither case are you really stopping the boat,
but you are allowing her to ride at a low speed while you solve your
problem.

Sailing at Night

Night sailing in good weather is one of the most pleasant things
you can do in a boat. With phosphorus sparkling in the bow wave
and wake, she seems to charge along at twice her normal speed in
her own small, quiet world. Boats a mere fifty yards away appear
like distant, skimpily decorated Christmas trees, and on board, your
shipmates' features become shadowy in the red glow of the binnacle
light as they lie back and silently gaze after stars and satellites. Yet,
while it can be extremely pleasant, night sailing also involves some
challenges to a sailor's eyesight and judgment that, if unmet, may
lead to an emergency.

The main problem is finding your way around the boat without
tripping over sheets, winches, and fittings. First off, lines should be
coiled and winch handles stowed so that decks are clear. A crewmember should walk the decks and examine all gear at least once
every two hours. And at least one bright flashlight should be handy
on deck for inspecting sails and rigging when night vision and the
moon do not combine to provide enough illumination. Plastic
household flashlights may be suitable, except that one hand is
needed to hold them and the helmsperson will be blinded if their
glaring and highly focused light is accidentally aimed aft. An excellent alternative, available in many chandleries, is a small, relatively
dim and unfocused light held in the mouth; to switch it on, bite
down. Everybody on deck can be issued one of these inexpensive
lights to avoid the time-consuming annoyance of passing a flashlight
from hand to hand for different chores. To protect the crew's night
vision, use white lights as sparingly as possible both on deck and
below. The steering (binnacle) compass must have a red light.
Ideally, a red bulb should be used over the chart table (if you can't
find a red one, simply rouge a white one with a red crayon). The

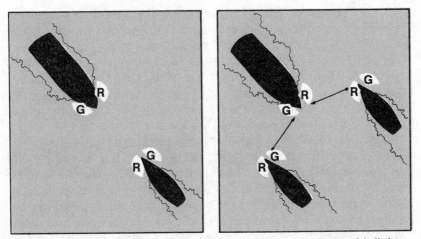

(left) A collision is likely if you see both the red and green sidelights on an approaching boat. Turn hard to starboard—"show her your red." (right) But if you see only one sidelight, you may safely hold your course.

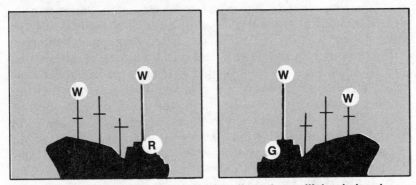

If the white range lights on a ship are aligned, a collision is imminent. But if they are not aligned, their relationship with a sidelight should indicate which way the ship is heading. Be careful: ships move a lot faster than they seem.

colors on charts were chosen to show up clearly under red.

The U.S. Coast Guard requires all boats sailing at night to carry a bright light for signaling other vessels. Larger boats carry exceptionally bright lights that run off the electrical system; smaller ones have large flashlights carried within reach of the helmsman. With either type, the best way to make yourself visible to an approaching boat is *not* to shine your light in the other fellow's eyes; it will only blind and confuse him. Rather, shine it on your sails, which will reflect brightly over a distance of hundreds of yards.

When another vessel does appear on the horizon (or closer), do your very best to identify her and her course and speed and to predict what your relative positions will be when you cross. This is easier said than done at night, when shore lights, poor visibility, and a crowded channel may make what is actually a very simple situation look very confusing. Lights on a big ship may be extremely misleading because they are set high in the air and far aft. Also, without a wake in sight, it's very difficult to judge the ship's speed. Remember the rule of thumb: she's heading at you if both her sidelights are visible. Whatever the situation, whatever kind of boat is approaching, if you have *any* worry that there may be a collision, assume the worst: the people on the other vessel are incompetents who have no awareness of your existence and no knowledge of the rules of the road. Turn away from them as fast and as far as you can, wait for them to pass, then resume your course. (See Chapter 10 for more on avoiding collisions.)

Steering at Night

When steering in the dark, try not to stare at the compass; your eyes and coordination will quickly blur and the spinning dial and dim light will mesmerize you. Instead, keep your eyes moving from side to side and up and down, occasionally glancing at the compass dial. Best of all, steer by a lighted landmark (make sure it's not another boat's stern light!) or a relatively stationary star (heading north is always easy since the north star moves only 2½ degrees daily). In a steady wind, you can keep to a fairly reliable course by steering by the apparent wind direction, using either the old-timers' technique of feeling the wind on the back of your neck or a more high-tech device such as a lighted masthead wind indicator or a lighted apparent wind indicator in the cockpit.

Taking Bearings at Night

Because a lighted aid to navigation at night is more conspicuous from a greater distance than an unlighted one, piloting at night is often easier than piloting during the day—assuming that you can find the aid in the first place. Still, taking accurate bearings at night is a major challenge, especially in rough weather when the boat's heading is never constant. Keep your eyes sweeping over the horizon, take at least two bearings each on at least two lighted aids roughly at a right angle to each other, and if you have any doubts, take the bearings again. Near shore, piloting at night can be a full-time job, sometimes for two people—one to take the bearings and the other to plot them.

Don't make night piloting any more complicated and dangerous than it has to be. Take advantage of the facts that white lights
can be seen from farther away than green or red ones, and that
lighthouses, being much higher in the air, have considerably greater
range than lighted buoys. In unfamiliar waters or when you're not
in a hurry, rather than sailing a straight-line course to your destination, plan a series of short doglegs toward the brightest aids to
navigation on the chart. This way you'll hopscotch between good
fixes and minimize error.

Getting Lost

In Chapter 9 we stressed the importance of systematic piloting;
the rules of thumb we laid out there are important whether or not
you know where you are. Even the most compulsively systematic
navigator sometimes is unable to say what his position is. When you
get lost out there, the vital first step is to *admit it*. Don't let false
pride talk you into denying what is patently the situation; you could
find yourself in even worse trouble. Second, don't get overly emo-
tional. Frustration, self-criticism, despair, guilt, and panic will only
lead to worse errors. Approach the problem with all the calm and
objectivity you can muster.

In good visibility, day or night, the quickest and simplest way
to get away from a tight spot—a shoal area, a rapidly approaching
shoreline, even a fog bank—is to turn around 180 degrees and
retrace your track back to an aid to navigation where you can refig-
ure your position and course. Meanwhile, take as many bearings on
charted objects as you can; even a single line of position will help.
If, on the other hand, you're out of sight of land and realize that
you're lost, head toward where you think land is and look for a
landmark or buoy.

But when the visibility is poor and you get lost on a moonless
night or in fog or rain, you may not be able to trust a reciprocal
course to get you away from nearby shoal waters. If that's the case,
stop or drastically slow your forward progress; drop the anchor if
you're very anxious. Pull out the chart and logbook, and using all
available evidence calculate your present position and the course
that got you to it. If your crew has any ideas or observations, hear
them out; some people have an uncanny intuition for position-find-
ing or a superb observational ability that functions independently
of maps and charts. Avoid the temptation of taking a simple, easy
action that could get you into hotter (or rather shallower) water.
This reexamination usually turns up a dumb error that you commit-
ted several hours before, back when you calculated or plotted the

course. Even very experienced navigators have been known to make one or more of the following gaffes:

✓ Referring to the wrong day in the tide table, or failing to add an hour for daylight time.

✓ Using the wrong mileage scale, or (my favorite boo-boo) carrying one chart's mileage scale on the dividers over to a chart with a different scale, say when moving from a small-scale general chart, showing a big chunk of water and shoreline, to a large-scale coast chart, which covers only a bay or sound.

✓ Over- or underestimating the boat's speed.

✓ Plotting the course using the outer, true ring on the chart's compass rose rather than the inner, magnetic ring.

✓ Using an old chart with outdated variation or an old buoy arrangement.

Fog and Bad Visibility

Piloting in the fog is like a blind person walking: it can be done just as long as you have a base point of departure and a system for measuring your progress from it. In piloting, the system is called *running out your time*. The departure point usually is the last buoy before you enter the fog. If you know how fast you're going (speed) and how far you have to go (distance), you can figure how long it's going to take (time) using this version of the speed/time/distance formula:

$$\text{time} = \frac{(60 \times \text{distance})}{\text{speed}}$$

Time is in minutes, *distance* is in nautical miles (or, on the Great Lakes, statute miles), and *speed* is in knots (or, on the Lakes, miles per hour). Be sure to add favorable tidal current to or subtract contrary current from *speed*.

If, for example, the distance from the departure buoy to the next buoy is 4.1 miles and the speed is 6.3 knots, it will take 39 minutes to make the leg. All the pilot has to do is punch the stop watch when the boat passes the first buoy and set the compass course for the second buoy. Thirty-nine minutes later, alter course to pass the second one; it's there even if it's invisible in the fog. From then on, continue running out your time as you work your way from buoy to buoy like a blind person counting steps between street corners. Used in conjunction with loran and radio devices,

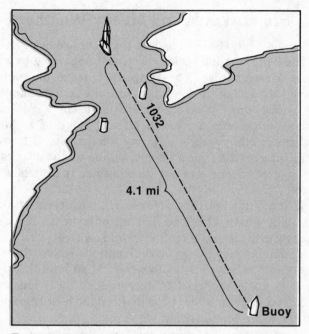

To "run out your time," calculate how long it will take to run a leg between two buoys. Then keep to the course and time the run with a stop watch.

running out your time should get you safely to your destination.

Sometimes, however, fog is so thick that you just can't trust to backtracking or running out your time. If that's the case, stop (unless you're in a channel crowded with big, fast-moving ships; if so, follow them) and wait for the fog to burn off. Keep a watch on deck and listen for and sound the appropriate horn or bell signals. Because clear hearing is important in fog, eliminate or cut down all unnecessary noise—luffing sails, chatter, clicking winches. It may be best to douse all sails, turn off the engine, and anchor. The appropriate signals are:

✓ **If under sail or unable to maneuver,** a long-short-short horn pattern at least every 2 minutes.

✓ **If under power and making way,** make one long horn blast at least every 2 minutes.

✓ **If under power but stopped,** sound a long-long horn pattern at least every 2 minutes.

✓ **If anchored,** ring a bell forward for 5 seconds every minute.

Fresh Winds and Heavy Weather

When the wind is so strong and the waves so large that you're fighting the helm, getting soaking wet, and beginning to wish for a quiet meal ashore, you're in heavy weather. It has more to do with comfort and the feel of the boat than with the actual strength of the wind in knots; small boats become difficult in wind conditions where many large ones are just beginning to come to life. Some people claim to enjoy sailing in heavy weather and a few of them actually mean it, but for most people, sailing on the edge of control and the edge of the boat is not pleasurable. It can, however, be manageable.

Handling rough stuff requires a slightly different attitude than sailing in light winds. Don't be passive; pull sheets, halyards, and the helm aggressively and forcefully. Hold on tight; use your safety harness. If you get seasick, go on deck and get active. Steer around large waves into relatively smooth water. Most important, be alert to the boat's angle of heel and balance. As the wind increases, reduce the heel angle and the speed (to keep the boat from pounding wildly in waves) in the following sequence:

Step 1: Depower the Sails

To reduce heel, weather helm, and speed, the first step is to moderate the side forces in the sails by depowering them. This is like putting a governor on an automobile engine to limit RPMs and horsepower. The first stage in depowering is to trim the sails flat. To flatten the mainsail when sailing close-hauled, tighten the outhaul and cunningham controls and pull the sheet down hard (leaving about 5 degrees of twist to leeward in the leech from clew to head). Trim the jib sheet in almost all the way, again leaving about 5 degrees of twist along the leech and a slight arc from leech to luff to provide some shape to redirect the wind; a board-flat sail is completely inefficient.

If there is still too much heel and weather helm, continue depowering by trimming the sails farther outboard (toward the rail). Let the mainsail traveler car down to leeward and trim the jib through a block to leeward of the normal lead—for example, a snatch block hooked to the rail. Upwind, moving the leads out decreases side forces while keeping forward forces about the same (it's standard procedure when reaching in all conditions).

If heel and weather helm remain a problem, try depowering the sails by letting them luff a little, trimming the sheets a couple of inches short of optimum. Or spill wind from the top of the sails, where the wind's heeling leverage is greatest, by twisting them off

Many boats will balance fairly well in heavy weather under a small jib or a deeply reefed mainsail alone, as this Taiwan-built Mao Ta cruiser shows.

more than the usual 5 degrees. To increase twist, move the jib lead aft a few inches and ease up on the mainsheet or boom vang. In gusty winds, you may always feather or pinch up (turn into the wind) a few degrees to temporarily depower the sails until the blast has passed on. In any case, keep the boat moving fast so that you can steer around waves.

Step 2: Shorten Sail

If depowering the sails doesn't work, you must shorten sail by either putting up a smaller jib, reefing, or lowering a sail, and in this way decreasing the exposed area. Whichever method you use, it's always better to shorten sail before it's absolutely necessary than to wait until the boat is badly overpowered, so stay alert to the wind strength and balance.

Changing jibs involves several steps and good coordination by the helmsperson and crew. It can be quite slow with a small crew working on the foredeck in very rough weather. First, take the replacement, bagged sail on deck and tie it to the windward rail near the mast. When the waves are big or heavy spray is flying, don't open the forward hatch unless you want to take water below;

instead, shove the bag up through the main hatch into the cockpit, then take it forward.

With a small or inexperienced crew, or in very rough weather, douse the old sail and put it away before working with the new one. Have two or more people sit on the foredeck (with their safety harnesses hooked on) and pull the jib down by the foot as the sheet and halyard are eased. The helmsperson can help by forereaching or by bearing off to a run so that the mainsail blankets the jib; the worst points of sail for dousing a jib are a beam and broad reach, when the jib foot is way to leeward of the bow and hard to grab. Once the sail is down all the way, the others hold it tightly while one sailor unsnaps the halyard and hooks it to the bow pulpit. The halyard is then tightened to keep it from tangling around the spreaders. The old sail is tied to the rail with nylon straps called sail ties. (Later, it may be dragged aft on the windward side, folded in big two- to three-foot flakes running from leech to luff, folded or rolled up, put in its own bag, and taken below.) Then the new sail is hooked onto the headstay—starting with the lower hanks (snap hooks) and working up toward the head—and its sheets are led properly.

I'm assuming that the sail is attached to the headstay with hanks (metal snap hooks). However, on many racer-cruisers the boltrope on the luff of the jib is fed into one of two grooves in a device attached to the stay, so the old sail is still up while the new one is hoisted. This arrangement works best when the old sail is doused to windward, inside the newly hoisted sail, which keeps it from blowing overboard. Once the old sail is on deck, it's attached to the boat only at the corners—by the halyard at the head, the tack fitting at the tack, and the sheets at the clew. By all means get this kind of jib tied down on deck as soon as possible.

Sheets for small jibs are usually led farther forward than ones for large jibs; the proper lead location should be marked on deck. Double-check all leads and the bowline used to tie the sheet to the jib clew. The loop through the clew should be small and tight and the tail of the knot should be at least four inches long. Then hook on the halyard and immediately pull the sail up. Somebody must usually stand on the bow keeping tension on the luff so the halyard aloft does not get slack and tangle on a spreader. Again, the helmsperson can take load off the sail by forereaching or running. Keep a little tension on the sheet as the sail goes up to prevent violent flogging, but don't trim it properly until the jib halyard is all the way up. Finally, take the empty sailbag below and leave it in some visible place—for example, tie it to the companionway ladder—and tell everybody on deck where it is (few frustrations are greater than that of losing a sailbag).

With better or larger crews, and in more benign weather, you may dump out the new sail and get it ready to hoist before dousing the old one. Tie the new one to the leeward rail with bow knots in sail ties. After the first sail is doused, tie it down and free and hoist the new one. While leaving a sail on deck may seem safe, prudence requires folding it in large flakes and stowing it below. All too often a wave may drag it overboard, ripping out stanchions and lifelines along the way.

Reefing (making a sail smaller) is most commonly done using the tie-in system in the mainsail. Before reefing, ease the mainsheet until the sail luffs and tighten the topping lift (a line running from

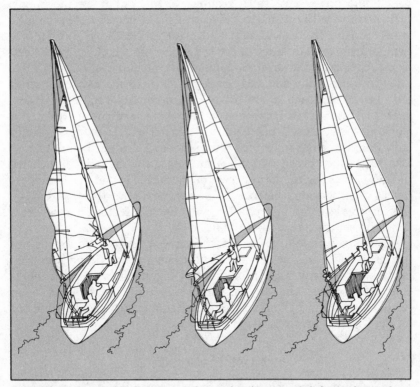

(left) To tie in a reef, first ease the main sheet and tighten the main boom's topping lift. Then lower the halyard until the luff cringle (ring) is at the tack. (center) Hook on the cringle, tighten the halyard, and haul in on the leech reefing line to pull the leech cringle down to the boom. The leech line should pull the sail both out and down. (Right) Ease the topping lift, trim the main sheet, and tie up the loose sail with some light line or sail stops. Finally, neaten all the lines you've been adjusting.

the boom's end to the top of the mast). Then lower the halyard and, with the boom supported by the topping lift, pull down on the luff until an eye called a cringle can be inserted over a hook near the tack. (Sometimes the luff cringle is pulled down tight with a line.) Next, pull in on a line already running from the boom up through a cringle on the leech until the cringle is lying on the bunched-up sail. Tighten the halyard, ease the topping lift, and trim the sheet again with the sail area reduced by about one-third. To keep the reefed part of the sail from flying about, lash it to the boom with light line led through small eyes in the cloth. It's a good idea to always keep the first reef line led through the lower leech cringle so you're ready to tie it in. If you're anticipating very rough weather, rig the second reef line, too.

Some boats have roller-reefing systems either on the boom, which is rotated to wind up the foot of the mainsail, or on the luff, where a wire inside the mast and near the headstay is rotated to wind up the forward edge of the sail. With the second system, keep some tension on the sheet so that the sail rolls up evenly.

Lowering one sail and not replacing it, while it doesn't work on all boats due to different balance requirements, can be the easiest and quickest way to shorten sail. Most boats can run or reach and some can sail close-hauled under mainsail alone, though traveler adjustments or reefs may be required to ease weather helm. The jib can sometimes be carried alone on a reach without too much lee helm. The closer the largest part of the sail is to the mast, the less effect it will have on balance, so in very heavy weather many boats sail quite nicely on any point of sail under a reefed mainsail or a small jib set just forward of the mast.

You may be tempted in heavy weather to douse all the sails and proceed under engine power. Unfortunately, the rough seas that always accompany high winds almost inevitably make this inefficient: few boats' engines are sufficiently powerful to push them through rough seas, and with all the pitching, the propellers are out of the water as much as they're in it.

Lost Halyards

Sometimes the shackle end of a halyard will get loose and fly around just out of your grasp. One way to deal with this embarrassing problem is to shin up the mast, grab the halyard, and slide back down with it. Or at least it *seems* like a solution until you try it and get stuck partway up. You'll need tough hands, a pole-vaulter's shoulder muscles, and viselike knees to climb more than ten feet.

Another solution is to pull somebody up the mast on another

halyard using a bosun's chair. Lead the halyard to the biggest winch on board. One crewmember turns the winch drum with the handle while the other tails, carefully watching that the person going aloft isn't pulled into the spreaders or stays. Nobody should stand under the trapeze artist—he may drop any tools he takes up—and nobody but he and the tailer should issue any orders. On the way down, the line should be eased out in long, steady, milkmaid's motions so that the chair and its priceless contents drop smoothly. Don't haul anybody aloft in rough seas; the end result will be bad bruises or fractures due to banging on the mast.

A less acrobatic way to retrieve a lost halyard blown out from the boat by the wind is to sail the boat under it. This requires making tight circles to try to get the halyard to swing directly into the waiting arms of a crewmember on the foredeck. Whether accidental or otherwise, the maneuver is guaranteed to stimulate a mood that, like the pendulum you're trying to create, will swing inexorably from fierce tension to genial hilarity. A helpful tool during this tricky exercise is a boat hook (a long rod with a hooked end), for grabbing the shackle as it flies around just out of arm's reach.

Torn and Flying Sails

Every now and then, you'll hoist a jib only to see its clew fly way out to leeward unencumbered by a sheet. Or a hastily secured sheet shackle or improperly tied bowline will come undone. Or a sail will rip. What to do? You can head up into the wind to bring the clew back over the deck and have one, two, or more crewmembers (the number depending on the amount of wind) snag and hold it while somebody tries to hook the sheet on. Inevitably, it takes so long to do this that the boat loses all steerageway and the bow swings off before the knot or shackle is fixed. The sail either pulls somebody into the water or flies out to leeward so that you're right back where you started. Therefore, if your crew is eager to show off their strength this way, use the engine to keep her moving directly into the wind. A less dramatic but much more effective way to retrieve a flying sail is to luff into the wind, drop the jib on deck, bear off to sail under mainsail alone until the sheets are put back on, and then hoist the sail again. Pulling a sail up and down a couple of times is a lot easier than dragging a shipmate out of the drink.

If it's the spinnaker that has dropped a sheet, bear off to a run and, using the other sheet, pull the spinnaker right behind the mainsail so it's blanketed. In light wind you should be able to hook the lost sheet back on; otherwise, drop the sail, rig it properly, and set it again in the mainsail's blanketing zone so that it doesn't fill until it's all the way up.

To prevent sheets from falling off in the first place, make sure they're put on correctly. Tie a bowline with a long tail to keep it from undoing itself while it tightens under first tension or shakes during a tack. Wrap a shackle with a turn of tape after clipping it into the sail.

Dragging Anchor

A lot was said about anchoring in Chapter 11, but since dragging anchor is not unusual, it's worth saying more about the problem here. Usually the anchor digs in and stays dug in all day, night, or week until you're ready to go. Sometimes, though, the wind shifts in the middle of the night, the boat swings, and the hook lifts out and doesn't reset. A sound sleeper may not know all this until somebody on another boat yells *"You're dragging!"* at the top of his lungs at two in the morning—or, worse, until the keel bangs on the rocks. If you're like me, however, you don't sleep soundly aboard a boat under your command, at least not for the first two or three nights until your senses are attuned to the feel of the boat—to the firm bobbing of the bow that means the hook's set firmly and the gurgling, wilder pitching and sluicing about that indicates she's dragging. When the motion changes, anybody below (and especially anybody sleeping far forward) will sense that something's amiss and probably wake up.

When you get the bad news, wake another competent person, rush on deck, and start the engine and leave it in neutral; you may need it on very short notice to help reset the anchor or move. Then evaluate the situation. If there's no immediate danger of running aground or banging into another boat, go up on the bow and inspect the anchor rode. Perhaps a tide rise has pulled the hook out of the bottom, or a wind shift has spun the hook out. If that's a possibility, throw out several yards of rode to increase the scope and narrow the angle between the rode and the water. Cleat the rode and go aft and back the boat down under power for about fifteen seconds (or tell somebody in the cockpit to do it). If the anchor sets, the boat should go almost straight backwards and the bow will resume its reassuring bob-bob-bob. But if it keeps dragging, the bow will swing from side to side and continue pitching. As she goes back, look around for an object ashore (such as a streetlamp or house light) or on the water (like a buoy or even a piece of weed or wood) to use as a guidepost after the engine is put back into neutral gear. If the object seems to move and the bow continues to rise and fall sharply, you're still dragging, so heave out more rode and back down again.

If the anchor does not reset itself after a couple of attempts, or if you're worried about running out of room astern, weigh anchor as we described in Chapter 11, move to another part of the harbor, and reanchor. But check the chart first; I once ran aground only five feet outside a channel in the Massachusetts harbor of Cutty-hunk while reanchoring in the middle of the night. If you have a depth sounder and loran electronic navigation device, turn them on. The depth sounder is your eyes below the water, and the loran, with a nighttime accuracy of plus or minus a couple of hundred feet, may be your best eyes on deck. Before dropping the hook, make sure your new location has good holding ground, with a sandy or mud bottom, and is protected from wind and waves by a spit of land or a reef. Don't automatically assume that the weather won't change; after all, it probably was a big wind shift that caused you to drag in the first place.

If there is any chance of a storm's building, seriously consider dropping a second anchor, leaving one or two crewmembers on deck on anchor watch, or even stowing the hook and heading out away from land. You'll lose some sleep, but otherwise you could lose your boat. In 1982 a gale surprised several dozen yachts in the Mexican harbor of Cabo San Lucas and drove them ashore before their crews could escape, while a handful of skippers who had heard the weather forecast safely rode out the storm in the Pacific.

A frequent cause of problems in crowded anchorages is the boat's dinghy. Left overnight at the end of a painter (bow line) astern, it may capsize or tangle in another boat's rode. (Granted, any harbor that packed is too crowded for a safe, quiet night's stay, but sometimes you have no choice.) If the dinghy can't be deflated or pulled on deck, shorten the painter as much as you can or tie her alongside, protecting the boat's topsides with fenders. In any case, remove all oars, floorboards, and other gear before leaving the dinghy for the night, for if she capsizes her equipment will be lost.

Running Aground

Every now and then, you'll make a small steering or piloting mistake and run your boat's keel or hull up on the rocks, sand, or mud. Rarely is running aground very dangerous; in fact, in shallow waters like Chesapeake Bay it is so common as to be unremarkable. If you're lucky, you can sail or power her right off; otherwise, you must pull her off one way or another. How long you stay "on the bricks" is usually determined by how fast you ran into the bottom, how soft it is, and the state of the tide. Expect a long wait after

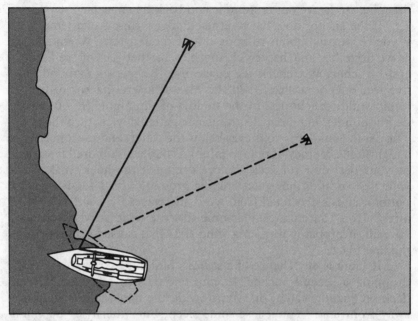

If you're aground and can't get off by sailing or powering, row or swim out a light anchor and try to pull yourself off using your largest sheet winch. Be sure that the rode doesn't chafe on anything, and stay away from it; the load is big and if the rode breaks, its backlash will be dangerous.

running hard into soft mud when the tide is going out, a short one after slicing slowly into hard sand on a rising tide, and no wait at all after bouncing off some rocks (though your keel may be dented).

Even if they are not guarded by buoys, shoals can often be spotted from a near distance. One piece of evidence is the number and shape of the waves, which are more and steeper over shallow areas than over deep ones. The water color changes as the bottom nears the surface, getting darker over mud, weed, and rocks and lighter over sand. Fishermen almost always set out lobster traps, oyster stakes, and fish weirs in shoal areas, following the cue of gulls and other birds, which usually hunt their prey in shallow water.

Getting off on Your Own

To get off on your own, you must decrease the boat's draft while aiming her away from the shoal area. Turn the helm to steer her back to deep water, then put the engine into forward gear and trim the sails to spin her on her keel, trimming the jib and easing the mainsail to spin to leeward and vice versa to spin to windward.

Increase the angle of heel by moving all the crew to the leeward side, even hanging them off the boom if possible. If she remains stuck, put the engine into neutral, ease the sheets, and have the crew run back and forth across the deck to rock her and break the suction of the bottom on the keel, then try sailing and powering off once again.

If sailing and powering off doesn't work, or if the tide is ebbing and there is little time, spin the bow by *kedging off*. Take the anchor out into deep water in a dinghy (or swim it out) and lead the rope rode through a large block shackled on the bow (it provides a better lead than the chock) and back to a big winch. With the help of the sails and engine, trimming the rode while the boat is heeled should swing the bow around. The rode will be heavily loaded and can whiplash dangerously if it snaps, so have everybody stand clear.

Towing Off

When you can't get off yourself, you'll probably require a tow. If a nearby boat is not willing to give it, call the Coast Guard on channel 16. They won't charge you for the service, but if a commercial towboat appears on the scene, the government officers will allow it to take over. Settle on terms (if any) before handing over your tow line, which should be your nylon anchor rode secured to the strongest fitting on board—a through-bolted bow cleat, the mast (using a bowline), or the biggest winch—and carefully protected from chafe with rags or pieces of split hose. The towline should be kept short and the pull moderate as the bow is gradually spun toward deep water. Heel the boat to decrease her draft and the resistance between keel and bottom.

If you need a tow home later on, lengthen the line considerably so that your boat rides comfortably in the trough of the third wave behind the tow boat, and steer to prevent the line from chafing on the headstay.

A Stalled Engine

Just like every other mechanical device, a boat's gasoline or diesel engine is a blessing when it works and a curse when it doesn't. While your best guide for getting a recalcitrant engine started is the owner's manual, several problems recur so frequently that we'd like to discuss them and their solutions here, with the obvious caveat that if you can't get the machinery working again you shouldn't panic. Your boat, after all, does have sails that will take her just about everywhere there is open water and wind. Alternatively, you can anchor, call for a tow, or change your plans. But you should not give up just because the engine won't turn over. One capsize that resulted in a sinking and three deaths was due at least partially to the crew's becoming discouraged when the engine packed up; they went to bed just when their boat needed careful handling in a gale. Don't allow that to happen to you and your crew.

With gasoline engines, found most often on outboard-powered boats, the spark plugs are the source of most malfunctions. If the engine won't start or if it runs rough, unscrew the spark plugs and clean off the accumulated carbon deposits with a fine abrasive like emery paper or even cardboard. If the points are badly worn or widely spread, replace the plugs. You should use a special spark plug wrench and install plugs about one-quarter turn harder than hand-tight.

With inboard engines—which in modern sailboats means diesels—voltage losses and shorts are the main electrical problem. This isn't surprising considering the humidity of the marine environment and the typically circuitous, hidden wiring systems that are so hard to inspect. Carry along some rags to wipe off moisture, a can of silicone spray (which displaces moisture), and some plastic-coated tape to cover exposed wires. If the starter doesn't work, spray silicone into the key hole and over all the terminals. Then try running the rag the entire length of the wires between the key and the block and clean off the terminals, using emery paper on corrosion. Tape over any worn spots. Look especially carefully around the engine, whose heat can play tricks with the wiring. I once spent half a day trying to trace down the cause of a starter failure, calling every manufacturer's representative listed in the owner's manual, before one of my shipmates noticed that the insulation on a wire had melted from contact with the hot engine block. She quickly cut away the damaged wire, spliced in a replacement, and secured the wire away from the engine. We were soon on our way.

If all you get is silence when you turn the key, the solenoid may be stuck or malfunctioning. A device that makes the connection between the engine and starter, the solenoid is located in a small tube or box, usually near the starter motor. First try freeing it with a sharp blow with a light tool. If that doesn't work, you can bypass it. Run a large-gauge wire around the solenoid from the terminal for the wire from the ignition switch to the terminal for the wire to the starter. Or hold a pair of pliers or channel locks or a screwdriver so that there is metal contact on those two terminals (making sure there's insulation between your hand and the metal) while somebody turns the ignition key.

Perhaps the battery is low. On some boats you can charge the batteries by plugging into an electrical outlet at a marina; otherwise, you must take them to a gas station. While you're lugging the things ashore, try to figure out why they drained to begin with. Modern electronic devices like speedometers and loran instruments draw some current, but the main culprits are electric lights and hot and cold water systems—frequently those within reach of children. When the navigator isn't referring to the loran set, switch off its lighted display, which may draw more juice than the receiver itself. During the day and between meals, turn off the master switches to lights, pressure water, and other unneeded accessories. Most cruising boats larger than about 30 feet have two batteries that can be used either in line or separately and are both charged by the engine. One battery should be reserved solely for starting the engine; use the other for lights and accessories when under sail or at anchor. Keep an eye on the ampere gauges and charge up when necessary by starting the engine and running it at fairly high RPMs for an hour or so. (Regular use at high speeds also keeps lubrication oil properly circulated.)

A common cause of engine problems is blockage in the fuel line, which is announced by a stall like the one that happens when the tank is dry. Fuel may be contaminated with water or dirt when it comes aboard, or it may pick up sediment kicked up from the bottom of the tank by the boat's motion. Modern fuel filters will separate dirt and water at both ends, but they are less effective at clearing air locks caused by bubbles in a near-empty tank. To clear air locks, you must bleed the fuel line and pump, opening access holes and turning over the engine until unadulterated fuel spurts through.

So much for relatively minor problems. Now, in the final two chapters, we'll look at what you should do if you're ever caught in a downright emergency.

CHAPTER 17

Seamanship
and Health
Emergencies

Compared with such challenges as skiing and driving an automobile in a big city, sailing is marvelously safe. It's so safe, in fact, that when the Coast Guard warns about boating dangers, many people become embarrassed, as though somebody has made a social *faux pas*, and try to change the subject to a more cheerful topic. In response, the authorities and their few followers who are deeply concerned about boating safety become increasingly strident, which only stimulates more yawns. That's a shame. Sometime, somewhere, just about every sailor is going to face the possibility of getting into serious trouble, which means that the studied indifference that many sailors show to boating safety is potentially very dangerous. It also denies the normal, instinctive fear of the wind and water that sheer human cussedness won't allow most of us to admit, even to ourselves. The first step toward avoiding a catastrophe on the water is to confess that the sea is not the warm, embracing creature that bad poets (who have never left land) believe we can shape to our own ends. To quote Lord Byron, a great poet who did go to sea,

> *Roll on, thou deep and dark blue ocean—roll!*
> *Ten thousand fleets sweep over thee in vain;*
> *Man marks the earth with ruin—his control*
> *Stops with the shore.*

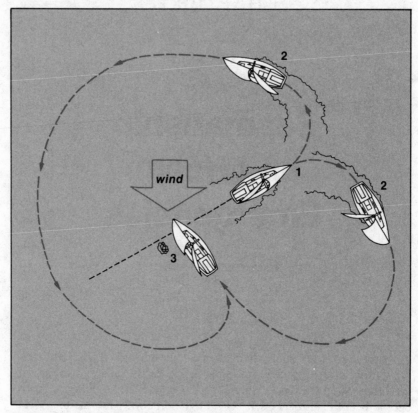

If somebody falls overboard, immediately stop the boat's forward progress, turn back, and make the approach on a close reach. Pick the swimmer up on the leeward side unless the water is very rough and there's a danger of the boat sliding into him or her.

While we can't eliminate a macho sailor's hubris, perhaps we can more firmly ground expectations in reality by describing ways to handle the most common emergencies that occur on boats. In this chapter we'll first tell how to deal with five serious seamanship and health problems—man overboard, hypothermia, seasickness, sunburn, and capsize. Then we'll describe how to call for help. And in Chapter 18 we'll analyze some yachting catastrophes to identify seven ways sailboats typically get into life-threatening situations.

When Someone Falls Overboard

In Chapter 8 we showed ways to avoid falling overboard by moving around on deck carefully and hooking on with a safety harness, but if somebody does take a tumble, the following procedure should lead to a prompt recovery. During the precruise safety orientation (described in Chapter 5), talk this routine over step by step with your shipmates. You might even practice it using a buoyant cushion as the victim.

1. **Stop the boat's progress away from the swimmer.** This is the most important step to take. Luff the sails, head up into the wind, turn 90 degrees to either side and proceed slowly—do whatever must be done to stay near the swimmer. You can make a drastic, sudden course alteration even with a spinnaker up in fresh wind—granted, with a little chaos, but considering that a life may be at stake some confusion can be tolerated.

2. **Assign one person to look and point at the swimmer.** This should be that crewmember's only job. In poor visibility, take a compass bearing on the victim and throw buoyant objects (special man overboard poles, cushions, or paper towels).

3. **Turn on the engine.** But don't put it in gear unless you must use it to get back to the swimmer (say, in a calm) and until you are sure that no lines are dangling near the propeller. However, don't plan on depending entirely on the engine to get you back to the swimmer in rough seas and when the boat is heeling, when an outboard engine's propeller will rarely be in the water and even an inboard's propeller won't be much help.

4. **Swing back toward the swimmer, aiming just upwind of him or her.** Under sail, make your approach on a close reach, on which you can quickly increase speed by bearing off slightly or slow down by heading up. As you approach, luff the sails until you just have steerageway. To keep the speed low and improve visibility to the swimmer, you may have to douse the jib. Under power, make the final approach dead into the wind, but if the waves stop your forward progress, approach across the wind and seas.

5. **Retrieve the victim over the downhill, leeward rail.** Trim the sails to heel the boat. Haul the victim onto the leeward deck. Nobody should dive in after the swimmer unless the swimmer is unable to help him- or herself and the rescuer is connected to the boat with a line. Playing hero here may well kill two people instead of saving one. If you are unable to sail or power to within grabbing distance, get upwind of the swimmer, throw a line with a buoyant object on the end, and retrieve him or her by hauling in the line.

When Your Fingers Get Numb and Your Mind Gets Vague

If a normally alert crewmember suddenly complains of numbness, becomes disoriented, and begins to move and work clumsily, the chances are that he or she is hypothermic. *Hypothermia* is severe loss of body heat, and it can happen even on warm summer days if you're drenched. As the body is chilled, it automatically cuts off blood circulation in the extremities—the hands, head, and feet—in order to protect the vital organs. The circulatory deficiency may lead to poor dexterity and bad judgment; this is serious business for sailors, who must be agile and clear-thinking if they are to perform jobs like steering, sail trimming, and piloting. As he or she becomes colder, the victim becomes less and less competent—physically and mentally—until, at the worst, body temperature drops to about 85 degrees and the victim dies.

The only sure, safe cure for hypothermia is for the victim to be warmed *gradually* in a sleeping bag or blankets or with the affectionate help of another body, meanwhile drinking warm, sugary, noncaffeinated liquids. *Do not* try to induce rapid warming and blood circulation by rubbing the numb extremities, exercising, drinking hot drinks, or taking stimulants such as liquor or caffeinated drinks. Any or all of these may have been prescribed by your grandmother, the old-time navy, and various other sources of common wisdom; even grandmothers can be wrong, as the following documented story suggests. A few years ago off the British coast, ten men were picked out of a lifeboat after their ship sank in a winter storm. All ten were issued the traditional English medicine of a couple of glasses of brandy, which stimulated their circulatory systems so efficiently that the cold blood in their extremities raced into and stopped their hearts. If their body temperatures had been brought back to normal through gradual warming, they probably would have survived.

When You Get Seasick

Before ever stepping on a boat, most people know if they're susceptible to motion sickness. If they are, they should have thought about and looked into the different types of available medication, most of which need to be taken at least a couple of hours before going aboard. The problem with most older pills has been that they induce drowsiness, which is conducive neither to pleasure nor to good seamanship. Nonsedating treatments include a two-pill combination originally designed for use by astronauts (one pill eases motion sickness and the other keeps you alert), a medication that is absorbed through the skin from a patch adhered behind the ear, and ginger pills. Some people who have used all three report success; others report none. Frankly, I wouldn't know which medication works best. The closest I've ever been to contracting the messy malaise was when a shipmate lit a cigar in the poorly ventilated cabin of a boat rolling like a log in a flat calm and long swell. The ship's cigars were of such high quality that their supplier, the captain, insisted that they not be smoked out in the wind. This reasoning made good sense one way and lousy sense another.

Cooks are most liable to seasickness because they spend more time below than most sailors and their systems are assaulted by a wide variety of smells and motions as well as by confinement. Some cooks in our survey say they don't get sick at all, but others not blessed with cast-iron stomachs and built-in gyroscopes make several helpful recommendations, among them, "If the feeling comes on me suddenly in the galley, I try to go topside for a while and take the helm or busy myself up in the fresh air. That helps more than anything." Perhaps steering serves as a remedy because it makes you focus on the horizon, the only immovable object in a boat's galaxy. Other advice included abstaining from liquor for a night or two prior to heading out, avoiding greasy and spicy foods before and during rough weather, and munching on something simple (like dry pilot crackers) to keep food in your stomach when you're too queasy to eat a real meal. During a rough reach across the Caribbean, my shipmate Donald Starr kept himself going by periodically downing a raw egg flavored with Worcestershire sauce —perhaps not your idea of a tasty meal, but nutritious all the same.

When the Sun Is Hot

Sunburn is an occupational hazard for anybody who spends time outdoors when the sun is high. For many years a dark tan was honored as a badge of the good life, but too many people have paid the price with skin cancer. I know one former winner of the America's Cup who is not allowed outdoors without full-length clothing and a huge sun bonnet. Pharmaceutical companies market whole lines of sun lotions for different skin sensitivities using a standard called the sun protection factor, which ranges from 1 to 15. A lotion with a low S.P.F. offers minimal protection against burning rays in order to promote tanning. One with a high number screens out almost all rays; it won't help your tan but it will protect against burns. Dark-skinned people can use a lotion with an S.P.F. below 5 or 6, but fair people should stick to one in the 12 to 15 range.

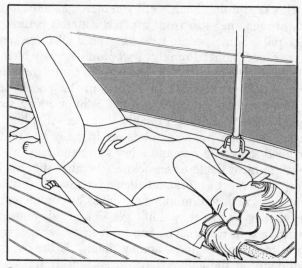

Sunglasses and a sun lotion with the right sun protection factor for your skin are essential if you want to enjoy the sun while avoiding its bad effects.

These lotions are widely available in good drugstores.

If you're blond and prone to burning, consider using zinc oxide as a sunscreen. While it's greasier than normal sun lotions, and while its white color isn't very stylish, zinc oxide is inexpensive and has the added benefit of being an effective first-aid cream to use on cuts, scrapes, mosquito bites, and other open wounds. Its color has one advantage: you'll know it's time to smear on some more cream when the white has rubbed off.

To work right, sun lotions must be applied assiduously whenever the sun is out. Burning probably is more likely on hazy days than on bright, clear ones. Goop the stuff on early, before you are distracted by the mechanics of sailing the boat; later, add layers as you perspire and rub up against gear. Be especially attentive to the extremities that are so vulnerable as you look up at sails—the nose, ears, and forehead. Don't forget the back of the neck or the inch or two of tender skin that may seem to be protected by shirt and pants cuffs but will be exposed when you stretch your arms and legs to steer or trim sheets.

While modern lotions are efficient when used in a timely manner, the most reliable sunscreen is a layer of long, loose, light-colored cotton clothing pulled on when the sun is high, between brief tanning sessions. A sweatshirt and a pair of the now-fashion-able drawstring pants will cover the body without stifling it; a big sun hat (or even a baseball cap) will protect the forehead.

Besides sunburn, the hot sun can cause severe eyestrain—a bad problem on sailboats, where the sheen off the slick water, white sails, and bright deck can be torturing. Eyestrain can lead to fierce headaches and accompanying depression and bad judgment. Many boatowners equip their boats with cockpit awnings and low-glare brown sails, but the simplest protection is a good pair of sunglasses. Polarized lenses are especially worthwhile because they pick up and highlight the color differences on the water between shallow and deep areas and wind puffs and lulls.

When Your Boat Capsizes

Although large keel boats can tip over or swamp (fill with water) or even sink in extreme, hurricane conditions, these words on capsizing are directed mainly to people who sail dinghies and small keel daysailers, whose flotation tanks or blocks of foam will keep them buoyant.

The worst that can happen—and too many times has happened —is that the crew becomes separated from the swamped boat and drowns. Therefore the most important guideline is to *stay with the boat*—even if you can't right it, even if there's an inviting beach only a half mile away. A half mile can quickly turn into a very long swim in rough seas and a strong current. Most modern, high-per-formance (fast and tippy) dinghies capsize easily and are righted just as readily. They're also self-bailing; their small, shallow cockpits capture little water, and that is easily drained (when the boat is sailing fast) through retractable sluices in the bottom called self-bailers. To right a dinghy, stand on the fully lowered centerboard, grab the rail, and lean back. You may have to lower the sails to decrease the water's resistance to your leveraging action. If some-body on a passing powerboat offers to help, have him pull up on the tip of the mast as you bounce on the centerboard. The mast must be pointed downwind during a righting; otherwise she'll flip right over again when she's upright.

Once the boat is upright, climb aboard, collect any objects floating around, trim the sails, open the bailers, and head off on a fast reach. The cockpit should be dry in a couple of minutes. Some older boats have large, deep cockpits that don't self-bail; the crew must bail the water out with buckets or have a powerboat tow her slowly back to shore.

When You Must Call for Help

There are two ways to call for help: with visual signals and with radio transmissions. Not surprisingly, the Coast Guard and other government agencies have established rigorous rules not only about how signaling equipment must be built and rigged, but also about the form the signals take.

Visual Signals

Any sailor on any boat can make a visual signal. Simply standing up and slowly and repeatedly waving your arms is internationally interpreted as meaning "Help!" Other improvised signals include flying the national flag or ensign upside down, waving an orange or red flag, showing a rapidly flashing strobe light, throwing dye marker in the water, and firing a loud explosive device. The

If you're in distress, you don't need an official signal to alert other people to your predicament. Wave your arms or an orange flag, fly the national flag upside down, or show a bright light.

Coast Guard requires that most boats carry certain approved flares for day and night use; these are described in the appendix.

A frequent problem with flares is that nobody on board knows how to ignite them. The precruise orientation, when you also review man overboard and other emergency procedures, is a good time to learn how to fire off the visual signals. Several visual signals are so compact and so little used that they may get lost in the tons of food, clothes, navigation equipment, and sailing gear stowed aboard. Preparing for an overnight delivery from Monterey to San Francisco, California, three other men and I spent two hours tearing the boat apart looking for the flares. They finally turned up in a locker that we all had gone through at least half a dozen times. The style-conscious manufacturer had cleverly made them so compact and attractive that we all thought they were a presentation pen and pencil set.

Radio Distress Signals

Most cruising boats are equipped with a Very High Frequency/FM (VHF/FM) radio that can transmit and receive signals within about forty miles. *Channel 16 is reserved for emergency calls when you get into a life-threatening situation,* for example, when you: run hard aground and are unable to get off on your own; lose both the mast and the engine; develop a bad leak that your boat's pumps cannot keep up with; suffer an uncontrollable fire; or experience a bad injury. *Do not use Channel 16* if you: can get to port on your own; run out of gas or wind in a channel crowded with potential tow boats; or have some other non-life-threatening inconvenience.

After turning the transmitter on to Channel 16, here's how to make a distress call:

1. **Press the radio's alarm signal button for 30 to 60 seconds.** This alerts the Coast Guard and others monitoring Channel 16 that a distress call is imminent. (The radio may not have such a button.)

2. **Say "Mayday" three times, then the name of your boat three times, then the radio's call sign.** *Mayday* is the pronunciation of the French word for "help me," *m'aidez.* The call sign is printed on the license, which must be posted near the radio.

3. **Give your position and briefly describe your situation and requirements.** The position should be given as a bearing and distance from a charted object or as latitude and longitude.

4. **Describe the boat, giving at least her size, type, and color.**

You should hear from the Coast Guard soon, but until you receive an acknowledgment, keep repeating those four steps. The Coast Guard requires that you write down the time and a summary of any emergency transmissions concerning safety that you make, receive, or overhear, and that you sign the entry.

I hope that you'll never have to use any of these emergency procedures, but you should know them just in case. In the next and last chapter, we'll examine seven factors that can turn emergency into disaster.

CHAPTER 18

Seven Ways Boats Get into Trouble

For several years, in the course of my career as a yachting journalist, I have studied and described several catastrophes involving pleasure sailors and pleasure boats. Not a pleasant task, you may think, but in its own way a valuable one, for while examining the tragedies of, for example, the 1979 Fastnet Race and a storm that killed several people off America's southeast coast three years later, I assembled enough grim detail to isolate some factors—seven in all—that often come into play when boats get into deadly trouble.

The sad story of a boat called *The Sting* summarizes many of these factors. In the New Orleans Lightship Race of March 1983, while reaching in a gale and very rough seas in a shallow part of the Gulf of Mexico, this 29-foot sloop was knocked over on her side. Two men on deck, who were either not wearing harnesses or not hooked on (accounts are unclear) were washed overboard. One man grabbed some trailing lines and was recovered. The other drowned in the 59-degree water as his shipmates tried unsuccessfully to get man overboard gear to him and then, after finally turning the boat, to power and sail back to him through ten-foot seas.

Later, an official inquiry by the Gulf Yachting Association found that, while *The Sting* was both seaworthy and properly equipped with safety gear, the crew was not prepared. Among the words that figured prominently in the inquiry committee's report were "panic," "confusion," and "indecision." Though exceptionally talented racing sailors, the six young men of *The Sting* were, to quote the committee, "inexperienced in ocean racing in extended heavy weather conditions." By the time of the accident, "the crew had experienced severe seasickness and were extremely fatigued after twenty hours at sea in deteriorating gale force weather conditions." Yet at no time during those twenty hours did the skipper discuss man overboard procedures or issue a direct order requiring the wearing of life jackets and safety harnesses. The inquiry also determined that, except for the absence of a life jacket, the drowned man had been dressed as if for dinghy racing, in a one-piece foul-weather jumpsuit whose cuffs were taped around his sea boots—an outfit guaranteed to retain water and pull a swimming body down and under with the efficiency of an anchor.

After reading such a tragic account and before engaging in a rage of sanctimonious finger-pointing we should remember how frequently *all* boats get into trouble—usually much less serious, to be sure, but trouble all the same. A boat's crew is human, hence prone to making mistakes. Her environment is natural, hence surprising and sometimes startling in its changeableness. And a boat's own nature and driving forces are complex, hence unpredictable to everybody except a few gifted, widely experienced seamen. For most of us, then, sailing mistakes are inevitable. Sooner or later, anyone can dress poorly and become hypothermic; miscalculate the boat's position by a few hundred yards by using the wrong chart scale; steer the wrong course because the right one was garbled in transmission from the navigator; let out too little rode and drag anchor; carry on too long in rough weather without shortening sail; misidentify a buoy or harbor in a hurried sighting; and so on. In normal conditions these errors often are quickly discovered and their consequences usually are trivial. Fortunately, most sailboats are so slow that if their crews are reasonably alert and follow a cautious routine of double-checking, none of these (and hundreds of other small errors) will have dangerous consequences. Every now and then, however, serious problems if not disasters result from a combination of errors or accidents—generally, but not always, in heavy weather.

My study of more than a dozen capsizes, sinkings, and abandonments indicates that it is human error rather than breakdowns in the boat and her rigging that usually leads to fatal disasters. Some of the accidents I have analyzed involve only two or three of the seven key factors, but most involve at least four. For more about these catastrophes, see my book *"Fastnet, Force 10"* (New York: W. W. Norton, 1980) and my article in the May 1983 issue of *Sail*.

A Rushed, Ill-Considered Departure

An important factor in many accidents is that the crew is pressured to meet a schedule imposed by somebody else. As a result, they are forced to start out in threatening weather, with unfinished repairs, or with shortages of storm equipment, food, water, ice, tools, and other necessities.

Races obviously impose this kind of pressure. Not many of the 300 boats entered in the 1979 Fastnet Race would have headed out into England's western approaches under the prevailing forecast for a mild gale if the race hadn't started when it did. But they came to race, and as it turned out, a storm of near-hurricane proportions swept them all, killed fifteen sailors, and sank four boats. Cruises may also begin prematurely because the crew is sailing under the gun of a short vacation imposed by a boss or some other obligation. Airplane and tide tables may also force a crew to key their departure to the chronological clock rather than wait for decent conditions.

Lesson 1: The only timetable that ultimately counts is the one imposed by the weather.

The Route Is Potentially Dangerous

Some sailing areas in some seasons are predictably risky. The vernal and autumnal equinoxes in late March and September always seem to be surrounded by a month or so of sudden storms. The fall is most dangerous in the western Atlantic, the Gulf of Mexico, and the Caribbean because that's the hurricane season; even boats hugging the shore to stay close to ports can get in terrible trouble when they're surprised by gales. In an Atlantic gale in October 1982, a 58-foot ketch, *Trashman*, fell on her side off a huge wave and sank about sixty miles off the Carolina coast (later, three people died in her life raft) and a 42-foot yawl, *Scrimmage*, was rolled over and almost sunk within sight of a Maryland resort town (fortunately, with no loss of life). It takes a big gale indeed to cause so much trouble for such large boats.

Even at other times and in other places, before heading off on a cruise keep track of weather changes by reading the newspaper weather maps and listening to National Weather Service short- and long-range forecasts on VHF/FM Channels 1, 2, and 3. You'll also learn a lot by getting to know a local commercial fisherman.

Lesson 2: Choose routes that take you through areas of predictably decent weather.

The Route Has No Alternatives

Survival in rough conditions often depends on the ability to choose an alternate course away from bad weather or shoal water. The seaman's traditional fear of a lee, or downwind, shore is based as much on the "no exit" sign that the land sticks high in the air as it is on the wretched prospect of being dashed onto the beach. The main problem that *Scrimmage* faced in the October 1982 gale was that she was pinned against the Middle Atlantic coastline by a strong northeasterly wind. She could not beat out into the Atlantic against the storm, and with huge seas breaking at channel entrances, she was unable to sail into a protective harbor. *Scrimmage* was eventually blown over a shoal area where breakers capsized her. A crewmember was lost overboard when his safety harness tether snapped, and only through extraordinary seamanship and courage (plus a bit of luck) was the boat saved and the man recovered.

Lesson 3: Whenever possible, put yourself in a position where you may choose alternate courses.

The Crew Is Unprepared

A crew that is too small, untalented, untrained, or unhealthy is frequently involved in bad sailing accidents. Let's go through those adjectives one by one.

An excessively small and untalented crew is one that is not prepared to handle the boat safely in the worst conditions expected for a cruise, race, or passage. As a rule of thumb, there should be enough good sailors on board so that at all times the boat is adequately steered and navigated, the sails are safely handled, and everybody gets enough rest and food. For a day's sail, it may be sufficient to have only a competent skipper and at least one crewmember who can steer a compass course and handle sails. For an overnight sail during which everyone will need a few hours' sleep— and they will if their good judgment is to stay intact—you'll need at least two people who are competent skippers plus at least two good helmsmen and sail handlers.

An untrained crew may be talented and large, but because the skipper has not oriented its members to the boat's emergency equipment and routines, they may not be prepared to handle life-threatening situations. Besides training expert sailors to work together in emergency procedures, a skipper should also train beginners in one or two basic skills, like steering in good weather and (if they're good with electronics) radio navigation. Too often, a novice's intelligence, eagerness to learn, and skills go underutilized.

An unhealthy crew is one not physically or psychologically prepared to take the rigors of the worst possible weather that can be

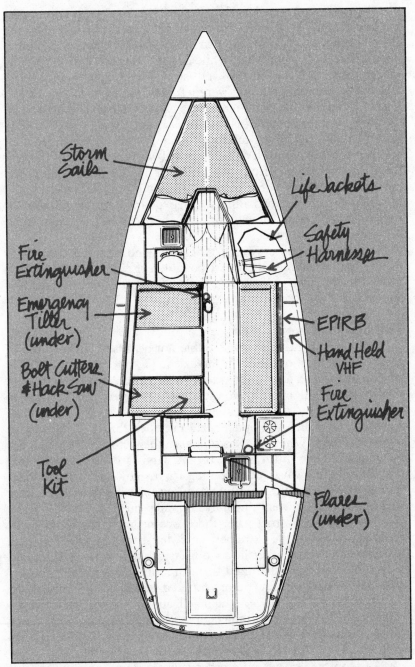

Storm
Sails

Life Jackets

Safety
Harnesses

Fire
Extinguisher

Emergency
Tiller
(under)

EPIRB

Hand Held
VHF

Bolt Cutters
& Hack Saw
(under)

Fire
Extinguisher

Tool
Kit

Flares
(under)

An emergency equipment chart like this one will save you and your shipmates a lot of time should you ever get into trouble. This is also a good system for keeping track of food and supplies.

met on a cruise or voyage. Here we're concerned with endurance, not knowledge. On *Grimalkin*, one of the boats hit hardest by the 1979 Fastnet Race storm, the two most talented sailors had permanent physical problems that, while not affecting strength or performance in normal conditions, were so debilitating in the cold gale that both men collapsed and were left for dead by their shipmates. One of these men, the first mate, was badly arthritic and did in fact die of exposure soon after his shipmates abandoned the boat in a life raft. The other, who was mildly epileptic, eventually regained consciousness to find himself alone on board with the corpse of the first mate. Interspersing periods of work with periods of rest, he determinedly pumped the boat out, and signaled for help until rescued by a helicopter. Serious illness, sleep deprivation, hypothermia, hunger, and nicotine, alcohol, or drug abuse can be harmful to good judgment and endurance.

Lesson 4: The crew must be large and talented enough to handle the boat under the worst possible conditions; they must be trained in the boat's routines; and they must be in sound health—and stay that way.

The Boat Is Unprepared

Boats frequently get into trouble not because a major piece of gear, like the mast or the helm, breaks down, but because relatively small damage or a seemingly minor oversight creates a chain effect that leads one link at a time to catastrophe. For example, *Trashman* was an extremely strong boat with an Achilles heel—large glass windows, for which the builder had provided thick, Plexiglas protective shutters. When she was caught in the October 1982 gale, her crew installed the shutters only on the windward side because that was the side the waves were coming from. However, she fell sideways off a wave onto the unprotected leeward windows, which were smashed open. She went down five minutes later.

In the 1979 Fastnet gale, there was no way that some crews could get in out of the extremely cold, harsh weather since storage batteries, tools, and other heavy objects broke loose during knockdowns and capsizes, shattered furniture, and made cabins dangerously inhospitable. A few sailors suffered serious head injuries; one man was hit by the stove, which fell out of its gimbals during a rollover. Forced out into the cockpit, the sailors were worn down to the point where many could see no alternative to abandoning ship in life rafts—a decision fatal to six of them.

Lesson 5: Try out all emergency and storm equipment well before you have to use it, and keep a "worst case" state of mind when you install gear.

The Crew Panics After an Injury

Often, a crew handles bad weather well and confidently until somebody is injured. Then panic sets in, storm tactics are changed, and instead of actively engaging with the boat and the storm, the crew becomes passive and even gives up. Well before her windows were stove in, *Trashman* was surviving reasonably well by running before the waves. Then a crewmember (whose safety harness tether was attached to the binnacle in the middle of the cockpit) was thrown entirely across the boat and badly injured. Fearing for her, the skipper immediately ordered the engine turned on and *Trashman* headed toward the Carolina shore. After a couple of hours, the engine's cooling system burned out. The exhausted, discouraged crew took to their bunks, leaving the boat to fend for herself, lying beam-to breaking seas. Soon after, she was fatally damaged. Perhaps if the skipper had focused more on the larger issue of survival, he would have held his course.

In the Fastnet storm, a few sailors suffered serious and frightening injuries; again, in most cases, the focus of the crew's concern and energy shifted from the boat's seaworthiness to the injured person's welfare. As morale plummeted, mistakes began to be made. On some boats, within an hour or two there was a capsize, a rollover, or a hasty decision to inflate the life raft and abandon ship in order to get the injured person away.

Lesson 6: Do not allow a crew injury to distract you from the job immediately at hand, which is to get the boat and the whole crew safely through the storm.

The Command Structure Is Unclear

For most of us, pleasure sailing is a volunteer activity that's meant to be fun. Much of the time, a good crew can function well in a relatively informal way with commands coming in the form of suggestions and with many crewmembers taking part in decision making. If the pastime were otherwise, it would lose half its adherents. But when emergencies threaten, strong leadership and a well-defined command structure are required. People lacking experience and confidence will feel and perform better if they can trust the skipper and his lieutenants to exercise decisive judgment. This is where laid-back attitudes about discipline and organization may very well be counterproductive, regardless of their contributions to the happiness of normal life.

Bad weather is no time for leadership by committee or for a skipper who is not respected by his crew. The most competent and experienced people on board—those women and men who have seen a gale or two and can handle responsibility—must be placed in charge, even if they are not the titular skipper and watch captains. Orders about essential safety procedures and gear must be firm, clear, and frequently repeated both in anticipation of an emergency and during a rescue operation. Leaders must not simply retire to the helm and shout commands. They will be much more effective if they mix with the crew and set an example—by wearing and using safety harnesses, by sharing (even taking the initiative in) the toughest jobs, and by resting and eating when they can.

A backup chain of command must also be established. In the Fastnet Race gale at least two boats were needlessly abandoned, with resulting loss of life, after the skippers were lost overboard and frightened crews impulsively inflated the life rafts. In both cases, if a clearly designated, well-respected second-in-command had immediately asserted leadership and reduced the level of panic, the rafts might have remained in their canisters and the men would have remained on the yachts—which, though damaged, succeeded in surviving the storm.

Lesson 7: The command structure must be firm, competent, and clear in dangerous conditions.

In Summary

Most of what we have discussed makes common sense, but some of it goes against human nature; ignoring an injury to a friend does not come easily even to soldiers in combat. The problems that we have described are so terrible and occur so rarely that most skippers and crews are tempted not to discuss them at all out of fear of frightening each other or causing bad luck. Yet these issues are substantial, and while we don't recommend preparing for them with such perfectionist vigor that sailing becomes more a chore than a pleasure, no crew should head out into open water without talking them over, inspecting vulnerable gear, and preparing for exigencies.

The sailing lifestyle that we have described in these pages is by turns pleasurable and challenging, romantic and trying, soothing and thrilling. This is as it should be with a pastime so fulfilling, so rich in its encounter with nature, and so overflowing with tradition. For sailing to be all these things, and for you to get the greatest reward from them, you the sailor must go about it consciously and thoughtfully, with due respect for the forces involved. Whether you're buying foul-weather gear, or navigating into a luscious Caribbean cove, or reefing the mainsail, or cooking a three-course banquet to eat in the cockpit, or anticipating bad weather—whatever you do on or concerning a boat, do it with regard to the consequences and do it well. Of all the hundreds of rules and hints and skills covered here, this one is always the most important.

APPENDIX

Eighty-two Things You Must, Should, and Want to Have When You Head off on a Cruise

T he government, common sense, and personal taste dictate what equipment must and should be on board any boat heading off for more than a day. A checklist will make preparations a little easier; here are lists of required and "should have" safety equipment, plus a list of suggested "nice to haves" that can make life aboard more pleasurable.

Once aboard, all this equipment can be easily lost in the boat's rabbit warren of lockers, bins, nooks, and crannies unless there's some kind of guide. You can keep things straight by making a list of items in alphabetical order. For example:

> Fire Extinguishers—in galley and on mast
> First-Aid Kit—in head locker
> Flares—in red box under companionway stairs
> Games—in green canvas bag, forward cabin
> Life Jackets—in forward starboard hanging locker

Better yet, use a clearly labeled schematic diagram. Yacht designers and builders produce overhead drawings called accommodation plans to show how the bunks, lockers, tables, and other furniture are arranged in the cabins. Photocopy this plan, mark the location of all important equipment on the copy, and photocopy *that* document. Prominently post one copy of this treasure map or your alphabetical list over the chart table and store another one in the chart table in the same waterproof folder where the ship's registration papers and other valuable documents are stowed.

"Must Have" Gear

At various points in the text we have referred to U.S. Coast Guard regulations concerning safety equipment. Many are (or at least should be) satisfied by the boatbuilder. Among these are navigation lights of sufficient brightness for the boat's length; a proper ventilation system and backfire flame control device for an inboard gasoline engine; an oil discharge placard posted near the engine compartment; and a legal toilet (called a *marine sanitation device*, or M.S.D., in bureaucratic mumbo jumbo). Outside of insuring that the light bulbs, engine blower, and toilet are functioning, the owner or charterer must usually take it on faith that the builder has met the requirements.

But there are six "must haves" for which the owner or charterer bears sole responsibility. The owner is liable to warnings and fines if any of these items are found to be lacking or in poor repair by a Coast Guard officer. This is a threat not to be taken lightly, for while the likelihood of a Coast Guard inspection of a pleasure boat was once extremely slim, rising official concern about boating safety and drug smuggling has been abetted by a United States Supreme Court ruling that the Coast Guard may stop and board a boat without a subpoena. Recently, a boat I know well was boarded off the Massachusetts coast and cited for not carrying proper papers and a copy of the rules of the road. We have space only to outline the six requirements, which are covered in much greater detail in *The Annapolis Book of Seamanship* and in several publications distributed by the U.S. Coast Guard and the U.S. Coast Guard Auxiliary.

The best way to guarantee that you're legal and safe is to ask your local Coast Guard Auxiliary flotilla for a free courtesy inspection, which covers recommended "should have" safety equipment as well as required "must haves." If your boat passes the examination, you will be given a special decal to stick on a window or port. As its name suggests, the Auxiliary is a civilian organization with close ties to the Coast Guard. The Auxiliary's 40,000 members are affiliated with more than 1,300 flotillas, which sponsor boat inspection and boating instruction programs. For more information about the Auxiliary and its programs, find your local flotilla's telephone number in a waterfront town's directory, or write to: U.S. Coast Guard Auxiliary, U.S. Coast Guard, Washington, DC 20593.

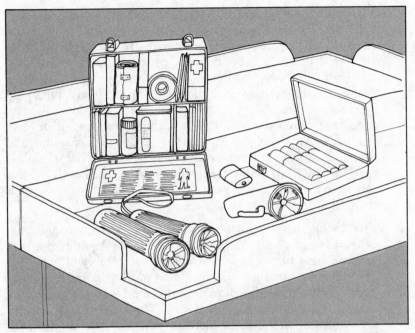

All cruising boats should carry a complete first-aid kit and a variety of flashlights, some in waterproof cases. They also must carry approved flares, here shown in a waterproof box.

Here are the six required items that any boatowner or charterer is responsible for:

✓　**A life jacket for every crewmember.** The life jacket—or, in bureaucratic jargon, *personal flotation device* or PFD—must be Coast Guard–approved (look for a prominent official label) and be a suitable size for the wearer. For normal use there are three types of PFD—I, II, and III—with Type I being the most buoyant and bulky and Type III the least buoyant and bulky. Boats larger than 16 feet must also carry a Type IV PFD, which is a throwable cushion or life ring. The Coast Guard does not require that PFDs be aboard sailboards, kayaks, and rowing shells, but state or local laws may.

✓　**A sound signal.** Boats larger than 16 feet must carry a whistle or horn for signaling under the rules of the road; those 39 feet and larger must also have a bell to sound in fog. A Freon-powered horn is suitable for smaller boats (remember to take a spare Freon canister) but may not be loud enough for boats longer than 39 feet.

✓ **Visual distress signals.** Under Coast Guard regulations, signals specified for *day use* must be carried on all boats with the exception of engineless sailboats smaller than 26 feet, all boats smaller than 16 feet, boats participating in races or parades, and manually propelled boats. Approved day signals are three orange smoke signals (either floating or hand-held) and an orange flag with a black square and circle. In addition, all boats used *at night* must carry a bright flashlight or some other electric light. Approved *combination day and night* signals include three parachute red flares or three hand-held red flares. Unless they are carefully stowed in a dry locker, preferably with a moisture-absorbing gel pack, flares will quickly become so damp that they will malfunction.

✓ **Fire extinguishers.** All boats with inboard engines, and outboard-powered boats larger than 26 feet or having compartments where fumes may be trapped, must carry at least one *charged* fire extinguisher designed to put out a fire in a flammable or combustible liquid. This kind of extinguisher is known as a B-type and is so labeled. The number and capacity of required extinguishers increase with the boat's size. Fire extinguishers generally must be recharged annually.

✓ **Registration papers.** Under the Federal Boat Safety Act of 1971, each state has its own boat registration system. Many boats larger than about 30 feet are also eligible for a federal registration system called *documentation*. Either way, the official papers must be aboard. A safe way to carry them and other important documents, like the radio license and the engine owner's manual, is in a well-sealed plastic attaché case stowed in the chart table or under the skipper's bunk.

✓ **The rules of the road.** All boats 12 meters (39.4 feet) long or longer (for some reason the dividing line for many requirements) must carry a copy of the rules of the road. This requirement may be satisfied by carrying Coast Guard publication M16672.2, *Navigation Rules, International-Inland*, available for $6.50 from most official nautical chart sales outlets, or any book that includes the complete text of the rules of the road, such as William P. Crawford, *Mariner's Rules of the Road* (New York: W. W. Norton, 1983), and William H. Tate, *A Mariner's Guide to the Rules of the Road* (2nd edition; Annapolis, Md.: Naval Institute Press, 1982). (All three of these publications may be purchased by mail order from The Armchair Sailor Bookstore, Lee's Wharf, Newport, RI 02840.)

"Should Have" Gear

The required equipment satisfies the government's legitimate concern for marine safety, but it won't meet all your needs. At the end of Chapter 3 there's a checklist for personal gear to take aboard. Below is one for minimum equipment that each cruising boat should have before heading off on a cruise that will last a weekend or longer.

1. General
✓ a water-repellent—preferably waterproof—jacket for each crewmember
✓ a sleeping bag or bedroll for each crewmember
✓ full fuel and water tanks (if the tanks are small, carry a jerry jug of each, too)
✓ several canvas and string bags for stowage and shopping
✓ two buckets
✓ a dozen clothespins
✓ loose mosquito netting to tape over open hatches and windows
✓ an accurate, compensated compass
✓ two suitable anchors and at least 150 feet of rode and chain
✓ four 20-foot lengths of heavy docking line
✓ three large fenders
✓ a swimming ladder
✓ a snorkel and swimming mask
✓ a dinghy or life raft
✓ a piloting and sailing instructional book
✓ a bosun's chair

2. Tools and Spares
✓ a tool kit with at least a sharp knife with a spike, a pair of pliers, a large crescent wrench, a small crescent wrench, a screwdriver for each type of screw on board, a large hammer, a hacksaw, a hand drill, and a variety of cotter pins, stainless steel machine screws, nuts, and washers
✓ a can of oil
✓ a tube of light waterproof grease
✓ spare engine coolant
✓ spare engine oil
✓ a small can of gasoline for cleaning grease off lines, fenders, shoes, etc.
✓ two rolls of heavy waterproof tape (preferably duct tape)
✓ a small sail-repair kit (including light tape)
✓ twenty feet of marline or other light line

Tools, fastenings, lubricants, tape, a voltmeter, and a bosun's chair for going aloft may all come in handy some day.

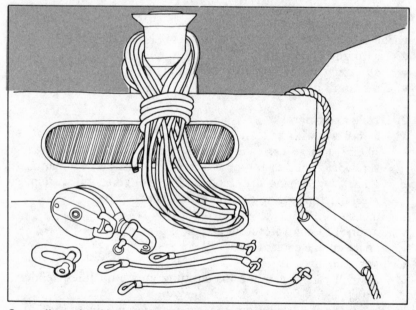

Spare line, shackles, and blocks are good to have along, as are some lengths of shockcord, for furling sails, and a rubber chafe guard to slip over the anchor rode where it passes through the bow chock.

✓ light shockcord
✓ a spare main/jib halyard
✓ spare jib sheets
✓ spare mainsail battens
✓ two spare blocks
✓ four spare shackles
✓ a spare or emergency tiller, in case the tiller or wheel breaks

3. The Galley
✓ full cooking fuel tanks
✓ large garbage bags
✓ food storage bags
✓ plastic wrap
✓ freezer tape
✓ five rolls of paper towels
✓ three emergency meals in cans
✓ pots and pans: at least a frying pan, a large pot, a small pot, and a tea kettle
✓ implements: at least a spatula, a serving spoon, and a fork and spoon for all
✓ ice tongs
✓ an ice pick and ice bucket
✓ liquid dish soap
✓ a dish scrubber
✓ a corkscrew

4. The Head
✓ five rolls of toilet paper
✓ three bars of Ivory soap (it floats!)
✓ air-freshener spray
✓ a large first-aid kit and manual. An excellent manual is Michael Martin Cohen, *Dr. Cohen's Healthy Sailor Book* (Camden, Me.: International Marine, 1983).
✓ nonprescription seasick pills
✓ several tubes of sun lotion, at least one a highly protective sunscreen with a sun protection factor (S.P.F.) of 12 or more

5. The Chart Table
✓ coast and harbor charts covering the largest possible area you'll cruise in
✓ a plotter
✓ dividers
✓ a large notebook (or log)
✓ a box of #2 pencils and a small sharpener

✔ a tide table
✔ an accurate watch with stopwatch function
✔ a copy of the *U.S. Coast Pilot*, or a local cruising guide, describing harbors and hazards to navigation
✔ a radio to receive weather broadcasts
✔ binoculars
✔ a hand bearing compass

6. Lights
✔ a battery-powered, 360-degree, white anchor light to hang from the headstay when anchored outside a Special Anchorage
✔ four standard flashlights (preferably with waterproof rubber or plastic casings) with spare batteries and bulbs
✔ an extremely bright large flashlight
✔ spare bulbs for all navigation and cabin lights
✔ a voltmeter to test wiring circuits

"Nice to Have" Gear

Here are a few take-aboard options that, while they don't make sailing any safer or easier, certainly make living aboard more interesting and fun.

✔ a field guide to local wildlife

✔ escapist reading material

✔ a tape player with earphones and a wide variety of cassette tapes

✔ a sketch pad, drawing pencils, and a manual like *Drawing on the Right Side of the Brain*

✔ two decks of playing cards with the same backs (some cards will inevitably fall into the bilge)

✔ a game, such as a magnetized chess or Scrabble set

✔ a guitar, harmonica, or recorder—and a musician who can play

✔ a Frisbee, football, tennis ball, or soccer ball for shore exercise

Glossary of 500 Important Sailing Terms

(With a Sample of Curious Derivations)

One of the most complicated and challenging aspects of sailing is its arcane and complex terminology. It drives some people mad: why not say *left*, *right*, and *front* instead of *port*, *starboard*, and *bow*? One reason is that if you use landlubber terms in a boating context, your shipmates who already know *port*, etc., won't have the slightest idea what you're talking about. The language is already in place, so just try to do your best to master it. Experience, reading, and patient shipmates will be your best teachers.

Here are the definitions of some 500 common sailing terms in general use today. The entire sailor's language has a much larger vocabulary—one special dictionary, René de Kerchove's classic *International Maritime Dictionary*, is a thousand pages long—but this is all you'll need on the decks and in the cabins of today's pleasure boats. For trivia and crossword puzzle buffs, after the main glossary we'll look more closely at the thirty terms that make up the hard core of the sailor's language.

A

Aback. With sails backed, or trimmed to windward.

Abaft. Behind.

Abeam. At right angles to a boat.

Aboard. On a boat.

Adrift. Unsecured.

Afloat. Floating.

Aft. Toward the stern.

After. A prefix denoting location toward the stern.

Aground. Stuck on the bottom in shallow water.

Aid to navigation. A buoy, lighthouse, or other channel marker.

Air. Wind.

Alee. To leeward, away from the wind. "Hard alee" is the command for tacking.

Aloft. In the rigging above the deck.

Alongside. Beside.

Amidship(s). In the middle of the boat, where she's widest.

Angle of Attack. The angle between the sail and the apparent wind or the rudder or centerline and the water flow.

Apparent wind. The wind felt on the moving boat.

Appendage. A rudder, keel, centerboard, or skeg.

Astern. Behind the stern.

Athwartships. Across the boat.

Auxiliary. A sailboat that has an engine.

Aweigh. Describes an anchor unhooked from the bottom.

B

Babystay. See **Jackstay**.

Back. (1) To trim a sail to windward; (2) counterclockwise shift in the wind direction.

Backstay. A stay running aft from the upper part of the mast, either permanent or running (adjustable).

Backwind. Wind flowing from a forward sail into the leeward side of an after sail.

Bail. To remove water with a bucket.

Bailers. Sluices in the bilge of a small boat to remove water when she's underway.

Balance. The degree to which all the forces on a boat are symmetrical so she sails with slight weather helm.

Ballast. Weight in the keel or on the windward side that restrains the boat from heeling too far.

Ballast-displacement ratio. The numerical ratio between the ballast and displacement in pounds.

Barber hauler. A sail control for changing the athwartships lead of the jib sheet.

Barometer. An instrument that shows atmospheric pressure in inches or millibars of mercury.

Batten. A wooden or plastic slat inserted in the leech of a sail.

Beam (bm). A boat's greatest

width.

Beamy. Wide.

Bear away. To head off, away from the wind.

Bearing. The angle to an object in relative or compass degrees.

Beat. A course sailed as close to the wind as is efficiently possible, or a close-hauled course.

Below. Beneath the deck.

Bend on sails. To install sails on the boom and headstay.

Berth. (1) A boat's position at a pier or float; (2) a "wide berth" is a large margin of safety; (3) a bed in a boat.

Bight. Any part of a line between the ends.

Bilge. The lowest part of the boat's hull.

Binnacle. A support or pedestal into which a compass is secured.

Bitter end. The end of a line.

Blanket. To come between the wind and a sail so the sail is not full.

Block. A nautical pulley made up of a sheave that rotates on a sheave pin (or center pin) or on ball bearings and hung from metal or plastic sides called cheeks.

Board. (1) Abbreviation for centerboard; (2) to go on a boat; (3) a leg or part of a course.

Boat hook. A pole with a hook on its end.

Boat speed. Speed through the water.

Boltrope. The line along the luff and foot of a mainsail and the luff of a jib.

Boom. The spar that extends and supports the foot of a mainsail.

Boom vang. A tackle or hydraulic system that restrains the boom from lifting.

Boot top. The painted band on the boat's topsides just at the waterline.

Bottom. (1) The submerged land; (2) the boat's hull under the water, or underbody.

Bow. The most forward part of the boat.

Braided line. Line or rope made up of a hard core inside a soft woven cover.

Breeze. Wind or air.

Broach. To get out of control and head up sharply, usually when sailing off the wind.

Broad off. About 45° to (the bow or stern); sometimes "broad on."

Bulkhead. A wall separating a boat's cabins that provides athwartships support for the hull.

Bunk. A bed in a boat; sometimes "berth."

Buoy. A floating object marking a channel or a mooring.

Buoyancy. The upward force that keeps a boat floating.

By the lee. Sailing on a run with the wind coming over the quarter on the same side that the boom is trimmed, making a sudden jibe likely.

C

Cabin. A room in a boat.

Calm. Little or no wind. A "flat calm" is totally devoid of wind.

Canvas. Sails or sail area.

Capsize. To turn over.

Cardinal points. North, east, south, and west. The intercardinal points are northeast, southeast, southwest and northwest.

Carry away. To break.

Cast off. To let a line go.

Catamaran. A multihull with two hulls separated by a deck or crossbeams from which a trampoline is suspended; abbreviated "cat."

Cat boat. A wide, shallow boat with a large mainsail and no jib.

Cat rig. A single- or two-masted boat with no jib.

Caught aback. With the sails backed, or trimmed to windward.

Centerboard. A retractable appendage that increases or reduces the draft and the lateral area of the underbody.

Center of effort. The point in the sail plan that is the balance point for all the aerodynamic forces.

Center of lateral resistance. The point in the hull's underbody that is the balance point for all the hydrodynamic forces.

Centerline. An imaginary line that runs down the middle of the boat from bow to stern.

Chafe. Abrasion or wear.

Chain plates. Straps on the hull to which stays are secured.

Chandlery. A marine hardware store.

Channel. Water sufficiently deep to sail in.

Chart. A nautical map.

Charter. To rent a boat.

Chine. The intersection between the topsides and the boat's bottom.

Chock. A fairlead for the anchor rode and docking lines.

Chop. Short, steep waves.

Chord. An imaginary line drawn between the luff and leech of a sail. The chord depth is an imaginary line drawn to the deepest part of the sail from the chord. The ratio of chord depth to chord length represents the sail's draft—a high ratio indicates a flat sail; a low ratio, a full sail.

Circumnavigation. A voyage around the world.

Cleat. A wooden, plastic, or metal object to which lines under strain are secured. There are two kinds of cleats, horn and quick-action.

Clevis pin. A large pin that secures one fitting to another.

Clew. The after lower corner of a mainsail, jib, or mizzen, and either lower corner of a spinnaker.

Close-hauled. Sailing as close to the wind as is efficient; also "beating" and "on the wind."

Coaming. A low wall around a cockpit.

Cockpit. A recessed area in the deck containing the tiller or wheel.

Coil. To arrange a line in easily manageable loops so it can be stowed.

Companionway. Opening leading down from the deck to the cabin.

Compass. A magnetized card in a glass dome that indicates the direction to magnetic north.

Compass rose. A circle on a chart that orients it to north.

Cotter pin. A small pin used to secure a clevis pin and to keep turnbuckles from unwinding.

Course. (1) The compass direction that is steered; (2) the sequence of buoys rounded in a race.

Cradle. A frame that supports a boat when she's hauled out of the water onto shore.

Crew. Everybody who helps sail a boat.

Cringle. A large reinforced eye in a sail.

Cruise. Two or more days spent continuously on a boat that is underway, with stops for the night.

Cruiser-racer. See **Racer-cruiser.**

Cruising boat. A boat used only for cruising.

Cunningham. A line controlling tension along a sail's luff, invented by Briggs Cunningham.

Current. Horizontal movement of the water caused by tidal change or wind.

Custom boat. A boat built specifically for one client, as against a stock boat.

Cut. The shape or design of a sail.

Cutter. A single-masted boat that flies two jibs at a time.

D

Daggerboard. A centerboard that is retracted vertically rather than hinged.

Dampen. To cause to moderate.

Danger sector. The fixed red part of a lighthouse's light shining over shoals.

Daysailer. A boat without a cabin that is used for short sails or racing.

Dead. Exactly.

Dead-end. To secure an end of a line to an object.

Dead Reckoning (D.R.). The calculation of a boat's position based on course and distance run.

Deck. The top of a hull.

Depower. To lessen heeling forces by making sails less full or allowing them to luff.

Deviation. A compass error caused by metal objects on board.

Dinghy. A small, light sailboat or rowboat.

Displacement. A boat's weight—more accurately, the weight of the water she displaces. A "light-displacement" boat is relatively light for her length.

Displacement boat. A relatively heavy boat that cannot plane.

Distance run. The mileage covered during a given time period.

Dock. (1) The water next to a float or pier; (2) to bring a boat alongside a float or pier.

Docking line. A line securing a boat to a float or pier.

Dodger. A fold-up spray shield at the forward end of the cockpit.

Double-bottom. A watertight compartment between the bottom and the sole, or floor.

Douse. To lower.

Downhaul. A line that holds an object down.

Downwind. Away from the direction from which the wind blows.

Draft (or draught). (1) The distance between the waterline and the lowest part of the keel; (2) the amount and position of fullness in a sail.

Drag. (1) Resistance; (2) when an anchor breaks out and skips along the bottom.

Drift. A current's velocity.

Drifting. In a calm, to be carried by the current.

E

Earing. A reefing line led through a leech cringle.

Ease. (1) To let out (a sheet); (2) to reduce pull on (the helm).

Easy. Without undue strain, smooth.

Ebb. The dropping, outgoing tide.

Eddy. A circular current.

End-for-end. A reversal of a line.

EPIRB. A small, buoyant transmitter for sending an emergency, position-indicating radio beacon.

Estimated Position (E.P.). A best estimate of a boat's position based on her dead reckoning plot and one bearing.

Eye. A loop.

Eye of the wind. The precise wind direction.

F

Fairlead. A fitting through

which a line passes so chafe is avoided.

Fairway. The middle of a channel.

Fair wind. A reach or run.

Fake. To make large loops on deck with a line in order to eliminate kinks.

Fast. Secure.

Fastenings. The screws and bolts that hold a boat together.

Favor. To ease or help.

Feather. To spill wind from the sails in a wind gust by suddenly heading up from close-hauled to a fore-reach.

Feel. The helmsman's sense of how well the boat is sailing.

Fender. A rubber bumper hung between the boat and a float or pier.

Fend off. To push off.

Fetch. (1) To sail a course that will clear a buoy or shoal, also "lay"; (2) the distance between an object and the windward shore.

Fish. To repair with turns of light line.

Fitting. A piece of a boat's gear.

Fix. A certain position based on two or more crossed bearings.

Float. A floating platform to which boats may be tied.

Flood. The rising, incoming tide.

Flotation. Foam blocks or air tanks that keep a swamped boat afloat.

Fluky. Unpredictable and weak.

Following sea. Waves from astern.

Foot. (1) The bottom edge of a sail; (2) to steer slightly lower than close-hauled in order to increase boat speed.

Force. A measurement in the Beaufort scale.

Fore. Prefix indicating location toward the bow.

Fore and aft. Everywhere on the boat.

Forepeak. A stowage compartment in the bow.

Forereach. To carry way while heading almost into the wind.

Foresail. A jib.

Forestay. A stay running from the foredeck to the mast, on which a jib is set.

Foretriangle. The area bounded by the mast, foredeck, and headstay.

Forward. Toward the bow.

Foul. (1) To tangle; (2) to violate a racing rule.

Foul-weather gear. Water-resistant clothing and boots.

Founder. To swamp or sink.

Fractional rig. A rig whose headstay goes partway up the mast.

Free. (1) On a broad reach or run; (2) a freeing wind is a lift, or a shift aft.

Freeboard. The distance from the deck to the water, or the height of the topsides.

Fresh air. Wind of about 16–22 knots.

Front. The approaching edge of a high-pressure or low-pressure system.

Full. (1) Not luffing; (2) with deep draft.

Full and by. Sailing close-hauled with sails full.

Full sail. All sails set.

Furl. To roll up and secure a sail to a boom.

G

Gadget. A specialized piece of gear.

Gaff-rigged. With a four-sided mainsail, whose top edge is supported by a spar called a gaff.

Galley. A boat's kitchen.

Gangway. An opening in the lifelines to facilitate boarding from a float or another boat.

Gear. Generic term for all equipment on a boat.

Genoa. A large jib whose clew overlaps the mast and mainsail.

Gilguy. A line or length of shock cord that holds a halyard away from the mast when the sails are not set.

Gimbals. Supports that allow a compass, table, or stove to remain level as the boat heels.

Give. Stretch.

Give-way vessel. Under the rules of the road, the vessel that must take action to avoid the vessel that has right-of-way.

Gooseneck. The fitting securing the forward end of the boom to the mast.

Gradient. The relative proximity and barometric pressure of adjoining isobars on a weather map.

Grommet. A small metal ring set into a sail.

Ground tackle. The anchor and anchor rode.

Gunwale. A boat's rail at the edge of the deck, pronounced "gun'l."

Gust. A strong puff of wind.

Guy. A line controlling the position of a spinnaker pole; the after guy pulls the pole back and eases it forward and the fore guy restrains it from lifting.

H

Halyard. A line or wire rope that hoists a sail and keeps it up.

Hand. (1) To lower; (2) a crew member.

Hank. A small snap hook that secures the jib luff to the headstay.

Harden up. To head up.

Hard over. As far as possible in one direction.

Hatch. An opening in a deck, covered by a hatch cover.

Haul. To veer, or shift direction clockwise.

Haul In. To trim.

Haul Out. To pull out of the water.

Head. (1) The top corner of a sail; (2) a boat's bathroom.

Headboard. The reinforcement in the head of a sail.

Header. A wind shift requiring the helmsman to alter course to leeward or the crew to trim sheets.

Heading. The course.

Head off. To alter course to leeward away from the wind; also "bear off," "bear away," and "come off."

Headroom. A cabin's height.

Headsail. A jib.

Head sea. Waves from ahead.

Headstay. The stay running from the bow to the mast.

Head to wind. With the bow heading dead into the wind.

Head up. To alter course to windward, toward the wind; also "harden up," "come up," and "luff up."

Headway. Forward motion.

Heave. To throw.

Heave-to. To sail along slowly with the jib backed.

Heavy air. Wind of gale force, stronger than 28 knots.

Heavy weather. Rough seas and gale-force winds.

Heel. A boat's athwartship tip.

Helm. (1) The tiller or steering wheel; (2) the boat's tendency to head off course: with weather helm, she tends to head up, with lee helm, to head off.

Helmsperson. The person who is steering.

High. (1) Several degrees more than the required course; (2) pinching, or sailing too close to the wind.

High cut. With the clew high off the deck.

High performance. Very fast.

Hike. To lean over the windward rail to counter the heeling forces on the sails.

Hiking strap. A strap in the cockpit that restrains a hiking sailor's feet.

Hockle. A kink.

Holding ground. The bottom in a harbor. Good holding ground, such as mud, grabs an anchor securely.

Hounds. The location of the jib halyard block on a mast.

House. The roof of a cabin extending above deck.

Hove-to. In the act of heaving-to.

Hull. A boat's shell, exclusive of appendages, deck, rig, and cabin.

Hull speed. A boat's theoretical maximum speed determined by multiplying the square root of her waterline length by 1.34.

I

Inboard. In from the rail.

In irons. Head to wind with no headway or sternway.

Isobar. A line on a weather map marking points of equal barometric pressure.

J

Jackstay. A stay running from the foredeck to the mast solely to support the mast; also "babystay."

Jackwire. A wire on deck onto which safety harness tethers are clipped.

Jib. A sail carried on the headstay or forestay.

Jibe. To change tacks by heading off until the sails swing across the boat.

Jiffy reef. A reef that is tied in.

Jumper strut. A strut sticking out from the mast near the jib halyard block (the hounds) of a fractional rig; over the strut passes the jumper stay, which when tensioned helps keep the top of the mast straight.

Jury rig. An improvised replacement for damaged gear.

K

Kedge off. To use an anchor to pull a grounded boat back into deep water.

Keel. A deep appendage, or fin, under the hull whose lateral area counteracts leeway forces and whose weight counteracts heeling forces—usually permanent but sometimes retractable.

Ketch. A two-masted boat whose after mast, the mizzenmast, is shorter than the forward mast, the mainmast, and is also located forward of the rudder post.

Kink. A temporary twist in a line.

Knockdown. A drastic increase in the angle of heel.

Knot. One nautical mile per hour.

L

Laid line. Line on rope made up of large strands (usually three of them) twisted around each other.

Land breeze. A wind blowing from the shore to the water.

Landmark. An object on the shore that can be helpful when piloting.

Lanyard. A short line.

Lash. To tie.

Launch. (1) To move a boat into the water from land; (2) a powerboat used as a ferry between land and a moored boat; also "shore boat."

Lay. To sail a course that will clear a buoy or shoal; also "fetch."

Layout. The arrangement of gear on deck or of furniture in the cabin.

Lazy. Not in use.

Lead. (1) A block for a jib sheet; (2) to pass a line through a block.

Lee. Short for "leeward."

Lee bow. To have the current pushing the boat to windward.

Leech. The after edge of a mainsail, jib, or mizzen, and both side edges of a spinnaker.

Lee helm. A boat's tendency to head off, away from the wind, unless checked by the tiller or wheel.

Lee shore. Land onto which the wind is blowing and which is to leeward of the boat.

Leeward. Downwind.

Leeway. Side-slippage to leeward.

Leg. A part of a passage or race sailed between two buoys or aids to navigation.

Length. Length overall (LOA) is the distance between the tip of the bow and the end of the stern. Waterline length (LWL) is the distance between the most forward and most aft points touching the water when the boat is at rest.

Lifeline. A coated wire, supported by posts called stanchions, that encircles the deck to restrain the crew from falling overboard.

Life raft. An inflatable boat for use in emergencies.

Lift. A wind shift allowing the helmsperson to head up, or alter course to windward, or the crew to ease sheets.

Light. (1) Describes a sail that is luffing; (2) an illuminated aid to navigation or boat's navigation light.

Light air. Wind less than 8 knots.

Light line. Line smaller than ¼ inch in diameter.

Line. Any length of rope that has a specified use.

Line of Position (L.O.P.). A compass bearing to a charted object.

Loose. To let go.

Low cut. With the clew near the deck.

Lubber's line. A post in a compass used to determine the course or a bearing.

Luff. (1) The forward edge of a mainsail, jib, or mizzen, and the windward edge of a spinnaker; (2) bubbling or flapping in a sail when it is not trimmed far enough or is being backwinded by another sail, or when the course is too close to the wind.

Luff curve. A convex (in a mainsail) or concave (in a jib) curve in a sail's luff to account for mast bend or headstay sag.

Lull. A relatively calm period between wind gusts.

M

Magnetic. Relative to magnetic north, as against true.

Mainmast. The mast, or the tallest of two masts.

Mainsail. The sail hoisted on the after side of the mainmast, pronounced "mains'l."

Mark. A buoy used in a race course.

Marline. A general-purpose tarred light line.

Marlinspike. A pointed tool on a sailor's knife used to pry open knots, start holes in wood, and accomplish other odd jobs.

Mast. A wooden or aluminum pole supported by standing rigging from which sails are set.

Masthead. The top of the mast.

Masthead fly. A wind direction indicator at the masthead.

Masthead light. A white light illuminated when powering at night, located *not* at the top of the mast but about two-thirds of the way up the mast; also "bow" or "powering" light.

Mast step. The support for the bottom (heel or butt) of the mast.

Millibar (mb). A unit of atmospheric pressure, with 1 mb equal to 0.03 inches of mercury.

Mizzen. The small, aftermost sail on a ketch or yawl, set on the mizzenmast.

Moderate air. Wind of about 9–15 knots.

Mooring. A permanently emplaced anchor with a pendant and buoy to which a boat may be secured.

Motion. The degree of instability of a boat's deck while she sails in waves.

Motor sailer. An auxiliary sailboat with an especially large engine and spacious accommodations.

Mousing. A length of light line or wire that secures a pin in a shackle.

Multihull. A boat with two hulls (a catamaran) or three hulls (a trimaran), or one hull and an outrigger.

N

Nautical mile. The unit of geographical distance used on salt-water charts (statute miles are used on Great Lakes charts), where 1 nautical mile = 6076 feet, or 1.15 statute mile. Therefore 1 statute mile = 0.87 nautical mile. One knot = 1 nautical mile per hour.

O

Obstruction. A buoy, vessel, shoal, or other object requiring a major course alteration to pass to one side.

Ocean racer. A boat with minimal accommodations used for racing overnight or long distances.

Offshore. (1) Out of sight of land; (2) from the land toward the water.

Off the wind. Reaching or running.

On board. On a boat.

On even keel. Not heeling.

Onshore. From the water toward the land.

On the beam. Abeam.

On the bow (stern). To one side of the bow (stern); also "off the bow (stern)."

One-design. A racing boat, usually a daysailer, designed and built to the same specifications as all other boats in her class.

Open boat. A boat without a deck.

Outboard. (1) Out toward and beyond the rail; (2) a portable engine on the stern.

Outhaul. A sail control that secures the clew of a boomed sail, and adjusts tension along its foot.

Overhang. The distance the bow and stern extend beyond the waterline.

Overhaul. (1) To tighten a lazy (unused) line or the tail of a line in use in order to check that the lead is fair and that there is no chafe; (2) to overtake.

Overlapping. Alongside of; an overlapping jib extends aft of the luff of the mainsail, and an overlapping boat has her bow or stern alongside another boat's stern or bow.

Overnight. For two or three days.

Overpowered. Heeling too far and difficult to steer.

Overrigged. Having too much sail area; also "over-canvassed."

Overstand. To lay or fetch a buoy or shoal with room to spare.

Overtaking. Coming up from astern and about to pass.

P

Padeye. A metal loop to which blocks and shackles are secured.

Painter. A bow line on a dinghy.

Part. (1) To break; (2) one of the sections of line in a tackle.

Partners. The deck opening for the mast.

Passage. More than 6 hours spent under way.

Pay out. To ease.

Pendant. A short length of wire or line used as an extender on a sail, halyard, or anchor rode, pronounced "pennant."

PFD. Personal Flotation Device, the official term for "life jacket."

Pier. A platform on posts that

sticks out from the shore.

Piloting. Navigation within sight of land.

Pinch. To sail too close to the wind when close-hauled.

Pitchpole. To somersault.

Plane. To skip up and across the bow wave at high speed.

Planing boat. A light boat that planes in fresh winds at speeds exceeding her theoretical hull speed.

Play. (1) To trim a sheet assiduously; (2) a loose fit.

Plot. To draw a boat's course and position on a chart.

Point. To sail close to the wind.

Points of sail. Close-hauled, reaching, and running.

Pooped. Smashed by a wave breaking over the stern.

Port. (1) The left side, facing forward; (2) a small round window; (3) a commercial harbor.

Porthole. A small round window; also "port."

Pound. To smash down heavily on waves.

Preventer. A line that restrains the boom from jibing accidentally.

Puff. A quick, local increase in wind velocity.

Pulpit. A stainless-steel guardrail around the bow or stern.

Q

Quarter. The after sections of the rails and topsides.

R

Race. (1) An especially strong, turbulent current; (2) an organized competition between boats.

Racer-cruiser. A boat comfortable enough for cruising and fast enough for racing.

Rail. The outer edge of the deck.

Rake. The tilt of a mast.

Range. (1) The difference in water level between high and low tides; (2) the full extent of a light's visibility; (3) two objects that, when aligned, indicate a channel or the course of another vessel.

Reach. (1) To sail across the wind; (2) a channel between the mainland and an island.

Reef. (1) To decrease a sail's size; (2) a shoal composed of rocks or coral.

Reeve. To lead a line through a block or cringle.

Regatta. A series of races in which cumulative scores are kept.

Render. To run easily through a block.

Rhumb Line. The most direct course between two points.

Rig. (1) The spars, standing rigging, and sails; (2) to get a boat ready for sailing or prepare a sail or piece of gear for use.

Rigging. The gear used to

support and adjust the sails: standing rigging includes the spars, stays, and turnbuckles; running rigging includes the sheets and halyards and their blocks, as well as sail controls such as the outhaul and boom vang.

Right-of-way. The legal authority to stay on the present course.

Roach. The sail area aft of the imaginary straight line running between the head and the clew.

Rode. The anchor line.

Roller furling. A way to stow sails by rolling them up at their luff.

Roller reef. A reef secured by rolling the sail up on itself.

Rudder. An underwater flap that is adjusted by the helm to steer the boat. It pivots on the rudder post.

Rules of the road. Laws that, when observed, prevent collisions.

Run. (1) A course with the wind astern; (2) distance covered.

Running lights. The navigation lights illuminated at night on the starboard and port sides and on the stern.

S

Safety harness. A web or rope harness worn on the upper body and attached to the deck with a tether to prevent a sailor's falling overboard in rough conditions.

Sailboard. A surfboard rigged with a sail that the standing sailor holds up.

Sail controls. Lines, tackles, and other gear used to hold a sail in position and adjust its shape, such as the sheets, traveler, outhaul, cunningham, and boom vang.

Sail cover. A protective cloth tied over a furled sail to protect it from ultraviolet rays and dirt.

Sail handling. The hoisting, trimming, and dousing of sails.

Sail ties. Straps used to secure a furled sail or to lash a doused sail on deck so it doesn't blow away; also called "stops" and "gaskets."

Schooner. A boat with two or more masts, the forwardmost of which, the foremast, is shorter than the aftermost, the mainmast.

Scope. The ratio between the amount of anchor rode let out and the depth of the water.

Scow. A fast, flat-bottomed daysailer raced on lakes.

Scull. To propel a boat by swinging the helm and rudder back and forth.

Scupper. A deck or cockpit drain.

Sea. (1) A wave; (2) a body of

salt water smaller than an ocean but larger than a sound or gulf.

Seaboot. A rubber boot with a nonslip sole.

Sea breeze. A wind blowing from the water to warmer land, filling the space left by rising heated air.

Sea cock. A valve opening and closing a pipe through the hull.

Sea condition. The size and shape of the waves.

Seakindly. Comfortable in rough seas.

Sea room. Enough distance from shore and shoals for safe sailing.

Seaway. Rough water.

Seaworthy. Able to survive heavy weather.

Secure. To fasten or cleat.

Self-bailing. Automatically draining.

Self-steering. Automatically steering without a helmsperson.

Set. (1) To raise (a sail); (2) a current's direction.

Set up. To rig.

Shackle. A metal hook that secures a line to a fitting, a line to a sail, or a fitting to a fitting.

Sheave. The roller in a block.

Sheer. The curve of the rail as seen from alongside.

Sheet. (1) The primary sail-control line, which pulls the sail in and out; (2) to trim.

Shifty. Frequently changing direction.

Shoal. Dangerously shallow water.

Shock cord. Elastic line.

Shoot into the wind. To head directly into the wind.

Shorten down. To set a smaller sail.

Shorthanded. With a small crew.

Shroud. A side stay.

Singlehanded. Solitary.

Sisterships. Boats of the same design.

Skeg. A small, fixed fin attached to the underbody near the stern.

Skipper. The person in charge of a boat.

Slack. (1) Not moving; (2) loose; (3) to ease.

Slat. To roll in a calm with the sails slapping back and forth noisily.

Slicker. A jacket for foul weather.

Slip. A dock between two floats in a marina.

Sloop. A single-masted boat that flies one jib at a time.

Slop. A confused seaway.

Small boat. A daysailer less than 30 feet long.

Snap hook. A spring-loaded hook used as a hank and for other small jobs.

Snub. To wrap a line once around a winch or cleat so most of its pull is absorbed.

Sole. A cabin or cockpit floor.

Sound. To measure depth.

Spar. Any mast, boom, or spinnaker pole.

Speed made good. A boat's speed as measured by her progress relative to land, factoring in her speed through the water and current.

Spinnaker. A light, ballooning sail used when sailing off the wind.

Splice. To make an eye in the end of a line or link two line ends together by interweaving strands.

Spill wind. To allow a sail to luff.

Spreader. An athwartships strut holding shrouds out from the mast and providing lateral support.

Stanchions. Metal posts supporting lifelines.

Stand-on vessel. Under the rules of the road, the boat with right-of-way.

Starboard. The right side, facing forward.

Stay. A wire supporting the mast either from forward (headstay, forestay, and jackstay), from athwartships (shrouds), or from astern (backstay and running backstay). Upper stays providing athwartships support are called intermediate stays and those supporting the mast fore and aft over jumper struts are called jumper stays.

Staysail. A small jib tacked down partway back from the headstay.

Steer by. Use as a guide when steering.

Steerageway. Enough speed through the water to allow efficient steering.

Steerer. The person who is steering.

Stem. The forward edge of the bow.

Step. To install a mast in a boat.

Stern. The aftermost part of the hull.

Stern way. Motion astern.

Stiff. Resistant to heeling.

Stock boat. A boat with many sisterships built by the same manufacturer from the same design, as against a custom boat.

Stop. A sail tie.

Stow. To put in the proper place.

Strong air. Wind of about 23–27 knots.

Surf. To slide down the face of a wave.

Swamp. To be filled with water.

Swell. Long waves created by prevailing winds or a distant storm; also "groundswell."

T

Tack. (1) With the wind coming over one side or the other; (2) to change tacks by heading up until the sails swing across the boat; (3) the forward lower corner of a mainsail, jib, or mizzen, or the lower windward corner of the spinnaker.

Tack down. To secure the sail's tack.

Tackle. A mechanical system of line (parts) and blocks that increases hauling power, pronounced "taykle."

Tail. (1) To pull on a sheet or halyard behind a winch; (2) the section of the sheet or halyard behind the winch and cleat.

Tang. A metal strap on the mast to which a stay or block is secured.

Telltale. A piece of yarn or ribbon either tied to the shrouds to help the crew determine wind direction or sewn to the sails to help them trim or steer.

Tender. Heels relatively quickly.

Thimble. A metal or plastic eye worked into an eye splice to protect the line or wire against chafe.

Three sheets to the wind. Drunk.

Tide. The rise and fall of water due to the moon's and sun's gravitational pull, as against current, which is the lateral motion of the water as the tides change.

Tide rip. A line of rough water where a fast-moving tidal current meets stationary or contrary-moving water.

Tied-in reef. A reef secured by tying cringles to the boom, as against roller reef; also called "jiffy reef" and "slab reef."

Tight leech. A leech pulled down so hard that it forms a straight line between the head and the clew.

Toggle. A metal fitting inserted between a stay and the mast or turnbuckle, or the turnbuckle and the chain plate, to keep the turnbuckle from bending.

Topping lift. A line or wire that holds up the boom or spinnaker pole.

Topsides. The outer sides of the hull.

Trailerable (or trailable). Capable of being towed behind a car on a trailer.

Transom. The athwartships-running surface at the stern.

Trapeze. A wire hanging from a racing dinghy's mast, from which a crew member is suspended in order to counteract heeling forces.

Traveler. An athwartships-running track on which slides a car connected to the main sheet blocks; by adjusting the location of the car, the crew can change the mainsail's angle of attack to the wind.

Trim. (1) To pull in (a sheet); (2) the set of a sail; (3) the bow-up or bow-down attitude a boat assumes when she's at rest.

Trimaran. A multihull with three hulls.

Trip. To break loose.

True. Relative to true north, as against magnetic.

True wind. The wind's direction and strength felt by a stationary object.

Tune. To adjust the standing rigging until the mast is straight.

Turnbuckle. A threaded fitting used to adjust a stay's length.

Twist. The amount that the leech sags off relative to the imaginary straight line between the clew and head.

Two-block. To raise all the way.

U

Under bare poles. With no sails set.

Underbody. The part of the hull that is underwater.

Under power. With the engine on.

Underrigged. With not enough sail set; also "undercanvassed."

Under way. Moving.

Unreeve. To remove a line from a block or cringle.

Unrig. To remove or disassemble gear after it is used.

Upwind. Toward the direction from which the wind blows.

USCG. United States Coast Guard.

USYRU. United States Yacht Racing Union.

V

Vang. (1) A boom vang; (2) to pull down on the boom with a boom vang.

Variable. Unsteady.

Variation. The local difference in degrees between true and magnetic north.

Veer. A clockwise shift in the wind direction.

Vent. A ventilator.

Vessel. Any boat or ship.

VHF/FM. A very high frequency radiotelephone.

Voyage. A long passage under sail.

W

Wake. The water turbulence left behind by a moving boat.

Watch. A part of the crew on deck or below according to a schedule; its leader is the "watch captain."

Way. Speed.

Weather. (1) General atmospheric conditions; (2) wind; (3) upwind; (4) to survive a storm.

Weather helm. A boat's tendency to head up, into the wind, unless checked by the tiller or wheel.

Wetted surface. The area of the underbody and appendages.

Whisker pole. A spar similar to a spinnaker pole used to hold out the jib when sailing wing-and-wing.

Williwaw. A violent gust of wind.

Winch. A geared drum turned by a handle used to pull halyards, sheets, and other lines under strain.

Windage. Wind resistance.

Windlass. A special type of winch used for pulling the anchor rode.

Windward. Upwind.

Wing-and-wing. With the jib and mainsail set on opposite sides when sailing on a run or broad reach.

Wing out. Set wing-and-wing.

Wire rope. Stainless steel or galvanized wire used in stays, halyards, sheets, and other gear.

Working sails. The mainsail and nongenoa jib.

Y

Yacht. A pleasure boat.

Yacht designer. A naval architect specializing in the design of yachts.

Yaw. To sail a wildly erratic course.

Yawl. A two-masted boat whose after mast, the mizzenmast, is shorter than the forward mast, the mainmast, and is located aft of the rudder post.

Y.C. Yacht club.

The Thirty Key Terms and their Derivations

Although the sailor's language is rich and complicated, the odds are that you can get through a typical day spent on the water in the average cruising boat using only thirty terms. All of them are defined in the main glossary, but because they're so important (and have such interesting histories) here we'll give them more space. Their etymologies may provide entertainment and may help your memory latch onto their meanings.*

Ends, Sides, and Directions

Bow. Pronounced like *now*, this is the front part of a boat, where she begins to narrow toward the extreme tip (the stem). The word is thought to be derived from the Old English word *bog*,

---

*The main sources for these derivations are W. A. McEwen and A. H. Lewis, *Encyclopedia of Nautical Knowledge* (Centerville, Md.: Cornell Maritime Press, 1953); René de Kerchove, *International Maritime Dictionary* (2nd edition; New York: Van Nostrand Reinhold, 1983); and *The Compact Edition of the Oxford English Dictionary* (New York: Oxford University Press, 1971).

prounounced *bough* or *bow* and meaning both "shoulder" and "bough of a tree." In a way the bow of a boat can be thought of either as her shoulder or as a boughlike extension.

Forward. Pronounced *f'ward*, this is the direction toward the bow and comes from the Old English adjective *foreweard*, meaning "in the front part."

Stern. Meaning the back part of the boat, it may be derived from the Old Norse and Icelandic *stjorn*, "steering," and the Old English *steoran*, "to steer," since the old-fashioned steering oar was usually in the back of the boat.

Aft. Derived from the Old English *aeftan*, meaning "behind," this word denotes directions toward the stern.

Starboard. In Old English, *bord* meant "side." Therefore, the side over which the steering oar—*steor*, "helm"—was hung was the "steerside" or *steorbord*, which was usually the right-hand side facing toward the bow.

Port. In Old English, the left-hand side of the boat was called the *baecbord* or "the back side" because the helmsman turned his back to it as he faced the steering oar on the right-hand side. That word was later replaced by *ladde-borde*, which was derived from *lade*, "load." To protect her valuable starboard-side steering oar from damage, the boat was always tied up for loading and unloading cargo with her left-hand side against the wharf or shore. *Ladde-borde* was eventually spelled *larboard* but pronounced *labbord*, which created problems because it sounded too much like *starboard*. The British Admiralty finally replaced *larboard* with the more distinguishable *port* (which, because it also means "harbor," equally indicates the side facing land).

Windward. In this term and the next, *ward*—from the Old English suffix *-weard*, "relative position"—locates an area relative to the wind. Since *wind* has meant "air in motion" in many European languages for more than a thousand years, *windward* is toward the direction from which the wind is blowing. (Interestingly, of all compass directions only the one for the wind indicates the source rather than the destination. A north wind blows from the north toward the south. Yet a north current flows from the south toward the north, and if you take a north bearing on an object, you are to the south of it.) In some areas, *weather* (or "toward the source of the weather," presumably the wind's direction) is used in place of *windward*.

Leeward. *Leeward* means "away from the wind's direction." When a boat is to leeward of an object she is protected from the wind, so it's not surprising that "lee" may come from words like the Old Swedish *hlea* and the Old Norse *hly*, which mean "shelter."

While *lee* sounds like *me*, the normal pronunciation of *leeward* is *looward*.

Parts of the Boat

Hull. The most important of the many parts of the boat, or pieces that make up the whole, is the hull, or shell. It consists of the bottom or underbody, which is the part underwater, and the topsides, which are the sides above the water. The word is derived from the Old English *hulu*, "husk," and is a distant cousin of the Old German *hulla*, "covering, cloak," and *hulsa*, "bean and pea shell." (To continue the container metaphor, mariners have traditionally called boats "vessels.")

Deck. The lid on the vessel, the top of the hull, is the *deck*, from the Middle Dutch *dec*, "cover, roof, or cloak."

Keel. This word comes down to us from the Old Norse *kjol*, the main timber running the full length of the hull's bottom—in human terms, her backbone (which is what this timber is often called). Today, when most boats are built of plastic or metal, the *keel* is the wing-shaped appendage hanging down from the hull to provide both lateral resistance so the boat doesn't slide sideways and a counterweight so she doesn't capsize.

Mast. This is the aluminum or wooden pole standing up from the deck and holding up the sails. In Old English, *maest* was either a tree trunk or a tree-grown fruit fed to pigs; it's not hard to tell which meaning our *mast* is derived from.

Boom. Spreading the sail on a horizontal plane is another pole called the *boom*, adapted from the Dutch *boom*, "pole, tree," and a close cousin to the English word *beam*. Masts and booms (and a special kind of boom called the spinnaker pole) fit into the generic category of *spar*, a word related to *spear* and similar words in many other European tongues.

Helm. The Old English *helma*, "rudder," and the German *helm*, "handle," give this one away. By definition the helm is the whole steering system. It includes the rudder (Old English *rother*, "paddle") and either the tiller (*teiler*, "wooden beam" in Old French) or the steering wheel that controls the angle the rudder makes to the water. However, most sailors use *helm* to mean just the tiller or wheel. *Windward* (or *weather*) *helm* describes the tiller's being held to windward so the boat stays on course; *leeward* (or *lee*) *helm* applies if it must be held to leeward.

Sail. The sail is the shaped cloth that catches and derives forward force from the wind. The name may or may not come from an ancient Indo-European root *segh-*, "to hold." More recently, the Scandinavian *segel* means what *sail* does today. A *mainsail* (pronounced *mainsul*)is the biggest sail, or at least it was until about 1965 when genoa jibs overtook them in area. A *foresail* or *headsail* is a sail set forward or on the head (or bow)—what we now call a *jib*.

Jib. Describing the sail set forward of the mast, this word has one of the most curious derivations of all sailing terms, even though it is found only in English. Apparently, it was applied to the highest and forwardmost of the many headsails set on a sailing ship because that sail hung as high as a criminal executed on a *gibbet*. Less gruesome is the history of the term *genoa jib*. The first big overlapping jib that could be trimmed efficiently for close-hauled sailing was set in a race off Genoa, Italy, in 1927 by a Swedish yachtsman named Sven Salen. Why it was not called the *Salen jib* and therefore added to the list of Scandinavian terms in the English sailing vocabulary is not known.

Spinnaker. The newest of all the terms in common usage, this is the name of the light balloonlike sail held out forward of the mast by a boom called the spinnaker pole when the wind comes over the side or stern. Although sails looking like it are seen in paintings and engravings of ships going back to the sixteenth century, this particular sail apparently first appeared in the 1860s on English racing yachts, one of which was named *Sphinx*. *Sphinx's spanker* might have led quickly to *spinnaker* (except that a spanker was a sail set near the stern, not forward over the bow). According to another tradition, the sail was first called a *spin-maker* because it made boats spin, or go especially fast. Both versions make good stories, if not entirely reliable ones.

Halyard. A halyard is a fiber or wire line (part of a rope) used to pull a sail up and hold it there. The word comes from the Middle English *hallyer*, "hauler," and the Old English *gyrd*, "stick." In the days of tall ships the line hauled up the *yard*, a boomlike pole that spread the squaresail.

Sheet. Although this word has been used to describe the sail itself, today it is the term for the line that adjusts the sail's shape and angle to the wind. The sheet is attached to the sail at or near its aft corner, the *clew* (derivation unknown). In Old English, the clew was called the *sceata* and the line attached to it the *sceatline. Sheetline* eventually was simplified to *sheet*.

Shackle. Lines, blocks, and sails are secured to each other and the deck, mast, and boom with metal, removable rings called shackles, whose name originated with the Old English *sceacul*, "fetter." Like many nautical nouns, it's also used as a verb: "Shackle the halyard to the jib."

Block. A pulley through which a sheet or halyard is led, the word apparently comes from the Middle German *bloch*, "an enclosed place." A block's shell encases and strengthens the turning part, the sheave. Some blocks are permanently fixed on the deck, mast, or boom, while others can be relocated using shackles.

Winch. On most boats longer than about 20 feet, the pull on sails is too hard for an unassisted sailor, so sheets and halyards are wrapped clockwise around a metal drum that is turned with a handle to trim the lines. The drum (and any gears inside) is called a *winch*, from the Old English *wince*, "reel, crank." The handle is called a *winch handle*. Lines are *winched in* when they are trimmed on a winch.

Cleat. A metal, plastic, or wooden object on or in which a line is secured so that you don't have to pull against its strain, a cleat is a modern version of an Old Low Germanic *klot*, a wooden wedge in which lines were stopped. Like *trim* and *shackle*, the word can also be used as a verb.

Maneuvers and General Terms

Head up. The bow was often called the *head* of the boat (in fact, a marine bathroom was first called a head because it was located on the bow), and *up* suggests climbing higher up the hill down which the wind is pouring. So this command means "alter course to windward."

Bear off. This is the opposite of *head up*. *Bear* here means "apply force"; to alter course away from the wind, a helmsperson must often apply considerable force to the tiller or wheel. Synonymous commands include *bear away* and *head off*.

Tack. This means (1) formerly, the windward fastening of the sail to the deck or a spar, and nowadays, the forward lower corner of a sail (or a spinnaker's windward corner)—this definition may come from the Old French *tache*, "nail"; (2) the relative angle between the course and the wind so that when the starboard side is the windward side, the boat's on the starboard tack and when the port side is to windward, she's on the port tack—this meaning originates in the first definition, since the side on which squaresails were tacked was the windward side; (3) to change course by heading up until the bow is directly in the wind, then bearing off with the wind on the other side, thereby *changing tacks*. Today, tacking in this last sense is often called *coming about*.

Jibe. Jibing entails changing tacks by bearing off until the stern is directly in the wind, then heading up with the wind on the other side. The word comes from the Dutch *gijben*, "to shift," and in Britain it is often spelled *gybe*. Either way, it rhymes with *imbibe*.

Trim. This word has four meanings: (1) A boat is *in trim* when she is floating just as she should and *out of trim* if she isn't. (2) The *trim of the sail* is the sail's angle to the wind and general shape. When the angle is narrow and the sail is relatively flat, the trim is flat; when broad and round, the trim is full. (3) To *trim sails* means to optimize the sail's shape and angle for the prevailing conditions. Finally, (4) to *trim sheets* is to pull in on the sheets, flattening the sails and narrowing the angle to the wind. All this overlapping derives from the all-purpose usefulness of the Old English *trymman,* "to strengthen or set in order." In fact, the adjective *untrum* meant "infirm," so a poorly trimmed sail or boat is, in a way, a sick one.

Ease. To *ease sheets* is the opposite of to trim sheets, for by letting out the sheets you make the sails more round and widen the angle between them and the wind. You can also lower the strain on any loaded line by easing it. The word is probably derived from the Old French *aaisier,* "to provide comfort" (originally, "to provide elbowroom").

Course. This is the direct heading to the destination, indicated usually by compass degrees (the *compass course*) but also by landmarks or buoys. You're *on course* when steering in the right direction. The word originates in the Latin *cursum,* "a running." Over the intervening millenia it has been applied to several types of running, among them the hunting of hares with greyhounds, the charge of two combatants in a medieval jousting tournament, a place where horses are raced, the flow of time, and the lower staysails run out on a squarerigger's yards.

Index

Note: Many technical sailing terms are defined in the glossary beginning on page 286.